CONTENTS

Introduction		*1*

SECTION A – FINDING WHAT WORKS: MODALITIES AND ADAPTATIONS

	Introduction	*9*
1	Autism in therapy: Monotropism, meditation and autistic flow *River Marino*	*11*
2	Training and working as an autistic cognitive behavioural therapist *Danielle Goddard*	*20*
3	Autism and the body: Dance movement psychotherapy *Kristina Takashina*	*30*
4	Art psychotherapy as an AuDHDer *Fiona Villarreal*	*39*
5	Finding what works *Sally Nilsson*	*51*
6	Art therapy, somatic experiencing and empathy *Chan Shu Yin*	*57*

SECTION B – TO BE THAT SELF WHICH ONE TRULY IS

	Introduction	*71*
7	Finding congruence *Natalie Furdek*	*73*
8	Don't be you *Leo Ricketts*	*80*
9	Trauma and the autistic therapist *Wendy Reiersen*	*88*
10	The journey from research knowledge to lived wisdom *Silvia Liu*	*97*
11	Befriending the beast: A therapist and her meltdowns *Debbie Luck*	*106*
12	Asian American autistic alien *Sharon Xie*	*115*

13	Working in one's own community: Self-disclosure and being 'that self which one truly is' *Max Marnau*	122
14	The autistic sense of justice and moral injury: Battling the system and blowing the whistle *Shirley Moore*	132

SECTION C – AUTISTIC THERAPISTS FOR AUTISTIC PEOPLE

	Introduction	145
15	Complex trauma, language and culture in autistic counselling *Katherine Balthazor*	147
16	To be the supervisor I wish I'd had *Amy Walters*	155
17	Making environments accessible: Permission to exist *Elinor Rowlands*	166
18	Neurodiversity-affirming supervision *Romy Graichen*	175
19	Kathryn's call: The lost generation *Wilma Wake*	183
20	Working with my neurokin *Kathy Carter*	189
21	The autistic therapist and chronic illness *Rebecca Antrim*	196

SECTION D – TRAINING, TRAINERS AND TRAINEES

	Introduction	207
22	The autistic trainer's perspective: Educating therapists *Interview with Vauna Beauvais and Eoin Stephens*	209
23	Our experiences as trainees *Katherine Balthazor, Danielle Goddard, Silvia Liu, River Marino, Max Marnau, Shirley Moore, Wendy Reiersen, Elinor Rowlands, Chan Shu Yin, Kristina Takashina and Amy Walters*	221
	About the contributors	231
	Name index	239
	Subject index	242

Praise for *On Being an Autistic Therapist*

This revolutionary, timely, necessary book is a must for all therapy trainers and organisations and I hope it finds its way into the hands of as many neurodivergent therapists and clients as possible. It's a readable, warm, wise mosaic of perspectives from autistic therapists who powerfully demonstrate a rainbow toolbox of ways they connect with clients, many of whom, like them, have felt different all their lives and flourish when their autistic language and culture is truly validated. I was inspired by the joyous inventiveness, myth-busting and hope I found in these pages. Therapy comes alive here as flow state, multi-sensorium, meditation, exploration, co-regulation and space of clarity, acceptance and safety in what has hitherto been a confusing world for both autistic therapists and clients. This book documents a changing paradigm in therapy and neurodiversity and I'm sure will also help lead and shape it.
Dr Kate Fox, poet, broadcaster, neurodivergent activist

This book is an important addition to the autism discussion: one that is particularly useful in confronting undeserved stereotypes about autistic adults, as well as opposing the notion that autistic people are supposed to be exclusively the recipients of therapy, rather than the professionals delivering it. It is loaded with valuable autistic voices worth listening to and learning from.
Chris Bonnello, autistic advocate, speaker and author

Ever since I started reading autobiographical accounts, I have thought that the best way of learning about autism is through the authentic autistic voice. One of the most distressing things I hear is when people assume that being autistic precludes the ability to be a therapist. Along with combatting many other equally nonsensical myths (such as the one declaring that autistics lack empathy), this book makes huge strides in addressing the levels of ignorance found in many autism texts. The world needs autistic therapists, and their stories in this great book will enable a better, deeper understanding of their experiences.
Dr Luke Beardon, senior lecturer in autism, Sheffield Hallam University

I love this book! Every chapter is a goldmine of insight. While the primary focus is on the experience of autistic therapists and the innovative ways the contributors use to do effective therapy with autistic clients, there are broader lessons here that are invaluable to the field of psychotherapy as a whole. Not only does this volume have the potential to transform professional practice, it may also be the final nail in the coffin of many archaic 20th century stereotypes and misconceptions about autistic people. It is a must-read for absolutely anyone involved in psychotherapy or adjacent fields, whether as a practitioner, supervisor, educator, student or client.

Nick Walker, PhD, professor of psychology at California Institute of Integral Studies and author of *Neuroqueer Heresies* **(2021)**

On Being an Autistic Therapist represents a moment in history and is a milestone. This anthology is timely, informative and compelling. I am very, very delighted to be a witness to this community of autistic professionals as they grow in confidence and self-expression.

Dr Catriona Stewart, OBE, MCPP, researcher, educator, ambassador and co-founder of the charity SWAN Autism Scotland

On Being an Autistic Therapist is a groundbreaking contribution to our field. These powerful, personal insights by autistic therapists challenge conventional but outdated views and provide fresh perspectives on what it means to be 'that self which one truly is', and how to create more inclusive, empathic spaces for both clients and practitioners. This is an invaluable resource for psychotherapists, educators and mental health practitioners, and I recommend it warmly. I hope it will slay many myths about what it means to be an autistic person working in the therapy arena.

Carolyn Spring, author, trainer, founder of the Trauma Recovery Community

For a very long time, it was considered inconceivable that an autistic person could be a therapist. This book features 23 of those people, whose unique and glorious journeys have led them to this work. Each of their stories is a fascinating joy to read, teaching me about them, myself and the rest of our tribe. The world of autism and therapy is a better place because of them.

Sarah Hendrickx, autistic and ADHD consultant, diagnostician and author of, among other books on autism and neurodivergence, *Women and Girls on the Autistic Spectrum* **(2nd ed., 2024) and** *Could I Really Be Autistic?* **(2025)**

On Being an Autistic Therapist shines a light on the prevalence of autistic people in a profession where many people still imagine our neurotype to be a problem, but where experiences that diverge from the norm are in fact invaluable. Like many minorities, autistic people often face social exclusion and misunderstanding; the experiences of this diverse group of authors should enlighten anyone who hopes to help in any way.

Fergus Murray, autistic writer, educator, community organiser and chair of AMASE (Autistic Mutual Aid Society Edinburgh)

ON BEING AN AUTISTIC THERAPIST

EDITED BY
MAX MARNAU

First published 2025
Product code – 022025500

PCCS Books Ltd
Wyastone Business Park
Wyastone Leys
Monmouth
NP25 3SR
United Kingdom

contact@pccs-books.co.uk
www.pccs-books.co.uk

This collection © PCCS Books, 2025
The individual chapters © the contributors, 2025
Illustrations © the artists, 2025

All rights reserved.

No part of this publication may be reproduced, stored in a retrieval system, transmitted or utilised in any form by any means, electronic, mechanical, photocopying or recording or otherwise, without permission in writing from the publishers.

The authors have asserted their right to be identified as the authors of this work in accordance with the Copyright, Designs and Patents Act 1988.

On Being an Autistic Therapist

British Library Cataloguing in Publication data: a catalogue record for this book is available from the British Library.

ISBN   paperback – 978 1 915220 56 1
            ePub – 978 1 915220 57 8

Cover design by EH6 Design
Cover illustration: 'Riding the Storm' © Fiona Villarreal
Typeset in-house by PCCS Books using Minion Pro and Myriad Pro
Printed in the UK by CMP, Dorset

This product has been assessed as low risk and can be used safely without safety information.

The manufacturer's authorised representative in the EU for product safety is:
Easy Access System Europe – Mustamäe tee 50, 10621 Tallinn, Estonia
gpsr.requests@easproject.com

Acknowledgement

I'm hugely grateful to all the contributors to this wonderful book, and particular thanks are due to Katherine Balthazor, without whose encouragement and help in the early stages this project would never have got off the ground.

About the editor

Max Marnau was born in London, the daughter of Austro-Hungarian refugees from Hitler's Nazis. In her late 20s she changed her first name to Maximilian, in honour of Maximilian Kolbe, the Polish Franciscan who gave his life for a fellow prisoner in Auschwitz, where her grandparents and other members of her family died.

Long before she knew she was autistic (self-identified in her late 50s, diagnosed in her early 60s), she knew she was different, but attributed that to being a 'second-generation exile' and so fitting nowhere.

University (both Cambridge and Oxford) suited her well, but thereafter, like so many autists (her word of choice), she 'lurched from one disastrous office job to another', with occasional respite periods working as a carer in residential homes and the community. She has also worked as a self-employed artist and gardener, and has published poetry, several articles and a novel. Circumstances made it possible for her to train as a counsellor in late middle age, having previously volunteered for Samaritans and Cruse Bereavement Care Scotland, and that was where she found her niche.

Since then, she has worked for various charities, for a university counselling service and, from 2013, in private practice. Since discovering that she is autistic (she says, 'so not "mad, bad, and dangerous to know", just wired differently!'), she has branched out into training, writing and, for her the most important of all after her work as a therapist, the foundation of the collective 'Autistic Counsellors and Psychotherapists'.

'Journeying Within' (watercolour, pen and ink on paper)
© Elinor Rowlands

Introduction

This book is unusual in that it is not about working *with* autistic people in the therapy room, but about working *as* autistic people in the therapy room.

It grew organically out of the collective Autistic Counsellors and Psychotherapists (ACP) – a group of autistic therapists who, through our work as therapists and our more general contact with the therapy world, came to realise two things: autistic clients were struggling to find appropriate therapy, and the stereotypes regarding autistic people, which we recognised to be outdated, were still very much alive.

The group exists as a response to those two facts. Our aim is to provide autistic clients with autistic therapists by being open about our own autism and creating a pool of therapists to refer people on to, and to counter the stereotypes.

We have written this book mainly for that second purpose. On the principle of 'Show, don't tell,' we have put together a collection of stand-alone chapters, each depicting an aspect of working as an autistic therapist. Although the chapters have been collected into four broad sections, each contributor had a completely free hand as to what they felt they could most usefully say on the subject of 'being an autistic therapist'. The chapters are mostly each a portrait of one autistic therapist (or two, in one instance) – how they perceive and process the world, and how they work with clients, with a final joint commentary on contributors' thoughts on how counselling and psychotherapy training, and access to it, can be improved.

So rather than seeing this book as single narrative, see it, perhaps, as a mosaic – a piece of art, almost. It is not insignificant that the first section, 'Finding what works', has contributions by three very different therapists who use art in their work.

ACP, and therefore this book, happened almost by chance, due to an extraordinary combination of circumstances. In early 2020, therapy changed, probably forever. From March, the Covid-19 pandemic imposed strict lockdowns and prohibitions on meeting in person, and therapists were faced with the choice of ceasing to practise or moving online. The university counselling department where I worked closed overnight, and did not reopen fully until the following academic year, and even then, it was mostly online. My new-found free time meant that I could accept a request from the Scottish Women's Autism Network (SWAN) to offer brief online therapy to autistic women in Scotland. Almost all those women told a story of desperately trying to find therapists who understood them. One said: 'There have been good therapists, nice therapists, but you are the first one who "gets it".' The difference was quite simply that I too was autistic. I adjusted my profile in the online Counselling Directory to make it clear that I am autistic, and within a short time my private practice was full, and I was starting to contact other autistic therapists and refer enquirers on.

My intention in seeking out other autistic therapists was not simply to have colleagues for onward referral, but for something much deeper and further reaching – to demonstrate, maybe in a limited way, that the stereotype that autistic people lack empathy, theory of mind (the capacity to recognise and understand the mind of the other) and self-reflection is manifestly untrue. So is the belief – which a distressing number of us have experienced, especially as trainees – that the concept of an autistic therapist is somehow problematic or even a contradiction in terms.

Because here was a group, small at first but ever-growing, of autistic therapists working effectively with both autistic and non-autistic clients.

In early 2021, that small group of autistic therapists created the Facebook group Autistic Counsellors and Psychotherapists (ACP). At the time of its creation, I fully expected that it would grow at most to a couple of dozen people, probably all from the UK. Today, at the time of writing (November 2024) there are nearly 1500 of us, all practising autistic counsellors and psychotherapists. We come from all the nations of the UK, and from Ireland, France, Belgium, Luxembourg, Germany, the Czech Republic, Hungary, at least 25 US states, Canada, Singapore, Australia, and beyond. Our modalities are person-centred, cognitive behavioural therapy, transactional analysis, Gestalt, Human Givens, acceptance and commitment therapy, psychodynamic therapy, and more. We are art therapists, music therapists, drama and dance therapists and equine-facilitated therapists. We do sand play, geek therapy, focusing, therapeutic life story work – and almost everything else you can think of. But we have one thing in common: we are all autistic.

The group grew rapidly, and about a year later I floated the idea of collaborating on a book about being autistic therapists. There were about 300 of us by then, with a wide variety of skills, trainings and interests. The idea was greeted with enthusiasm and several people put forward proposals for chapters. Eventually, 23 chapters were completed – and here they are.

We want you to meet us – 23 representatives of ACP: 23 of all the autistic therapists throughout the world. We are professional, ethical, empathic, creative, and very, very varied. And, as you will also see in the pages that follow, in this society we are disabled. We are all autistic; some of us also have other neurodivergences, such as ADHD, dyslexia and/or dyspraxia; some of us have physical health conditions; some of us are grappling with the effects of major trauma. You will find all this in our chapters. Sometimes our very strengths as autistic people can manifest as difficulties in this non-autistic world. Shirley Moore (Chapter 14) expresses this extremely powerfully in her chapter on the autistic sense of justice.

We have learned to adapt our lives to accommodate that. We have learned to use our differences to their best advantage. We have 'befriended the beast' (as Debbie Luck puts it in Chapter 11), but the fact remains: we might look as if we have it all together but, as Chris Bonnello, an autistic trainer, author and advocate, frequently says, 'We are "high functioning" …until we are not.' Please do not see us as somehow 'less autistic' than people with more obviously disabling co-occurring conditions or those living in even less autistic-friendly environments than we do. Luke Beardon's well-known 'golden equation' runs: 'Autism + environment = outcome' (Beardon, 2021, p.5).

In the first drafts of our chapters, many of us included the histories of our lives before we started training as therapists and/or recognised that we were autistic. The similarities were so common within a group of such diverse people that the stories became almost repetitive: we were all, effectively, saying the same thing. So, we decided to keep them in only a couple of the chapters where they were integral to the piece and reduce them to snapshots in the others. Those commonalities can be summarised as a pervasive feeling of difference, of confusion; the feeling that, as River Marino (Chapter 1) puts it, 'Everyone else got a manual aptly titled *How to be a Human in the World*, and unfortunately you didn't receive a copy'; the sense of inferiority, fear and shame that comes with that; the learning how to mask or camouflage, and then the dawning realisation that there was a reason for all this and that the reason had a name.

If it seems surprising that this realisation can take so long, remember that, unlike most minorities, we do not tend to grow up with an awareness of our tribe, our neurokin; we don't even have a sense that we might belong to a tribe.

So many of us grow up with the belief that we are the only one of our kind in the world. Wilma Wake (Chapter 19) says:

> Often, when a client is diagnosed/recognises their diagnosis, I'll ask, 'Who else do you know who is autistic?' Often, they will say, 'Only you.' Can you imagine the people of any other minority group not knowing each other? You have to meet 'your people'. You are part of a tribe.

That is what makes the difference, has made the difference, for us. It is interesting, in this context, to note that – with one exception – all the contributors were diagnosed in adulthood: in two cases, not until our 60s. The one who was diagnosed as a child tells a sad but all too familiar story: their parent was told by doctors that a diagnosis would 'severely impair the child's opportunities in education and having a life', and so it would be better not to diagnose them, because they were 'bright' and 'no one would notice'. It was not until they were adult that they themselves chose to seek diagnosis and to challenge the stigma that was still attached to autism in their family.

I started with the statement that this book is not primarily about doing therapy *with* autistic people but doing therapy *as* autistic people. However, we have all found, in one way or another, that our caseload is now largely autistic. And so, as it turns out, the book also offers suggestions of ways of working effectively with autistic people.

And that, really, explains the sections of the book and the order in which we have chosen to put them. With each section, I also offer a brief summary of the main themes discussed, to guide the reader.

Essentially, the aim of the book is the same as that of ACP itself: to provide incontrovertible evidence that the old stereotypes about autistic people have had their day; that the existence of autistic therapists, far from being problematic or even a contradiction, is quite simply normal. And that neurodiversity, just like biodiversity, enriches, broadens and benefits all concerned.

We are telling you this, but we are also showing you, by letting you into the workings of our minds, hearts, and therapeutic approaches. We are giving you the chance to meet us, to see us as humans, as therapists, as supervisors, in the hope that, in its small way, this collection may give readers – autistic, allistic, therapists and would-be therapists, clients and would-be clients – the understanding that they need in order to join us in changing the world.

To quote Danielle Goddard (Chapter 2), we:

> hope that other therapists find this helpful and autistic people aspiring to a psychological profession feel empowered to take that next step in

their career. We also hope that, with time, being an autistic therapist is normalised and celebrated.

Sally Nilsson (Chapter 5) hopes her journey:

> will encourage more therapists to actively want to add to their skill sets and that late-diagnosed neurodivergent therapists feel empowered to increase their client base and take positive steps for change in the therapy room.

And Katherine Balthazor (Chapter 15) speaks for us all when she writes:

> Autism is more than a diagnosis. It is a culture and language. It is diverse within itself, with subcultures and generally unlabelled dialects. Just as you can try to learn to speak a new language or learn about a culture, you can get to know us. You might like what you find!

References

Beardon, L. (2021). *Avoiding anxiety in autistic adults.* Sheldon Press.

SECTION A

Finding what works: Modalities and adaptations

'The Door is Open' (mixed media – greyscale reproduction from colour) © River Marino

Introduction

We very often hear the question 'What therapy works for autistic people?' Well, what therapy works for people? Autistic people are as varied as non-autistic people, and what works for me may not work for you. So here are six very different autistic therapists, each in their own way challenging the stereotypes.

One stereotype, for example, tells us that autistic people are not imaginative, are literal, and do not understand metaphor, imagery or figurative language. So, we begin our 'mosaic' with River Marino (Chapter 1), an artist and therapist, who gives us an insight into their autistic mind. They are not telling us about their experience so much as inviting us in, to look around and explore. Here we enter the mind of an artist, for whom everything has existence both as itself and as an image that points beyond. Introducing the chapter, they say:

> Here I am, one autistic person sharing their story through various lenses: the traumatised teen who discovered meditation, the monotropic experiences of an autistic therapist, the human who accessed the healing qualities of self-energy and some of the visual art created along the way.

Another stereotype is that autistic people are rigid, unwilling to look beyond the rules. Sally Nilsson (Chapter 5) trained initially in Human Givens, but as she learned more about her own autism and recognised neurodivergence in so many of her clients, she realised that:

> the way I did therapy would need to change significantly. My Human Givens model and general counselling skills were useful and important, but I needed to adapt and to become trained in other models that were more person-centred and humanistic and more geared towards sensory experiences. I also wanted to add to my trauma learning, as it was clear that people within the neurodivergent community often lived with trauma all their lives… out went the scripts and the pathologised way of treating the symptoms of stress, anxiety, trauma, addiction and depression. My new approach is a work in progress; it seems to chime with my neurodivergent clients.

One of the most damaging stereotypes for autistic therapists – and perhaps especially for autistic therapists in training – is that autistic people are not empathic. The opposite is in fact the case for most of us. This is what Chan Shu Yin (Chapter 6) says:

The stereotype that autistic people have no empathy couldn't be farther from the truth. Often, I feel highly empathetic and can feel the client's emotions viscerally in my own body. Perhaps keen observation of details, pattern-recognition skills and looking past social hierarchies allow me to see the person for who they are beneath their social mask.

Kristina Takashina (Chapter 3) says something quite similar:

> My body resonates all the time in the therapy space. I often get the feeling in my own body of where a sensation is in the other person – I am literally resonating. My bodily sensations are like a palette containing all the colours of the relationship. When working with people who are dissociated through trauma, this type of physical feedback seems to be particularly helpful for reconnecting to their bodies and regaining agency.

And Fiona Villarreal (Chapter 4) describes in detail how she responds 'with all [her] senses working in tune with each other' to her clients' artwork: what they make, how they make it, and what is left thereafter.

A different kind of stereotype is that CBT does not work for autistic people. There is some truth in this: CBT as it is usually delivered can seem like a mix of the over-obvious (because we tend to have analytical brains, we have probably already thought of most of the solutions offered by CBT, tried them and found them wanting) and the impossible. CBT can require an almost instant knowledge of what emotion the client is experiencing, and many autistic people either have alexithymia or express their emotions in a way that is completely different to the norm, potentially resulting in mutual incomprehension. Danielle Goddard (Chapter 2) has embraced CBT, recognising the ways in which it can play to her strengths; she does not, however, disguise the struggles she encountered during her training.

Max Marnau

Chapter 1

Autism in therapy: Monotropism, meditation and autistic flow

River Marino

> I wish I could show you, when you are lonely or in darkness, the astonishing light of your own being.
> Attr. Hafiz Shirazi (1325/26–1389/90) (Ladinsky, 2006)

Imagine standing on a rock cliff, high above a surrounding forest that is shrouded in fog so dense you can barely see the trees. It's a monochromatic scene of various shades of black and grey. You are entirely alone. The world around you is unknowable and you feel unreachable…

One of the most painful experiences in life, especially for many autistic people, is feeling deeply misunderstood and alone – an alien dropped into a world (allistic culture) that doesn't make any sense. It seems like everyone else got a manual titled *How to be a Human in the World* and unfortunately you didn't. Life is painted in broad brushstrokes of loneliness and confusion and the important details seem to be missing: who am I and where are the others like me? Where are *my* people?

Of course, I can only speak for myself and my experience of being autistic. There's a common saying: If you've met one autistic person, you've met one autistic person. Here I am, one autistic person sharing their story through various lenses: the traumatised teen who discovered meditation, the monotropic experiences of an autistic therapist and the human who accessed the healing qualities of self-energy.

Neurodiversity-affirming perspective of autism

> I understand being autistic to be a cultural identity and recognize #actuallyautistic people as experts on their own culture.
> *Janae Elisabeth (2020)*

Autism is often very misunderstood, so let's begin with what I mean when I say autistic or autism. Autism is a genetically based neurotype, not a medical disorder. Autism is simply the label given to autistic neurology, and the simplest definition of this neurology is this: Autistic people have a hyperconnected bodymind (meaning: nervous system and brain) (Rose, 2023).

> The complex set of interrelated characteristics that distinguish autistic neurology from non-autistic neurology is not yet fully understood, but current evidence indicates that the central distinction is that autistic brains are characterized by particularly high levels of synaptic connectivity and responsiveness. (Walker, 2021, p.81)

According to The Autistic Advocate, Kieran Rose, autistic people:

> actively process more sensory information than non-Autistic people and that can create big differences in processing speeds, communication styles and how we interpret and interact with the world. There is no negativity or positivity in this, just difference. (Rose, 2023)

Janae Elisabeth (2020) blogs on Trauma Geek:

> We have more neuronal branching than neurotypical people which means more opportunities for connection between parts of the mindbody that may not typically connect.

She goes on to say:

> Hyper-plasticity predisposes us to have strong associative reactions to trauma. Our threat-response learning system is turned to high alert. The flip side of this hyper-plasticity is that we also adapt quickly to environments that are truly safe for our nervous system.

Due to the hyperconnected nature of the autistic bodymind, the (allistic-centred) world can often feel overwhelming for autistics. Regularly experiencing states of monotropic flow can be essential for overall autistic wellbeing. I'll share more about monotropism later in the chapter, but first this: meditation found me in a meteor shower, and I need to tell you about it.

Meditation found me in a meteor shower

> If you need to rest, let the earth hold you.
> Lama Rod Owens (2021)

Meditation saved my life. I mean this almost literally. I had just turned 20 years old and was, without realising it, coping with symptoms of trauma that were causing significant distress in all areas of my life. Here's the long story short: in my late teens, I experienced two violent and very traumatic events. I didn't know much about meditation back then, and I certainly wasn't aware of the healing benefits of a mindfulness practice, but, quite mysteriously, meditation found me one night.

Let me set the scene. Remember that person standing on the rock cliff at the beginning of this chapter? We're back there again, but this time it's a comfortably warm summer night after my second year of undergrad. I'm lying on the rock cliff above a forest along the rustic shore of Lake Superior, deep in conversation with a close friend. We take turns sharing about our traumas, our fears, our doubts and dreams, while gazing up at a sky full of twinkling stars and an unexpected meteor shower that eventually cascades through much of the night sky. I begin to (quite unintentionally) enter a state of meditation.

If the days, weeks and even several years after that night on the rock cliff are a chapter in the 'story of my life', the most appropriate title is this: 'Meditation in Motion'. Quite spontaneously, and without effort, meditation became a daily practice – a valuable part of my routine. Most mornings, I would sit in states of contemplative meditation for hours at a time, but these meditative states weren't always the archetypal 'sitting perfectly still in lotus pose'. I'd also enter a meditative flow while painting, writing, reading or spending time in nature – essentially, any time I was captivated by something of interest.

Over time, the debilitating trauma symptoms began to recede into the background, and calm, creative, confident and courageous parts of myself began to step forward. Let me be clear here: I'm not reducing the healing of trauma to simply practising daily meditation – recovering from trauma is more complex and nuanced than that. What I am saying is this: these meditative flow states had a profound impact on me, both internally (the way I experienced and perceived myself) and externally (how I perceived and engaged with the world around me). I returned to studying a topic I'd been interested in since high school: what it means to be human. My curiosity with what creates trauma and what heals it was insatiable, eventually leading to a graduate degree in clinical social work.

Fast forward many years to now. I didn't always know I was autistic; I discovered this about myself two years ago. In the past couple of years, as I've learned about my autistic neurology, I've realised that the meditative flow states I experience while connecting with something (or someone) I care about can be explained by the theory of monotropism.

Monotropism and autistic flow

> Remember, the entrance door to the sanctuary is inside you.
> *Rumi (2004)*

Let's revisit that rock cliff, this time with a new perspective: I'll explain it through the lens of monotropism. That night, all of my attention was focused on the meaningful conversation and the streaks of light from the meteor shower. It was like being inside a cosy, protective bubble where only the conversation, the stars and the meteor shower existed. My attention was entirely absorbed in the *experience of each moment*, and it was as if nothing outside of that 'protective bubble' existed. Only the moment, and then the moment after that…

Let me explain it another way: imagine looking through a telescope and all you can see is what's on the other side of the lens. The direction of the telescope determines what you see. In Kripalu yoga teacher training, I learned a different way to put this: where attention goes, energy flows. This is the essence of my experience when I'm in a monotropic, meditative state.

Before I continue, let me give credit to the three autistics who introduced the theory of monotropism. Dinah Murray began exploring the concept of monotropism in the early 1990s (F. Murray, 2022), and in 2005 she, Wenn Lawson and Mike Lesser wrote about this theory in the journal *Autism*, in a paper titled 'Attention, monotropism and the diagnostic criteria for autism' (D. Murray et al., 2005).

Fergus Murray (Dinah is their mother) describes monotropism as:

> the tendency for our interests to pull us in more strongly than most people… It rests on a model of the mind as an 'interest system': we are all interested in many things, and our interests help direct our attention. Different interests are salient at different times. In a monotropic mind, fewer interests tend to be aroused at any time, and they attract more of our processing resources, making it harder to deal with things outside of our current attention tunnel. (F. Murray, 2018)

Matt Lowry, licensed psychological practitioner (LPP) and co-host of The Autistic Culture podcast, emphasises that 'monotropic focus is the outcome of having a hyperconnected Autistic brain' (Lauria & Lowry, 2022a). He explains that, due to autistic neurology, monotropic flow states can often come with ease for autistics when they're engaged in SPecial INterests (SPINs). Where attention goes, energy flows; when the telescope ('attention tunnel') is pointed towards something enthralling, it's difficult to step back and look away, and everything outside of your view disappears.

Lowry explains that, when autistic people are in monotropic flow, they truly are in a meditative state, and that it's actually a change in brain wave states, from alpha (brain waves when we're awake and alert) to theta (brain waves when we're deeply relaxed). He highlights that this shift to theta waves is what creates the experience of deep meditation that can be incredibly healing (Lauria & Lowry, 2022b).

The theory of monotropism suggests that autistic brains are monotropic and allistic brains are polytropic. If we continue using the analogy of the telescope, then polytropic attention is like stepping back from the telescope and casually glancing around at the night sky and shadowy scenery without focusing on anything in particular. Put more simply: polytropic attention is dispersed over many different things and monotropic attention is hyperfocused on the thing of interest.

Let's return for a moment to the concept of 'flow state' and give credit to the psychologist who coined it. Mihaly Csikszentmihalyi initially developed flow theory in the 1970s, and in 1990 wrote the popular book *Flow: The psychology of optimal experience* (1990). In his book, he describes flow as:

> a state in which people are so involved in an activity that nothing else seems to matter; the experience is so enjoyable that people will continue to do it even at great cost, for the sheer sake of doing it. (p.4)

Flow states are not unique to the autistic experience and can be accessed by allistic people but, due to monotropism, autistic people likely enter flow states more regularly and with greater ease. I often refer to the monotropic focus that autistics experience as autistic flow. Remember the saying, 'If you've met one autistic person, you've met one autistic person'? I can't speak to what other autistic people experience when in autistic flow, but my experience is one of hyperfocus, respite, retreat, passionate interest, insatiable hunger for more information about the SPIN, meditative flow, lack of distractions, singular focus, healing, restoration and being in my own (cosy and safe) world.

Looking through the lens of monotropism, it makes sense that I (quite instinctually) continued to seek meditative flow states after the night on the rock cliff. It's as if my brain knew that one of the antidotes to my overwhelm and emotional hurt was to focus monotropically – to intently 'point the telescope' towards what I care about, in order to heal.

SPINs can bring autistic people into flow, and three of my SPINs are therapy (what it means to be human), a type of therapy called Internal Family Systems (IFS), and learning about autism and autistic culture (most of my clients are autistic). One of my favourite things about being an autistic therapist is that, because of these intersecting SPINs, the process of therapy often becomes a flow state for me – meaning therapy sessions can be like looking through an extra powerful telescope towards the absolutely most fascinating part of the night sky.

Therapy as meditation

> Let the truth exist somewhere other than inside your body.
> *Della Hicks-Wilson (2021)*

I'm going to try to describe what feels like the indescribable: my experience as an autistic therapist. Before I continue, let me be clear: autism is a neurotype and doesn't need to be 'treated'. Autistic clients come to me for a variety of reasons, none of which include trying to make them 'less autistic'. If they're late-identified, like me, they may want to learn more about their neurotype or need support in affirming their autistic identity.

Therapy sessions with clients can often feel like that night on the rock cliff, except I'm meeting with each person online, not outside, under a starry sky. The screen provides us each a space in which to get cosy and comfortable – feeling safe is an important element of therapy.

As I enter monotropic flow, my vision focuses and the screen disappears; it's just me and the client sitting together, almost as if we are in the same room. My hearing focuses and it's easier for my brain to tune out distracting background sounds, so that I'm mostly only hearing the two of us. An important note: when I'm not in a monotropic flow state, I'm incredibly sensitive to sounds and often experience sensory overload if I'm not wearing noise-cancelling headphones or my Loop earplugs.

Just like the night on the rock cliff, the world outside of the client and me disappears; even my thoughts are incredibly focused. Remember: my brain is in 'telescopic mode', focused on the client, so I'm rarely distracted by thoughts unrelated to the session. I'm simply present in each moment and the session becomes a meditation of all the details: every word, every movement, every sensation, every feeling. Therapy becomes a meditation on seeing someone in all their complexity: all the nuances that make up a person, moment by moment.

To be clear, I'm not using meditative as a synonym for peaceful or relaxing – especially when the content of the session is grief, trauma or heartbreaking sorrow. In sessions with painful content (most sessions, in fact), monotropic focus draws me into the realness of the moment. Some sessions become a gritty meditation on grief and noticing all the subtleties that make up an experience that words often can't fully describe.

Some sessions are a meditation on witnessing what needs to be seen: the deep ache of a lifetime of feeling misunderstood. In these sessions, monotropic focus supports me in helping the other person to really feel seen, heard and understood. Sometimes this involves supporting and encouraging an autistic client to enter their own state of monotropic flow. In these moments, we enter a state of healing flow together as they enthusiastically (and unabashedly) infodump about a SPIN. It's important (and vital to the therapeutic relationship) that therapists create a safe space for autistic clients to share their SPINs (Lauria & Lowry, 2022c).

Entering a state of autistic flow with clients often increases the access each of us has to self.

Autistic flow and self-energy

> be easy.
> take your time.
> you are coming
> home.
> to yourself.
> *Nayyirah Waheed (2013)*

Self (often referred to as self-energy) is a concept from Internal Family Systems (IFS), a non-pathologising model of therapy developed by Richard Schwartz. Because this chapter is about my monotropic experience of therapy as an autistic therapist, I won't go into the details of IFS as a therapeutic model. Instead, I'll focus on my experience of the dynamic relationship between self-energy and autistic flow.

But first: what is self? I think of self as the wise and intuitive nature I was born with: essentially, who I truly am underneath all of the trauma, heartbreak and stress. In IFS, self is described as 'an innate presence in each of us that promotes balance, harmony, and nonjudgmental qualities' (Anderson, 2021, p.8). It is often referred to as the eight Cs: compassion, confidence, clarity, curiosity, calm, courage, creativity and connectedness (Schwartz, 2001, pp.33–48). This is an over-simplification but, essentially, in IFS therapy, accessing self-energy is integral to healing trauma and self is considered a 'state of being that can neither be created nor destroyed' (Anderson, 2021, p.8).

My experience of self-energy feels like calm, connected, intuitive, restoration, healing, compassion, creative, meditative flow, safe and cosy. You may notice that the words I use to describe my experience of self-energy are similar to the words I used to describe my experience of autistic flow. I often experience a dynamic relationship between self-energy and autistic flow. This means that, when I access self-energy, it's more likely that I will enter an autistic flow state, and when I'm in an autistic flow state, it's likely that I will experience more connection with self-energy.

The most meditative moments for me as a therapist are when I'm connected with self-energy. The more I'm able to access self when I'm in session with a client, the more monotropic the experience will be. When I have access to self-energy, it's like looking through that super-powerful telescope at an intriguing part of the night sky and feeling boundless compassion and immense calm.

The meditative flow I entered that night on the rock cliff gave me an opportunity to access self-energy. Connecting with self-energy sparked the 'meditation-in-motion chapter of my life' that followed, healing some of my trauma and ultimately teaching me the importance of autistic flow. This interplay between self-energy and autistic flow continues to inspire my work as an autistic therapist, writer and artist. I'll close this chapter with a specific type of meditative practice: metta meditation (often called loving-kindness meditation).

Finding safe refuge under a starry sky

Healing happens when we feel safe enough to show up exactly as we are.

Think back to the person standing on the rock cliff amidst a forest shrouded in fog. Have you ever felt this alone, this forgotten, this lacking in vibrancy and aliveness? Maybe I'm speaking directly to your current experience, or possibly to a younger part of yourself – maybe 'middle school you' or 'teenage you'. Whatever part of you may be standing on that cliff, anxious and alone, I hope, if any of the following words are supportive, they'll find their way to you:

> May you find a place – a someone – where all parts of you are welcome and where you feel safe enough to show up exactly as you are.
>
> May you discover within yourself a wellspring of curiosity, creativity and compassion.

May you have enough support to tenderly hold both grief and gratitude, sorrow and joy.

May you find your way into the deeply healing state of flow...

May you know that you are enough exactly as you are.

References

Anderson, F. (2021). *Transcending trauma: Healing complex PTSD with Internal Family Systems therapy*. PESI Publishing.

Csikszentmihalyi, M. (1990). *Flow: The psychology of optimal experience*. Harper & Row.

Elisabeth, J. (2020, November 6). Discovering a trauma-informed positive autistic identity. *Trauma Geek*. www.traumageek.com/blog/discovering-a-trauma-informed-positive-auisticnbspidentity

Hicks-Wilson, D. (2021). *Small cures*. Andrews McMeel Publishing.

Ladinsky, D. (2006). *I heard God laughing: Poems of hope and joy*. Penguin Books.

Lauria, A. (Host) & Lowry, M. (Host). (2022a, November 15). Industrial light & magic is autistic. *The Autistic Culture Podcast: Episode 4*. https://podcasts.apple.com/us/podcast/episode-4-industrial-light-magic-is-autistic/id1653171456?i=1000586282608

Lauria, A. (Host) & Lowry, M. (Host). (2022b, November 7). Poetry is autistic. *The Autistic Culture Podcast: Episode 3*. https://podcasts.apple.com/us/podcast/episode-3-poetry-is-autistic/id1653171456?i=1000585421120

Lauria, A. (Host) & Lowry, M. (Host). (2022c, November 29). Lemony Snicket is autistic. *The Autistic Culture Podcast: Episode 6*. https://podcasts.apple.com/us/podcast/episode-6-lemony-snicket-is-autistic/id1653171456?i=1000587943102

Murray, D., Lesser, M. & Lawson, W. (2005). Attention, monotropism and the diagnostic criteria for autism. *Autism, 9(2)*, 139–56.

Murray, F. (2018, November 30). Me and monotropism: A unified theory of autism. *The Psychologist*. www.bps.org.uk/psychologist/me-and-monotropism-unified-theory-autism

Murray, F. (2022). *Monotropism*. https://monotropism.org/2022/theory-vs-trait/

Owens, R. (2021, August 17). A shout out to all of us who are struggling today. [Facebook post.] www.facebook.com/photophp?fbid=994664111080681&id=1663593339111167&set=a.490560844824346

Rose, K. (2023). *The Autistic Advocate*. https://theautisticadvocate.com/autism-faqs/

Rumi, J. al-D. (2004). *The essential Rumi* (C. Barks, Trans.) (Expanded ed.). HarperOne.

Schwartz. R. (2001). *Introduction to the Internal Family Systems model*. Trailheads Publications.

Waheed, N. (2013). '- the becoming/wing'. In *Salt*. CreateSpace Independent.

Walker, N. (2021). *Neuroqueer heresies: Notes on the neurodiversity paradigm, autistic empowerment, and postnormal possibilities*. Autonomous Press.

Chapter 2

Training and working as an autistic cognitive behavioural therapist

Danielle Goddard

Before training in high-intensity cognitive behavioural therapy (CBT), I was an education mental health practitioner. As part of that role, I received training on how to adapt low-intensity CBT for autistic children and young people, delivered by the Anna Freud Centre in the UK. The training had been specially designed for my NHS service and I was a part of the first cohort to receive it.

The training took place over four days, with a number of speakers delivering modules. The speakers were either autistic themselves or had experience of their children being diagnosed autistic. Before this point, I had very little awareness of autism or neurodivergence. I was keen to learn more as I was finding that many of the children I was working with were neurodivergent.

During the training, I found myself asking the question, 'Isn't everyone a little autistic?', as I related to several of the traits that were being discussed.

I did not know at the time that this was an insensitive question. The speaker was upset as they explained that autistic people can experience severe difficulties due to the traits they experience, so, no, it is not the case that 'everyone is a little autistic'.

This left me feeling confused. Why did I relate so strongly to the traits of autism? I left the training with this question, which led to me researching autism in a lot more detail. I could recall times as a child where I had cancelled parties my parents tried to organise because I believed nobody would show up. I recalled having no friends through school and always struggling in class when asked to pair up; times I had cried in social situations because people had brushed past me and it caused me physical pain; sharing a room with my sister and becoming distressed every time things were not left where they should be; needing my books to be arranged in size order and grouped according to author.

I spent hours researching this. By the time I had applied and been accepted on the CBT training course, I had spoken to my doctor and requested a formal assessment for autism. This was not a pleasant experience, as I had to defend my wish to seek diagnosis at the age of 25, when I had been 'fine' up to this point. I was told that a diagnosis would not lead to additional support as I was not a child in school. I explained that I worked with neurodivergent individuals and receiving my own diagnosis might be beneficial in this setting, which seemed enough for the doctor. Realistically, I just wanted to understand my own experiences better.

The CBT course started long before I finally got a date for my autism assessment. I disclosed to my course tutor that I was going through assessment for autism and that I was concerned that I might struggle on the course. They were very understanding; indeed, they disclosed to me that they had a formal diagnosis of attention deficit hyperactivity disorder (ADHD) and were likely autistic themselves. Nonetheless, disclosing my possible autism was upsetting, as I was worried it would cause issues on the course.

The CBT training was extremely intense. There were six modules covered over a year's teaching period. Two days a week were spent in university and three days in a service delivering CBT to clients. The course I completed required the submission of six recorded sessions for marking, three of which counted towards the final degree mark. These videos were marked using a Revised Cognitive Therapy Scale (CTS-R) (Blackburn et al., 2000). I was also required to complete four case reports of 4,000 words and a 4,000-word literature review. Alongside all this work, I needed to keep track of every client that I had worked with and all my supervision hours for a final clinical portfolio. It was not a course for the faint of heart.

Despite the intensity of the course, I was determined. I had already decided I wanted to work with autistic and other neurodivergent clients in the future. A qualification and accreditation in CBT felt like one step towards this. I eventually wanted to undertake a doctorate in clinical psychology, so I considered CBT accreditation a helpful achievement.

In the first week of training, I searched for works written by autistic practitioners. Surely I was not the only autistic CBT therapist out there? I wanted to find some advice or guidance to help me navigate this part of my identity. I had started to follow several pages on social media sites, and even took to asking on these platforms if anyone knew of any research or writing on the topic. The closest suggestion I received was an article written from the perspective of autistic medical health care practitioners (Doherty et al., 2021). I was shocked.

In my year of training, I met and spoke with several therapists who disclosed their own neurodivergence to me. My supervisor for the majority of my training had ADHD. There are so many therapists out there, but I couldn't find any research or writings on practising as a neurodivergent therapist. Research is emerging regarding neurodivergence in therapeutic practice (Garrett, 2022), but there is currently a lack of writing around autistic therapists' experiences.

During my CBT training, I went for my formal autism assessment. The assessor had a very narrow understanding of autism and, due to my capacity for empathy and my ability to maintain a conversation during the assessment, decided that I could not be autistic. Initially that was upsetting, but after some time I realised that I did not need a formal diagnosis. I am fortunate to have the support of my family. Because certain groups (for example, women and people who do not have an intellectual disability) are significantly less likely to receive an autism diagnosis (Zener, 2019; Thurm et al., 2019), self-diagnosis is widely accepted in the autistic community and has received interest in the academic community (McDonald, 2020).

This experience gave me first-hand experience of the stigma and misunderstanding that still exists around being autistic (Turnock et al., 2022). As therapists, we are expected to show empathy and engage in conversations with clients, which surely (says the stereotype) no autistic person would be able to do. For every neurodivergent therapist I have met, I have met 10 neurotypical ones who still hold outdated and misinformed perceptions of neurodivergence. I am always careful whom I tell at work about my self-diagnosis of autism.

I have spent a lot of time during my CBT training reflecting on all the strengths and difficulties that come with being an autistic practitioner. I acknowledge that I have privileges (such as being a white heterosexual woman) that mean I am able to mask (Pearson & Rose, 2021) and function in the world of therapy. I have learned the importance of unmasking and giving myself space, after experiencing autistic burnout (Higgins et al., 2021).

I hope that other therapists find this account helpful, and that autistic people aspiring to a psychological profession feel empowered to take that next step in their career. I also hope that, with time, being an autistic therapist is normalised and celebrated.

Difficulties with CBT training

Ahead of the CBT training, I knew I might have issues with the way sessions were marked. The CTS-R (Blackburn, et al., 2000) measures competence in 12 aspects of a session that should be present and completed to a standard sufficient to deliver CBT. The CTS-R was first designed in 1980 and was revised in 1988 and 2001. There are no mentions of neurodivergence across the CTS-R marking scheme, and this can lead to some issues for those who are not neurotypical.

One example of this is item 5 on the marking scheme: 'Interpersonal effectiveness'. The therapist is marked according to how empathetic, genuine and warm they are. One given measure of this is that therapists should not look 'distant, aloof or critical'. During my low-intensity CBT training, I often struggled to get higher marks on this section. Once I began exploring my own autism, I started to connect the dots and understand this. I do not display empathy in a neurotypical way; I feel it and display it in an autistic way. I do not know where to look in sessions and feel more comfortable with a laptop in front of me, which I use to take notes. If my environment is uncomfortable, I have to use extra effort to stay fully present in the conversation. This is not a failure in empathy; rather, it is simply that I am being asked to demonstrate empathy in a way that is difficult and takes more energy for me to maintain.

I came across a post on a social media forum in which an autistic person described doing a 'mental search', which helped me understand my own process of empathy. If a client is describing a situation I have been in myself, I can do a mental search and find the emotions related to this and show empathy very easily. However, if the mental search comes up blank, I find it much harder to know how to show empathy in a neurotypical way. However, again, that does not mean I do not feel empathy – it just means I have to work harder in the session to show empathy in a different way to how I naturally experience it.

The markers were often not aware of my autism and the differences in how I might display empathy. When I raised this in supervision, my supervisor was clearly unaware of how empathy can be experienced by an autistic person. They were quick to try to help me with what they perceived as my 'lack of empathy', despite my explanation of the 'double empathy problem' (Milton, 2012). As Milton contends, I do experience empathy, but I may not demonstrate it in the way a non-autistic person might. That does not mean it is not equally valid and helpful to the client. To date, I have not had any client feedback that has indicated I am not empathetic.

Item 6 on the CTS-R explores 'eliciting appropriate emotional expression'. Many of my neurotypical colleagues had difficulties with this criterion. Being autistic potentially added to those difficulties. I have never understood my own emotions in neurotypical terms, and therefore struggle to label them in those terms. During training, I learned of alexithymia (Sifneos, 1996). This – a difficulty identifying and describing emotions, and specifically, in my case, doing so in neurotypical terms – has sometimes caused me difficulties with how my work is marked. Because it is not natural to me to express emotions in a conventional way, learning to identify them in a client does not come naturally either and has taken considerable work to achieve.

CBT sessions

In sessions, I could find it difficult to manage emotions in the therapy space. Subtle emotional cues from clients can be hard to read, especially when working remotely. Some clients chose to switch their camera off on a video call, which removed the visual cues. Even with cameras on, I often couldn't see a client's body language when only their face was visible.

Clients bring lots of emotion to the room and I find it difficult to know how to meet the neurotypical expectations of how to react to this. I found myself masking in order to give the client a reaction they might expect, to communicate empathy in line with neurotypical expectations. This might happen when clients cried or expressed sadness. After discussing this in supervision, I began adopting learned phrases like 'Would you like to get a tissue or to take a break?' because it seemed to me that was a neurotypical response. It does not come naturally to me to feel sadness with the client if it isn't a shared experience.

This also reflects my experiences of cognitive as opposed to affective empathy. When I did not have a shared experience with a client, I struggled to mirror the emotions they were expressing. My empathy was genuine, but it was cognitive and measured. However, when I could tap into the client's emotional responses from an experience I had been through, it felt easier to express empathy through my own emotions. This is an example of how the double empathy problem may arise in a clinical setting; I am empathetic, but this may not be communicated in a way that neurotypical clients expect.

When clients shared something that tapped into my own experiences, I could find that some of the client's distress could catch up with me later in the day. Sometimes clients would share a lot of information in one session, especially in initial sessions. It takes me some time to process everything from a session, so after the workday, if this had occurred, I would find myself taking the client's emotions home with me. I would spend evenings feeling anxious or upset.

It was not easy to discuss this with my supervisor, as their response felt very negative. I got the impression that if I could not separate the client's emotions from my own life, I should not be a therapist. On reflection, I do not agree with this stance. While I may struggle to process some emotions, I have learned to give myself more space between sessions and practise self-care if this occurs. I stim between sessions and have fidget toys in my workspace that I use to self-regulate between sessions. Experiencing emotions differently is not a deficit, and being able to address this and getting support in supervision mean I can be present for clients and build an effective therapeutic relationship.

At times clients expect the therapist to 'read between the lines' of what they are saying. They may not feel able to address a problem directly, or may not even be aware that something additional is going on. They may use sarcastic phrases or metaphors to express themselves. There may well be cues that I have missed or not been aware of, for this reason. Over time, I have learned to ask clients questions about what they mean and will rephrase things in a way that makes sense to me, to check I have understood. For example, if a client says, 'I felt stuck between a rock and a hard place', I might ask what they mean by 'rock' and 'hard place'. Such questions, which a non-autistic therapist might not feel the need to ask, can be invaluable in therapy and are a strength of neurodivergent therapists like us.

CBT sessions can also be difficult from a sensory perspective. Certain sounds, textures and temperatures can make me experience hypo- or hyperarousal and lead to overstimulation. Over time I have worked to understand my sensory profile better. I am more aware that, if a therapy room is too cold or too hot, too bright or uncomfortable, it may mean that I need to mask to hide my discomfort for the benefit of the client. Having these difficulties means I am more aware of how the environment can influence comfort, and I am more likely to ask clients whether they feel comfortable with an environment.

As a CBT therapist, I believe that it is important to practise what we work on with clients. At times, this work can be uncomfortable if it relates to differences between the neurodivergent therapist and their neurotypical clients. A particular example of this comes from my work with social anxiety. Attention training is part of the Clark and Wells social anxiety treatment protocol (Clark & Wells, 1995). Clients are given various sensory inputs (such as visual and audio) and are asked to work on their ability to switch their focus between them, with the understanding that their current internal focus is leading to increased social anxiety and we want to give them the skills to switch to an external focus. I used an auditory video in a session with a client and by the end of the day I had to go off sick due to a migraine. The video included several sounds playing at once, which I found overstimulating and distressing. Adaptations to CBT are needed for clients but should also be considered for therapists. After that experience, I still used the videos but now I knew I needed to mute my own computer.

Face-to-face training requirements

My CBT training was delivered using a blended learning approach. I had one day of teaching delivered fully remotely and one day when I was required to attend in person.

During the training we students engaged in conversations with the university about neurodiversity and the accessibility of the course. Autism,

ADHD and dyslexia were represented in the cohort and issues were raised relating to neurodivergence. One of the issues we raised was the requirement for those living near the course to attend face-to-face. We knew it was possible to attend the course remotely, as some of us were doing so already because it was accepted that they lived too far away to be reasonably expected to attend in person.

However, we were told that this was only due to their location and that everyone else had to attend in person, unless they had Covid-19.

This is not a logic I can understand, but it is not a unique experience. Accessibility in universities is a very significant issue (Accardo et al., 2019). I am grateful for the advances made as a result of Covid-19 restrictions (Heyworth et al., 2021). Working online from my own home suits me much better. I can control elements such as lighting and temperature, which makes me more able to concentrate. Working on a computer is easier for me, as I am not making direct eye contact but the people on the other side of the call are not necessarily aware of this. I can have several tabs open on a computer so I can, for example, use simple games to help me concentrate when attending an online lecture.

Being in a stark white room on a group training course for 7.5 hours in a day feels to me like torture. I am forced into social situations with other colleagues. Pleasant as these colleagues may be, this isn't a comfortable situation for me. I have to manage where I sit so nobody touches me. I have to concentrate on my body language and how I am sitting, if I am smiling, when to nod… it becomes an exhausting task of trying to learn while also being constantly alert to how I am being perceived socially.

Dealing with change can be difficult for me, as it is for most autistic people (Gillott & Standen, 2007), and it usually takes me a while to prepare for and process it once it occurs. In my course, I was required to manage several changes each term – for example, changing both my supervision and clinical skills groups. One of my course supervisors also left the course suddenly, which was another change to manage. I did not have the luxuries of time or consistency. I never got used to this and every term was a struggle.

As I do not have a formal diagnosis of autism, I was not able to access the university disability service to request reasonable adjustments. Ironically, my longstanding label of anxiety/depression turned out to be fortunate, as it meant that I was able to access the university mental health service and request reasonable adjustments that way.

Needing a formal diagnosis can be a barrier to students trying to get the learning support they need. Adjustments that may be very helpful to students and make minimal demands of the university include:

- allowing extensions on assignments
- allowing virtual attendance where possible
- giving lecturers information on students so they can help with participation in lectures/seminars/workshops
- making presentations universally accessible (off-white background, larger fonts)
- offering a range of seating options (standing desks, normal desks, floor space)
- normalising needing to leave for a break
- offering a quiet/sensory space on campus
- allowing students to listen to music while in lectures (as long as this does not interrupt other students).

Strengths with CBT training

Along with some difficulties, I also feel that being autistic gave me some strengths while on the course. When I spoke with my tutor at university about my concerns and difficulties, they helped me to explore how autism may also be a 'superpower'. This way of thinking was very helpful for me when I was focusing on all the ways I might be disadvantaged.

While colleagues struggled with structuring sessions, I did not find this overly challenging. I have learned that I thrive when I give myself a structure and routine, and over time have learned to do this in my daily life. I use to-do lists and planners to help me plan each day in advance and follow a set routine. CBT fits well with this, as each session has a certain structure that needs to be followed. I know every session will start with a brief check-in and review of the weekly measures, followed by a home practice review. The client will then have space to bring any content to the session, and usually I will introduce a change technique. Finally, we will agree a home practice for the following week and I will summarise the session. This kind of pattern feels comfortable and gave each session structure during my training.

I had been worried that I might come across as blunt or ask questions that would have felt obvious to the client. Because I understand emotions differently, I often ask people in my personal life 'What are you thinking?' When I discussed that with my supervisor, we agreed there was benefit in it for the client. Non-autistic trainees are perhaps more likely to make assumptions about clients' emotional experiences and cognitions and may find it harder to ask these types of Socratic questions. Since I often feel unsure about people's emotions and thoughts, I felt more comfortable asking the questions. Assumptions may be wrong! Knowing that I cannot assume and must therefore ask can definitely be a superpower.

While many autistic people say that they do not find CBT the most effective therapy for themselves, I find it suits me as a therapist. While training, we explored modalities such as mindfulness and meditation, but these modalities did not come as easily to me. CBT has a structure and routine to it that feels more comfortable to me as a therapist. I work with the client to set an agenda at the start of each session, which gives me a guideline of what we will talk about and how long for. I have learned that certain questions are helpful in CBT, which feels like learning a script, which I repeat with each client.

I tend to be more detail-oriented and can sometimes concentrate on smaller details rather than the bigger picture. In therapy, this isn't a negative. While having an overview of the client is helpful, CBT focuses on a specific aspect of a person's difficult experiences and understanding what is maintaining this. Being able to focus on a person's specific presenting problem helps me keep therapy on track and not digress into unrelated topics.

It is true that at times I can appear blunt, and I like to get to the point in a conversation. Small talk is not something I enjoy. In CBT, especially virtually, there is no time for small talk, and getting to the point keeps the therapy focused. Where non-autistic therapists might struggle to leave behind social norms and expectations, and might find it hard to ask direct questions, my autistic directness, structuredness and plain speaking can be just what is needed.

References

Accardo, A.L., Bean, K., Cook, B., Gillies, A., Edgington, R., Kuder, S.J., & Bomgardner, E.M. (2019). College access, success and equity for students on the autism spectrum. *Journal of autism and developmental disorders, 49*(1), 4877–4890.

Blackburn, I.M., James, I.A., Milne, D.L. & Reichelt, F.K. (2000). *Cognitive therapy scale – revised (CTS-R)*. Newcastle Cognitive and Behavioural Therapies Centre. https://ebbp.org/resources/CTS-R.pdf

Clark, D.M. & Wells, A. (1995). A cognitive model of social phobia. In G. Heimberg, M.R. Liebowitz, D. Hope & F. Scheier, *Social phobia: Diagnosis, assessment, and treatment* (pp. 69–93). The Guilford Press.

Doherty, M., Johnson, M. & Buckley, C. (2021). Supporting autistic doctors in primary care: Challenging the myths and misconceptions. *British Journal of General Practice, 71*(708), 294–295.

Garrett, C. (2022). 'There is beauty in diversity in all areas of life including neurological diversity' (Bella): A mixed method study into how new thoughts on neurodiversity are influencing psychotherapists' practice. *Zeitschrift für Psychodrama und Soziometrie, 21*(1), 1–15.

Gillott, A. & Standen, P.J. (2007). Levels of anxiety and sources of stress in adults with autism. *Journal of Intellectual Disabilities, 11*(4), 359–370.

Heyworth, M., Brett, S., Houting, J.D., Magiati, I., Steward, R., Urbanowicz, A., Steers, M. & Pellicano, E. (2021). 'It just fits my needs better': Autistic students and parents' experiences of learning from home during the early phase of the COVID-19 pandemic. *Autism & Developmental Language Impairments, 6*. https://doi.org/10.1177/23969415211057681

Higgins, J.M., Arnold, S.R., Weise, J., Pellicano, E. & Trollor, J.N. (2021). Defining autistic burnout through experts by lived experience: Grounded Delphi method investigating #AutisticBurnout. *Autism, 25*(8), 2356–2369.

McDonald, T.A. (2020). Autism identity and the 'lost generation': Structural validation of the Autism Spectrum Identity Scale and comparison of diagnosed and self-diagnosed adults on the autism spectrum. *Autism Adulthood, 2*(1), 13–23.

Milton, D.E.M. (2012). On the ontological status of autism: The 'double empathy problem'. *Disability & Society, 27*(6), 883–887.

Pearson, A. & Rose, K. (2021). A conceptual analysis of autistic masking: Understanding the narrative of stigma and the illusion of choice. *Autism in Adulthood, 3*(1), 52–60.

Sifneos, P.E. (1996). Alexithymia: Past and present. *The American Journal of Psychiatry, 153*(1), 137–142.

Thurm, A., Farmer, C., Salzman, E., Lord, C. & Bishop, S. (2019). State of the field: Differentiating intellectual disability from autism spectrum disorder. *Frontiers in Psychiatry, 10*. https://doi.org/10.3389/fpsyt.2019.00526

Turnock, A., Langley, K. & Jones, C.R. (2022). Understanding stigma in autism: A narrative review and theoretical model. *Autism in Adulthood, 4*(1), 76–91.

Zener, D. (2019). Journey to diagnosis for women with autism. *Advances in Autism, 5*(1), 2–13.

Chapter 3

Autism and the body: Dance movement psychotherapy

Kristina Takashina

Crazy Kristina, kangaroo Kristina, chaotic Kristina… Long after those epithets were first applied to me, it turned out that I am autistic and have ADHD. I am a UK-based dance movement psychotherapist and am currently in the final stages of a post-qualification diploma in vocal psychotherapy.

I have no idea how I got here. It's a wild coincidence, as I wander into the space sideways, backwards, leaves in my hair, chalk on my hands, chocolate round my mouth and inevitably toothpaste somewhere…

I can't help but follow my own interests. As I baby, I slept on a pillow covered in a cobblestone patchwork of books I had laid out underneath me – and no one could move them because I'd wake up very cross and put them back. I was reading the newspaper at age three. I was advanced a year at school in Year 2. I taught myself French from a book at age nine and loved to sit doing maths problems at the kitchen table in the school holidays. And yet so many things only made a surface sort of sense to me. I remember trying to work out what adults did all the time, acting things out. Everything was acting in a game I didn't understand.

When I was growing up, I didn't know that therapy as I practise it now existed. I'd learned how to move my body through watching TV and from my mother, who had been sexualised all her life. This meant I was expressing a sexual energy that I had no idea about from a very young age. My behaviour was just taken from movies and stereotypes – I had no idea what I was supposed to feel, or indeed that I was supposed to feel anything. In fact, much of what I felt was migraine, which I had over and over and over again, debilitating and confining me in dark rooms for days. I took on the accent and voice intonation of whoever I was with, and this meant I was many different people all the time. I had no idea who was underneath; I didn't even know there was anyone. It didn't seem to matter, unless I was with several people at once. Then it became easier to just be a bombastic sort of super character – loud, crazy, a bit wild.

Not surprisingly, I was exhausted – when I got home from school, I felt like a shrivelled party balloon, deflated and bruised from all the bashing up against humanity. I could literally feel the air go out of me as my tummy relaxed when I left any social situation. I remember asking my mother why my head made funny noises as I lay down in bed. Now I know that I was holding myself so tight that my muscles would crack as I lay down.

The lights and noise and touching at school really bothered me, as did the smell of the lunches, the perfumes, the people. Yet I did well academically, so no one really noticed. Indeed, I excelled. But I became a sort of box of a person, rigid on the outside but empty inside. When I started to explore my body, it turned out that this was physically true also – my core was not holding me up; my outer muscles were doing all the work.

I looked at my body from the outside because I didn't yet have an autistic experience to relate to, to get a sense of self from. I had no story except internalised neurotypicalness and an operatic attempt to mimic that. I'm not in fact sure if this is why I never learned to know my own feelings of fatigue or distrust, or if this was inherent in me because of my autism. Even when I was sexually assaulted several times, I had no idea that that was what had happened. Like all social experiences, it was just the way things were.

So how did I find myself working as a psychotherapist?

I thank my SPINs (SPecial INterests) for getting me here. At school I was always good at listening to and helping with people's problems. I often saw things from the outside and saw patterns in people's behaviour that others weren't aware of. I liked watching people and working out what was going on.

When I was 13, I heard my first opera and knew that was what I needed to do (I finally trained as a singer at the Royal Conservatoire of Scotland in my late 20s and still have lessons and perform when I have the inclination). My family weren't keen on opera or music and did not understand what it entailed or what the point of it was. Luckily, when I went to university, I met my husband, who loves music, and I started singing with a few others. I asked and asked for singing lessons but couldn't persuade my family to allow it; even at age 20, permission and support from my family seemed to matter. It was not until I enrolled on my first masters in literary translation that I decided to audition for amateur opera, and that was when everything started. I saw some musicians using the Alexander Technique, which is a way of working with our habits of movement and behaviour in order to use ourselves to our full potential (see, for example, Selhub, 2015).

And that was when I discovered that I had a body.

I continued to explore my connection to my body, and to agency and intention in particular, for many years through extensive workshops in singing, Alexander Technique, Feldenkrais, Reiki, dance of all types, yoga, gym, Pilates, mountain climbing… I liked sensing, being in my body, moving. I was constantly on the go.

Training

When I signed up for dance therapy training some 12 years ago, I genuinely thought I was going to be learning how to use my body better, and how to help others to do the same. The therapy part was foreign to me. I just knew I felt better when I moved.

When I walked into the training room on my first day of dance therapy training, the others had been together for about two weeks. I'd woken up late, having slept through my alarm, and had to rush to catch the train so wasn't properly washed or dressed. I remember thinking that I had no idea what they expected me to say when I introduced myself. I didn't get to hear their introductions. I was on the back foot and I kind of assumed that was why I didn't get what was going on.

My first few weeks were spent wondering why we did things the way we did. I couldn't understand why there was some sort of 'therapy' way of being and how everyone else knew what it was! Everything went slow and you had to take ages before you spoke, even when it was your 'turn'. You had to talk to take up space, even in dance and music therapy. Simply being there and existing as a human wasn't enough. But what seemed to be especially wrong was to speak first, as no one appeared to want to do it. There were certain messages you were supposed to convey that let the other person know this was therapy too, but nothing direct. As usual, I just didn't get the rules. There were accepted connections between causes and reasons and relevant things to say. There were accepted versions of what a boundary looked like or felt like. It was as if we were talking another language. I couldn't understand how that was different from everyday life – why people weren't just themselves, here and everywhere else. They seemed to have a therapy self and a normal self.

People weren't expected to listen to the actual words you said either; we were supposed to work out what the feeling was that went with them. The other thing was not to tell your own story back to the other person. Autistic women seem to resonate a lot with each other by giving examples of what we might have experienced that might be the same in some way. Apparently, that is a no-no in therapy training. My being just couldn't synchronise with the way things were done – I'd have a million different images if asked for one; I'd have things to say to everyone's experience but never the time or space to formulate anything.

Sharing neurodivergent spaces

I've since reconnected with my neurodivergent sense of sharing space, and I find telling anecdotes can be extremely effective with my clients. But then most of them are neurodivergent like me. We do feel connected when we know we have similar experiences to one another, but our experiences are genuinely different. I keep repeating to my client, 'There isn't one rule on how to be human'. I think the principle is the same as neurotypical therapy – to connect with another – but the means can be so different.

Being present as a therapist for me means really sharing quite a lot of myself. I know I can't relate to anything that isn't concrete. An abstract emotion just doesn't mean anything to me. I have found that in many of my clients. They need to see me as a whole person, with thinking processes that don't just magically arrive out of the air, with concrete life experiences, concrete doubts and so on. With many of my clients, I show them how what I'm saying relates to my training and where my training may be wrong, so that what I'm doing and why isn't abstract. It gives clients a sense of choice and control too. They can take or leave what they want. What they seem to want is clarity, and where neurotypical life seems vague to them, they can uncloud that with me.

One of the things that seems to help my clients the most is when I share my physical sense of what is happening through my own bodily sensations. My body resonates all the time in the therapy space. I often get the feeling in my own body of where a sensation is in the other person – I am literally resonating. My bodily sensations are like a palette containing all the colours of the relationship. When working with people who are dissociated through trauma, this type of physical feedback seems to be particularly helpful for reconnecting to their bodies and regaining agency.

My first neurodivergent group experience was so liberating – for the first time I understood Yalom's group therapy textbook (1995), and in particular the concept of 'universality' – the feeling of sharing the human experience. To see my experiences in another brought tears to my eyes and raised goosebumps on my skin – it was a visceral experience. I was so grateful to be given space to work with my own neurodivergent flow, my own processing speeds, my own deep-thinking processes, and to share them with other people like me. The language of therapy started to make more sense when I actually had an experience of what others talked about, but that experience needed neurodivergence at its core.

Neurodivergent trauma

In my opinion, there is a trauma that is specifically neurodivergent, just as there is racial and LGBTQI+ trauma. As neurodivergents, we often have very few positive mirrors for our experience in the world, and we are all very different too, so perhaps that also prevents us from finding mirrors to help us define ourselves. Finding the words to describe why I am different is so hard, and my own sense is that it is also a power relations issue, because it's almost shameful to admit just how hard it is to do simple things like take shoes back to a store, make a phone call and organise my piles of washing. But that's the tip of the iceberg for neurodivergents: it doesn't feel safe to be us a lot of the time, because our needs are still considered out of the ordinary and only to be granted in special circumstances.

Many of us have also grown up with parents who are unaware that they too are neurodivergent – parents who have failed to find a safe place within the world to be themselves fully as neurodivergent people. Perhaps they have been bullied and genuinely believe that it helps you to stay safe and alive if you pretend or force yourself to be normal, whatever that means to them. So effectively they reproduce the bullying that they themselves have experienced: don't be sensitive, don't be weird, follow a very strict line, put one foot in front of the other without thinking or feeling, because otherwise you risk revealing parts of you that would be dangerous to show. They may use ridicule and humiliation to 'harden you up' so you can handle it out there – it's a tough world outside! The result is that you can't inhabit your own body: it is theirs, not yours. You have developed no boundaries to protect yourself either, and you have nowhere to go home to when you're upset.

In therapy, the way I express the trauma of my experiences doesn't seem to get a response. Something about my way of talking means it sounds fake, even after years of therapy, so that even in my current training group people can't tell if I'm sad or stressed. I can't seem to provoke empathy in another person. It seems to be me that's wrong again. And it takes ages and ages to find out the root of it.

Attending to the physical

Talking never really helped me work out the world. Language doesn't resonate with me in that way; it seems to resonate way after the moment, sometimes years later, but I'm never processing language in the here and now enough to communicate, and this makes relationships using language as a medium particularly tricky. When I spend time with people, it's usually doing something specific, like going to see a show or playing a game, or most commonly working on a piece of music with someone, either in a lesson or towards a performance. I hate having to sit at a social function and just talk. I do like to dance though; I like to be in my body, reacting to the music.

I'm hypermobile, and this means in my experience that I don't get adequate feedback from my muscles to help me to regulate their tone and their location. I struggle with both proprioception, which is the ability to sense where my body is in space and in relationship to itself, and interoception, which is the ability to sense what is going on in my body, such as heart rate increases, when I'm full and when I'm tired. As much as the emotional learning from therapy, understanding and owning my physical body has been so beneficial to me as a neurodivergent person. I have learned to sense what intention is and how it feels in my body. I have explored autonomy, direction and decision through physical explorations with the ground, gravity, space and objects around me, including the walls in particular, which give me sensory feedback about where I am – a physical sense of self. My hypermobility and proprioception difficulties mean I find it difficult even to sense whether my joints are or should be moving at any one moment. I have needed another person to help me to learn this and it really affects how I am able to relate to the world, my sense of anxiety or safety, and my ability to form a sense of my own boundaries.

I'm also apparently alexithymic, according to my autism diagnosis – pretty shocking for a therapist who is supposed to know how to work with 'feelings'. Alexithymia is difficulty with recognising, describing and expressing one's feelings. However, it is a complex thing; it doesn't mean I don't *feel* emotions, but that I don't relate to my feelings in words (literally, 'not-speaking-heart'). I often call myself non-verbal because so little of my experience of the world has anything to do with words. I relate deeply to the work of the non-speaking autistic writer Naoki Higashida. I am experiencing the world somewhere other than at the level of words, so it's hard to relate to people there. I love being with dogs and cats because they use their bodies, pheromones and sound, moving around me to blend and separate from me in so many expressive ways.

My hypermobility means I can injure myself really easily when I try to do what are generally considered normal exercises, like lifting weights, which I love and which protects my hypermobile joints by providing stability, or running, which I sometimes love and sometimes hate. It feels like I have a relationship with my body that in itself is tricky because it doesn't seem to want to do the things I tell it to. I often need to trick it, or to focus in an entirely different way, an indirect way. In movement therapy, the focus is different – it's more on learning my own body's balance and relationship with itself. I have never injured myself through doing it.

My alexithymia can mean I injure myself emotionally, because I don't feel in the moment or recognise what has happened until much later – I take a while to process any given happening in therapy. Physical sensations allow me a different way of feeding back to the client that is much more immediate.

In my personal therapy over the past 12 years or so with two therapists consecutively, I tend also to be reacting to the sensory environment around me, so I have a complex relationship with the carpet and the rugs, the pictures on the wall, the temperature and the lighting; each day they are different, the colours and shapes resonating differently and having a different internal significance. I'm a sensory storm, in a way, moving from one thing to the other in connections that are relevant to me.

I need to sense my own flow in the space; I'm genuinely not that interested in conversing with the therapist. But I do want to be seen and contained as myself. The therapist being there is enough for me most of the time. I need them to honour me and my flow, my expression in the world, but it doesn't need to be much of a dialogue, or to be honoured with words, as sometimes words are so singular when my experience is so plural; so reductive when I'm in a complex relationship with space and time.

Dancer Martha Graham said:

> There is a vitality, a life force, a quickening that is translated through you into action, and because there is only one of you in all of time, this expression is unique. And if you block it, it will never exist through any other medium and it will be lost. The world will not have it. It is not your business to determine how good it is, nor how valuable, nor how it compares with other expressions. It is your business to keep it yours clearly and directly, to keep the channel open. (De Mille, 1991, p.264)

To me, this quotation really resonates with the neurodivergent experience. And it is why I feel therapy, as it is often written about, misses a trick. Group therapy in particular is often described as being about exploring the universal, the shared, the connections between people, and I addressed that earlier in relation to sharing neurodivergent experiences. But what has usually been more interesting for me and my neurodivergent clients is the ways in which we are different and allowing those parts to blossom. These parts are the ones that we often push back into the shadows in order to survive in a culture that requires us to conform.

The best moments for me in my dance psychotherapy training group were when I got to attend to myself, to my senses, and was left to my own devices but in a contained space. When I run group movement psychotherapy sessions, it is usually to encourage attenders to be present with their own bodies, their experiences, in the moment, and to notice what moments are brought there with them, past, present and future, both imagined and 'real'. Often, we use drawing as a means of reflection, and the need for words is minimal. We might use one another to help us work something out, but it's never about the dialogue itself, the sharing; it's always about the self, or maybe the self-energy. We learn how to allow that self to just be, without judgement. And to allow it to flow more and more into the space. The sharing is in the containment; being together itself is enough, as humans in the space.

When I work with trauma with clients one to one, it's not so different, except that I am there to help the regulation process. I help my clients to feel their different states and place those in their timelines, where relevant. I follow their flow; I share my flow with them, and I use my own energy to help them see and feel their own. It's often not about the content of any particular session, but more about something deeper, in an energetic sense, that allows their body to become a whole and relate to their environment in the here and now at any given moment.

A neurodivergent therapist?

I'm currently unsure whether to advertise myself specifically as a neurodivergent therapist. I value deeply my connection with clients who may not yet recognise themselves as neurodivergent.

The word 'autistic' in particular has so many connotations that it may not be helpful in the profile of a therapist. When I sought therapy to find my inner self, I did not know that autism and ADHD were at the root of so many of my difficulties. With an image of myself as deeply empathic – indeed, my friends were shocked to hear I was autistic because empathy seemed to be the first word that came to them when thinking of me – I doubt I would have gone to a therapist describing themselves as autistic because I wouldn't have identified with that label.

That stereotype needs to change, and people like us need to change it; the question is how.

Currently, I advertise myself as a therapist who works with autism, ADHD and neurodivergence, among other things. And the clients who find me mostly seem to be neurodivergent, even though I don't say that is what I am. That in itself is intriguing!

Having said that, I have clients who are diagnosed autistic or ADHD who love that I am also neurodivergent and wish they had known from the start, because having therapy with someone of their own neurotype has been very valuable to them. What they seem to value is that I support them as they are: I don't pathologise or seek to change their neurotype. I don't see all behaviour as a symptom of trauma or avoidance (in the way some therapists might); rather, I tune into their sensory need or difficulty.

I also, as described above, recognise the trauma inherent in the neurodivergent experience in the current social climate, where 'social skills' mean monolithically neurotypical social skills; where simply existing is often met with microaggression day in, day out. It is crucial to recognise that neurodivergence is a social and cultural issue and that this affects the body of those experiencing it, and that those experiencing it have different bodily experiences too. Much can be learned from the work of queer and feminist therapists such as Christine Caldwell (2013), whose article on assessing the diverse body in the therapeutic environment gets to the heart of where the body and culture intersect. Caldwell quotes another wonderful piece by Hanna (1990, p.118):

> Since the body is composed of universal features, most members of the medical and therapeutic professions erroneously assume that the body is experienced in a universal manner. Because time, space and energy are universals in human life, many professionals mistakenly believe all people experience them in the same way. However, assumptions concerning the psychic unity of humans ignore the facts of cultural learning.

It's a difficult balance currently for me, then, to be available for those who already know they are autistic and want an autistic therapist, as well as for those who need someone to help them to find themselves, which may or may not mean uncovering neurodivergence of some sort along the way. I don't have a ready answer for how to make that work yet, and my priorities may of course change. However, my hope is that, by coming out in the world as myself, with all my neurodivergences, I can create a safer space for more people like me to feel safer to be themselves.

References

Caldwell, C. (2013). Diversity issues in movement observation and assessment. *American Journal of Dance Therapy, 35*(2). DOI:10.1007/s10465-013-9159-9

De Mille, A. (1991). *The life and work of Martha Graham – a biography*. Random House.

Hanna, J. (1990). Anthropological perspectives for dance/movement therapy. *American Journal of Dance Therapy, 12*(2), 115–126.

Selhub, E. (2015, November 23). *The Alexander Technique can help you (literally) unwind*. Harvard Health Blog. www.health.harvard.edu/blog/the-alexander-technique-can-help-you-literally-unwind-201511238652

Yalom, I. (1995). *The theory and practice of group psychotherapy* (4th ed.). Basic Books.

Chapter 4

Art psychotherapy as an AuDHDer

Fiona Villarreal

'Self-portrait' © Fiona Villarreal, 2024

I didn't know I was autistic and ADHD when I was younger. I just knew I felt different from many people and navigating social situations felt very challenging. I have a very early memory of someone reminding me to make eye contact when talking. I was described as 'shy' at school, and so this is what I thought I was. I was nicknamed 'the little ballerina' as I walked on my toes. Childhood felt like a mix of daydreams, hyperactivity and anxiety. I grew up in a very loving, accepting home, and my 'quirks' were celebrated as I was cherished for being me. I was happiest being on my own in another world in the garden, listening to music or making art. I connected with family and close friends whom I felt comfortable being around. Everything else always felt a little detached or too much to process.

I spent a lot of time observing others. I felt the intensity of others' emotions when I walked into a room. Adolescent years felt heightened and emotional as I experienced social anxiety and low moods. It was a chapter in my life that spiralled out of control from a deep-seated sense of isolation from my peers, and I was lucky I found a way forward. There were good times in my formative years, but the formative years extended a little further as I needed more time to navigate life and find a way to feel comfortable in myself.

The difficult, chaotic times in my youth eventually led me down the path of discovering the power of art for healing. I was very lucky to have followed my intuition to go to art college. I met fellow creatives and felt comfortable. There was no need to try to fit into something others expected me to be – I could be myself. Creating art felt good. It felt cathartic. This little glimpse of what art could do in terms of releasing emotional pain, communicating emotions and finding connections laid the foundations of my path towards becoming an art psychotherapist.

I trained in fine art initially. My bachelor's degree focused on conceptual fine art. Still totally unaware of my neurodivergency, I found the spacious art studios and the social aspect of the degree course overwhelming. I would go to openings for exhibitions and not know what to do with myself once I had finished looking at the artwork. Apparently, I was meant to 'network' at these events. The social 'mingling' and 'chit chat' just seemed weird to me. Having conversations with a hidden purpose to the interaction just seemed forced and unenjoyable for me. I could socialise in my downtime but again this required unhealthy coping mechanisms to block out the anxiety I felt with conversation.

Throughout my studies I channelled the tension and unease I experienced into the art process. I studied myself and the human experience of feeling watched, observed and isolated within scrutiny. My focus became creating art that communicated the idea of discomfort in the environment. I spent most of my time absorbed in the reasons behind the art, the message conveyed in the piece. I immersed myself in learning about outsider art, architecture and psychology.

It was many years later that I began my masters training in art psychotherapy. I needed to feel it was the right time for me and that I had gained enough experience in the field of mental health. I was also preoccupied in the period between my undergraduate and postgraduate degrees with situations and relationships that would later become more lived experience that could inform my work. Training to be an art psychotherapist was the absolute best feeling. Although it was a masters training and a lot of work, it never felt like a chore. It was what I was meant to be doing. I was like a sponge, soaking up every bit of information I could. I got to hyperfocus on my interests in art, psychology, emotional expression, reading and writing. We were expected to be in personal therapy for the duration of the training. I saw an art psychotherapist throughout this time. Understanding art therapy from the perspective of being a client was invaluable to my learning. I had a lot to process from my clinical placement caseload and many layers to unpack as my own trauma surfaced. And yet I still had no idea that I was neurodivergent. It was missed throughout my entire training.

As a qualified art psychotherapist, I am constantly interested in what the next client session will bring. I work on general acute psychiatric wards, with adults in addiction treatment programmes and with children and adolescents needing social, emotional and mental health support in school settings. Much of my clinical practice has leaned towards working with people who have experienced trauma and/or are neurodivergent. I have found that autistic and ADHD people tend to be referred to me, and that the sessions and communication between me and these clients have a particular flow to them.

The qualities I offer as an AuDHDer art therapist include the richness of lived experience and an understanding of autism and ADHD. I bring an ability to hyperfocus on my work, to work to tight deadlines, as I need the sense of urgency to get motivated, and to stay very calm in high-intensity situations. I bring somatic empathy; I am acutely sensitive to noticing and feeling patterns; I have an intense focus on details, and I have a deep understanding of the need for autonomy. Elements of the work I find trickier are too many interactions with colleagues I don't know very well, lunchtime 'small talk', noisy environments when I am processing and writing notes, organisational changes and feeling the compassion fatigue in others.

Once I get to know colleagues, I find things much easier, and I can relax and be myself. It's the non-therapy part of my days that feels complex. If I have had a particularly challenging week, I tell myself I don't have to 'people' (be sociable) for that day. I preserve my energy for sessions or a few people I know well. Before I knew I was an AuDHDer, I would not understand why I would feel mentally exhausted after prolonged periods of time around people; why I would become hyperactive, or why my moods would be up and down. Diagnosed aged 35, I began knowing and equipping myself with lots of self-compassion and understanding. I am lucky that the work my neurodivergent mind led me into also led me to meet some professionals who would point out that I might be autistic and ADHD. I am grateful to the people who suggested this to me a few years after I qualified.

Art therapy feels very natural to me. I always forget that many people who are not trained in art psychotherapy do not understand what it is. I have this assumption in my mind that, because I understand it, others will too, especially in work settings. Then I am faced time and time again with the realisation that art therapy is often seen as a mystery modality that people mistake for other things. I feel so passionately about art therapy that, when others make wrong assumptions of what my role entails, I can get quite frustrated. Over time, my response has changed, and I try to remind myself now to be grateful that I am in a position to be asked what art therapy is. Yes, it can be tiring to have to explain numerous times what it entails, but it is what I have chosen and what I always wanted for myself.

I am trained in art psychotherapy with a focus on psychodynamic and attachment theory. I am also experienced in using other approaches, and so my work is often integrative. Sessions usually unfold in a non-directive way, but this will depend on the individual and what best supports them. I am looking to understand the person, the art image and the process and how this may link to their sense of self, to past experiences, to attachment relationships and to much more. I offer space for the client to reflect on what is surfacing from their subconscious. I may not always outwardly reflect on such things in the session, but these observations inform me. I put a lot of emphasis on holding space and trusting in the process. As I have gained more experience in my work, I have become more flexible and confident in using alternative approaches as and when needed. Often alternative approaches emerge in my group work, depending on the people attending the group, as their needs can vary a lot (Case & Dalley, 2006, p.248). Adult addiction groups are very different from groups on acute psychiatric wards, for example, where participants are likely to have varying needs and levels at which they can engage.

For me, the beauty in art therapy is that there are many layers to it that we can work with. As Shaun McNiff observes (1998):

> In art therapy, healing often occurs when we begin to make paintings and performances that engage the sources of our discontents. When I enact my angst and fears in an artwork, they become my partners in creation, and my relationship to them is transformed. (p.27)

If a person is needing to create mess and immerse themselves in it, I may offer some space to sound out what I am noticing from them that day – that they seem to be needing a space to be messy, to show me, to feel it and to connect with it. The mess may be a representation of traumatic experiences (Chong, 2015; O'Brien, 2004), and so I will go in with this very tentatively and use my experience to decide if the client needs to stay with the mess or if I need to be ready to offer some room for stabilisation through grounding techniques. Sometimes I explore the process verbally, as if an outsider is looking in and describing what they see. Sometimes the exploration is through the person inviting me into their world, asking me to place my hands in the mess and feel the sensory aspect of what is happening as if I am reliving it with them. Sometimes it can be through the person acting out through play; the art materials become the props, and I become a character in a narrative they are needing to make sense of. Art accesses emotional memories in the brain through sensory arousal (Chong, 2015). It is more of a feeling and a sensing within the process. Art can feel like play. Playing/acting out difficult feelings and life events allows the person to feel slightly removed from the threat/trigger of the actual event, and the art image/scene becomes a stage in which they can reframe their experiences. As trauma specialist Bessel van der Kolk puts it: 'Projecting your inner world into the three-dimensional space of a structure enables you to see what's happening in the theatre of your mind' (2014, p.299).

We are taught the importance of the therapeutic frame in psychotherapy, of providing a session that feels secure and safe for the client by establishing the boundaries of time, the therapy space, confidentiality and our own boundaries. If a person feels safe, secure and emotionally contained in their environment, it allows them to dare to trust, to explore their internal world and for their authentic self to emerge (Rogers, 1967, p.108). In art therapy, the therapeutic frame reaches out further to the materials that we offer clients and our consistency in showing up with the same materials every session. The boundaries can be seen in terms of how much of the art materials someone can use: do I need to let them know the limits to this? The client needs to know where my boundaries are, so they know where it is safe to explore their experiences. I have found that the boundaries I offer as a therapist also support me – I need consistency and predictability; the sameness allows me to see the differences and the patterns that emerge in the session; it allows me to notice the details. Working environments that offer a more secure, structured, scheduled and well-paced day allow me to offer the best version of myself.

It's important to consider how the sessions are contained (Casement, 1985). When we talk about containment, we mean emotional and psychological containment. We provide this through the therapeutic frame. It is also provided through how we model sitting with uncomfortable feelings. Not sitting with discomfort might manifest in actively tidying up the session space with the client present, so indicating it has become too 'messy'. Containment can be the art therapist taking care of the artwork, keeping it safe and confidential. Containment can look like allowing space for paint bottles to be squeezed and for the paint to spill out, but with the client knowing the boundaries of this. Containment can be within the boundaries of the paper/canvas/table – how much can it hold? What is it holding? Is the person testing out how much I can contain for them? Are they stuck with taking up a tiny space in the very centre of the canvas? Do they find it hard to take up space in real life? Or is the boundary hard to make out as the paint covers the edges or spills out onto the floor? The therapist's response will look and feel very different to that of a non-therapist professional, and the outcome of the session will be dramatically different too.

During sessions I feel like all my senses are working in tune with each other harmoniously. This is where I get to really use my hyperfocus to its full advantage. From the initial moment the person steps into the room, I am analysing and observing. I am sensing any transference/countertransference (Joseph, 1985) within the session. I am noticing subtleties in body language and facial expression. This doesn't stop until the person leaves the session. Even once the session is finished, I am processing what feelings I am still holding and my response to how the space and the materials have been left. I can't think of another job where I would get to experience this as part of my role.

In terms of the art process, I will be looking out for the materials the client has selected: how they are chosen, what they use, if they use any tools (e.g. paintbrushes, pens, clay tools), their sensory responses, whether they use materials that connect them physically to the image (e.g. soft pastels, finger painting), the colours they choose, the composition of the work, where they place certain subjects, whether they break the boundaries of the canvas, the neatness/messiness, what they have left out of the image (not just what they've put in) (Levens, 1989, p.145), the order in which they create the image, any metaphorical meaning associated with certain parts of the image, the textures they create, and layers, whether anything has been covered up, have they placed themselves within the image somewhere, have they projected, what developmental age does the art appear to represent, does the image link to any emerging themes, is the image a continuation from previous sessions, how does the client respond to what they may view as 'mistakes', is the person aiming any of the materials and mess at me, is the client inviting me in for joint engagement or are they keeping me as the observer, is the person blocking me somehow with borders/art resources, when would verbalisation be most helpful, if any…? To an outsider looking in, there may be many parts of the session that could look as if we are 'just painting/drawing/sculpting', but there is so much more going on in the room.

I keep sessions as neurodivergent-friendly as I can. As therapists, we are always mindful of how much we disclose to clients. I will offer some self-disclosure about being autistic if I feel it is appropriate and something that the client will gain from. It can be super-helpful when working with neurodivergent clients to open up conversation about sensory needs, that it's okay to use fidget toys in sessions, and that I accept and understand their need for silence to focus, or to get up and stretch from time to time. Many clients really appreciate the space to talk about the experience of being neurodivergent and to de-stigmatise and de-mask. There are many aspects to the sessions that can support neurodivergent people to feel more comfortable in the therapy space: for example, there tends to be minimal eye contact as we are focused on the art in front of us and making art alongside each other (therefore a different mode of connecting). The sensory nature of the work means art materials can often themselves be used for fidgeting with and stimming, and there is less expectation of verbalisation.

Throughout my career as an art therapist, I have continued to practise as an artist. Creating art regularly in my down time can help me to connect myself with my internal world. It offers me a place of exploration between the self and the art image/process. Sometimes I make art in groups alongside the participants. The art that I make in groups is very different from what I would make in my own time. When I am in groups, I am mindful of why I am making art and what the participants could gain from it. I am mindful of how much I could potentially be disclosing in the art and am seeking to find a balance with how much I am okay with sharing at that moment. Sometimes groups are themed, and so I can model an idea of how I interpret the theme to make it feel safe and boundaried for the participants. I have found that, when I make art in sessions, it helps me to process something of what I am feeling in the moment. At work, I can look for any themes that emerge in response to the group or to the given theme. I sometimes name the piece after the session in order to understand it further and establish closure.

My personal art can allow me to go deeper into my subconscious and explore my past, my identity and challenging times. It allows me to communicate my innermost feelings, my vulnerable self. The artwork I make in my own time stays separate from work. This chapter is the first time they are being seen together in one space, and the images I feel comfortable including have been carefully chosen.

> When a painter begins to work on something in the external world, the medium and the imagination work together to produce something not quite as one expected so that the artist has to come to terms with the 'nature inside'. (Case & Dalley, 2006, p.123)

'Sunrise Bringing Peace' (greyscale of colour image) © Fiona Villarreal, 2023

The above image depicts the contentment in my life from meeting my husband in 2023 and being in a relationship full of acceptance and embracement of self. The space within the image feels healthy and refreshing; the home is central and intriguing; the waves of the ocean are gentle and consistent. Having a personal life that allows for me to be myself in turn allows for me to offer so much more in therapy. After all, when we step into the therapy room, we are bringing ourselves, our energy and our presence into the space.

'Children Playing' (greyscale of colour image) © Fiona Villarreal, 2021

The image above was created during the pandemic when there were many layers playing out within group settings. Themes emerged around life/death in multiple ways. There is a sense of isolation and feeling cut off from the 'real' world. I have used oil pastels to frame the piece and create an additional sense of containment.

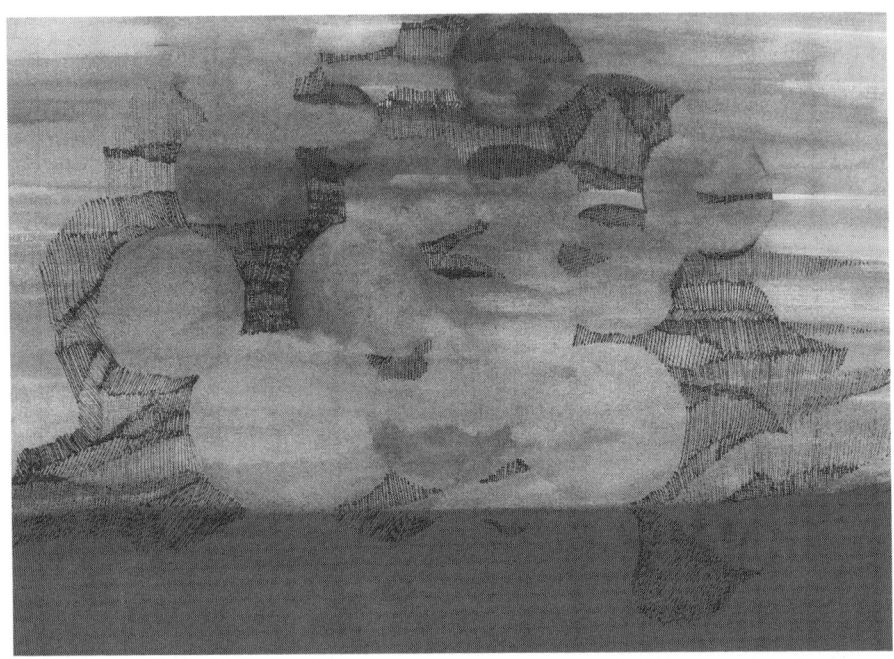

'Clouds Enmeshed' (greyscale of colour image) © Fiona Villarreal, 2023

This image was created earlier than 'Sunrise Bringing Peace' in 2023. It contains heavy emotions, as shown by the fine-liner tangled up around the circular watercolour clouds. The image depicts clouds trapped in web-like structures being weighed down into the deep water below. The art process helped me to sit with, recognise and release feelings of low mood and the experience of feeling stuck/trapped. Being able to use art to release such feelings helps me to process and understand my thoughts, situations and values and gives me a sense of ownership and empowerment of myself and my needs. Art has always been a very cathartic process for me in this way.

'The Container' (greyscale of colour image) © Fiona Villarreal, 2015

I thought I would end the chapter with an image depicting a container. This is a personal piece I created at the very beginning of my art therapy training. The person is holding a vase. The vase contains external 'flaws', as does the person. The person holds the vase awkwardly. We cannot see what is inside the container. Is the vase empty or full? Does the vase hold flowers for celebration or for grief? The container as a metaphor would not be fully realised until my training progressed. The image could represent the very humility that comes with journeying into a career as a therapist – the humbling reminder that, if the therapist is to provide containment to others, they need to equip themselves with a container of their own. Reflecting on this as an autistic therapist, I recognise that I offer the best of my self to my clients if I have the right manager, supervisor or therapist/life coach – one who understands my experience as an autistic individual and can act as that safe and supportive holding space, or container, which in turns allows me to safely express my authentic self.

References

Case, C. & Dalley, T. (2006). *The handbook of art therapy* (2nd ed.). Routledge.

Casement, P. (1985). *On learning from the patient*. Routledge.

Chong, C.Y.J. (2015). Why art psychotherapy? Through the lens of interpersonal neurobiology: The distinctive role of art psychotherapy intervention for clients with early relational trauma. *International Journal of Art Therapy, 20*(3), 118–126. DOI: 10.1080/17454832.2015.1079727

Joseph, B. (1985). Transference: The total situation. *International Journal of Psychoanalysis, 66*, 457–454.

Levens, M. (1989). *Working with defence mechanisms in art therapy*. Routledge.

McNiff, S. (1998). *Trust the process: An artist's guide to letting go*. Shambhala.

O'Brien, F. (2004). The making of mess in art therapy: Attachment, trauma and the brain. *Inscape, 9*(1), 2–13.

Rogers, C.R. (1967). *On becoming a person*. Houghton Mifflin.

Van der Kolk, B. (2014). *The body keeps the score: Mind, brain and body in the transformation of trauma*. Viking.

Chapter 5

Finding what works

Sally Nilsson

I have always been fascinated by people – the way they are and the way they behave. As a child, I would mimic others, and drama has played an important role throughout my life. I mirror others to build rapport, a bit like a chameleon. I know now that I adapted my behaviour from age eight, in order to fit in.

Education was a struggle. I discovered that I shone at art, music, drama and crafts, but struggled with maths and with processing multiple information streams. Once I entered the world of work, I discovered that I could get jobs – interviews were my stage, where I could show off my confidence and play-acting skills – but I could not keep them. Eventually, with two growing children and running my own, one-woman taxi business, I reached a watershed moment and knew I needed a reset. I wrote a book about my great grandfather, and the research for it changed everything.

My great-grandfather was the helmsman on Titanic when she hit the iceberg. He survived, and his life was both extraordinary and tragic. The 100th anniversary of the sinking was in 2012; I was writing in 2010, so I had a deadline, and saw this as just the challenge I needed. Much of the research I did for the biography was about his mental state. He was diagnosed with neurasthenia – PTSD was not recognised as a condition in 1912. It was this research that whetted my appetite to find out more about my own mental health and a growing desire to help others.

I began training as a therapist.

From 2016, I was practising as a hypnotherapist, and from 2018 as a Human Givens practitioner, but I still lacked one essential piece of information. It was another 'reset' that put me on the journey to discovering that piece of information.

In 2020, as the Covid-19 lockdown was lifting, I was approached by a local autistic charity to give mental health support to families who were themselves autistic. This connection sparked my interest in autism. Something was growing in my mind. I felt a familiarity with the autistic experience, but at this stage I couldn't join the dots.

And then, as we entered another lockdown, I broke both my ankles when simply walking out of my front door. Surgery and eight weeks at home recovering meant that I could only see my clients online. It was during this time that I started becoming more aware of my differences and began to believe I might be autistic myself. A colleague had recommended a book called *Divergent Mind* by Jenara Nerenberg (2021). I read it in one day and came away feeling a unique enlightenment. I could see in myself so many traits of autism that I made the decision to seek an assessment. If I was autistic, then I would specialise and 'go niche' with my counselling business.

I found an autistic coach and we worked together for four weeks. I booked an appointment with an autism specialist who was recommended to me, and was asked to write a 20-page account of my life, based loosely around 20 questions. A two-hour appointment followed. Result, I am autistic.

Getting this diagnosis was incredibly important. I had spent such a long time not knowing who I really was. I'd gone through imposter syndrome, grief for the little girl and woman who had felt so alone, so wrong, and feeling I didn't know where I belonged in this world. Now I threw myself into meeting new people, my people. I shouted from the rooftops that I was autistic and ADHD and began the process of changing my website and my directory entries and telling my professional bodies and institutions.

It wasn't long before neurodivergent clients started to book appointments. I was now openly a neurodivergent psychotherapist working with neurodivergent clients, and the rewards for this new work were great. I saw mainly women from age 16 up. Many came to me wanting to know who they were, believing themselves to be on a spectrum. I continued to study, focusing on educating myself, reading and taking courses, attending conferences and webinars and watching all manner of experts, to support me on my quest to help others who were struggling.

Since March 2021, then, I have worked as a neurodivergent psychotherapist and coach for neurodivergent clients. The transition has been all-encompassing. My clients bring many different challenges and the therapeutic support I give has been significantly adapted.

I became convinced that the way I did therapy would also need to change significantly. Every human is different, and every neurodivergent person is even more different in that they bring sensory, processing, communication and alexithymic and interoception challenges that I had not encountered in my non-autistic clients. My Human Givens model and general counselling skills were useful and important, but I needed to adapt and become trained in other models that were more person-centred and humanistic and more geared towards sensory experiences. I also wanted to add to my trauma learning as it was clear that people within the neurodivergent community often lived with trauma all their lives.

What I know now, after hundreds of hours of research and practice, is that I had seen clients in the past who, I now realised, were neurodivergent. I had had no training on neurodiversity. It appeared that models of therapy were being used the same way for every client – a 'one-size-fits-all' approach. I felt sad that I could have helped many more people, had I understood. I couldn't go back but I could move forward to ensure that every new client received tailor-made therapy, no matter whether they were autistic or had ADHD, dyslexia, dyspraxia, dyscalculia, Tourette's or obsessive compulsive disorder, or were otherwise traumatised from living their lives in a world where they felt they didn't fit.

Out went the scripts and the pathologised way of treating the symptoms of stress, anxiety, trauma, addiction and depression.

Now I work with clients who sometimes don't know or can't explain how they feel. They may not recognise when they are hungry, thirsty or in pain. Their emotions may be highly deregulated. They say, in an expressionless voice, that they are terrified of food or think about suicide every day. They report being unable to speak in stressful situations and becoming intolerably anxious about leaving the house in case someone 'out there' talks to them and they don't respond 'correctly'.

I recognise these feelings, and I now have more answers to many of these questions. I understand why I have been the way I am all my life – different, not broken – and I know I can help others like me. How do I do this and what do I do differently from what I did before?

My new approach is a work in progress, but it seems to chime with my neurodivergent clients. I call it MACC, and here is a sketch of how it works.

M = Managing traits

When I say 'managing traits', I do not mean 'changing behaviour'. My autistic clients have many traits, and while some may be benign, others may cause difficulties in everyday life. Through experience and research, I have become familiar with these traits, and we can look at strengths and limitations and find tools and techniques to make the limitations more manageable. For instance, an autistic person may say they struggle to understand other people's feelings. I help clients recognise what other people might be feeling by their body posture and facial expressions, and I have found that this can also help them understand their own mind, body sensations, thoughts and feelings. It is unfortunately still true that neurodivergent people are expected to do most of the understanding and adapting. It is to be hoped that in the future the neurotypical majority will make more of an effort to speak our language and understand our way of being.

Other traits that may be problematic for an autistic client are sleep differences, unusual eating preferences and explosive anger or crying. We can work on turning down the dial and lowering stress levels so that the client has more capacity to cope.

A = Acceptance

Our spectrums and traits are part of who we are as neurodivergent humans. We are different, but we are not broken, diseased, damaged or abnormal.

Acceptance means a lot for clients. They may come to therapy wondering if they may be autistic, and we go on a journey together. When I saw clients in the past, I did not recognise many of the life experiences and traits that now, as a neurodivergent therapist, I can hear and see as likely to come under the neurodivergence umbrella.

It is not for me to assess or diagnose but, gently and over time, we can explore the possibilities of difference, with full acknowledgement that our journey might go in the direction of getting an assessment and diagnosis and the possibility of a new and happier life thereafter. At every one of these steps, neurodivergent people need specialist support and understanding, including a great deal of listening and validation. My previous therapeutic approach would have been inadequate; the Human Givens model of therapy is brief and solution focused. I discovered that this way of supporting clients was not so successful with my neurodivergent clients. The journey is much longer now: previously I was seeing clients for an average of four sessions; I now see them for many months. When these clients come to the end of our therapy journey, they have accepted their differences and have a useful toolbox of techniques to help them not only survive but to thrive and fit in as they choose, without compromising their true identity.

C = Challenges – good and not so good

I'm not keen on words like 'issues', 'problems' and 'difficulties'. I like the word 'challenge' because it can be used positively as well as negatively.

Our emotional needs are very important. In my model of therapy – Human Givens – we work around attention, control, security, community, intimacy, meaning and purpose, privacy, learning and achievement. We use a scaling tool called the Emotional Needs Audit to see which emotions are not being met in balance. It helps us identify and then focus on particular areas where challenges occur.

I have learned some important things as a diagnosed autistic person and as a psychotherapist.

First, anyone can experience mental health challenges, whether they are neurodivergent or not. Bereavement, illness, failure in work or relationships – these can happen to anyone.

Second, neurodivergent people are dealing with these things like everyone else, but we are also dealing with communication difficulties, which tend to be presented as our fault; with sensory sensitivities and social confusion, and with the resulting overwhelm and burnout. We are susceptible to gaslighting from others and to our own perfectionism from a lifetime of receiving the message that we are somehow wrong.

Related to that are the effects of how society views and treats those who are different from the perceived norm. As mentioned above, the onus to conform tends to fall on the shoulders of those who are different, and there is often little support or understanding from the majority.

It is hardly surprising that therapy for our community is particularly complex and requires particular patience and understanding, as well as very specific training and education.

C = Celebrate

My therapeutic work is more productive and beneficial now that I also work as a coach and mentor. It allows me to show clients how they can feel proud, or even just a little happier, about their achievements. I can help them see that their many thoughts and ideas and what they perceive as unusual behaviours are who they are and are natural and okay.

These valued and fascinating clients tell me about their lives. They sometimes dismiss or minimise their achievements or emphasise their failures rather than their successes. They share their experiences of ADHD paralysis and a lifetime of autistic masking. I love to hear about their passions and interests but am struck by how often they cannot see how those interests can be turned into job opportunities or fulfilling hobbies.

No one likes toxic positivity but there are indeed things to be celebrated. Sometimes it may just be a question of shining a light on the hidden depths of what it means to be so wonderfully different.

I mirror my clients to build rapport and help them feel at ease. I actively listen and validate what they tell me. I show them that they are not alone. For me, meeting my new tribe feels like coming home. I feel as if I have returned from a long, arduous journey and, now that I'm home, I can speak my own language, which other neurodivergent people seem to understand without effort. We are a growing culture, and that is something truly worth celebrating.

In the past four years since being diagnosed, I have taken action to educate myself on how to support my clients with all the new things they bring to my therapy room. I will always be learning. I too was ableist and judgemental once. Much of this came from childhood conditioning and from learned experiences and biased teachings.

I realise that many of my judgements came from a place of curiosity. I observed and made judgements as to what I thought was 'normal' and 'correct'. I was wrong. I've had my own therapy to overcome this and have ditched the shame and guilt I have felt for so long.

I am aware that very few counsellors and psychotherapists have any training to work with neurodivergent clients – as, indeed, I had not – and I hope, more than anything, that those who work with neurodivergent people will decide to educate themselves further.

I have never felt so rewarded as I do now in the work I do within my exceptionally varied and wonderful community. I hope that my story will encourage more therapists – perhaps especially other late-diagnosed neurodivergent ones – to actively add to their skill sets and feel empowered to take positive steps for change in the therapy room and beyond.

Reference

Nerenberg, J. (2021). *Divergent mind: Thriving in a world that wasn't designed for you.* HarperOne.

Chapter 6

Art therapy, somatic experiencing and empathy

Chan Shu Yin

The journey of being an art therapist has enriched my life in more ways than one, and it was from this journey that I discovered I was autistic. Like the chicken-and-egg analogy, I feel the strengths of being autistic have been advantageous in my work as art therapist and the converse is also true – the vocation of art therapist has been a good fit for me. Certainly, autism is a wide spectrum, and I can only speak for myself and my presentation. In this chapter, I will share my experience as an autistic art therapist and how it allows me to craft my own career path. I will begin with the context of my practice, and elaborate on my personal route through life and how it has taken me to this unique position. I will expand on the joys and challenges of being an autistic art therapist, and how art therapy as a profession can be beneficial both for the therapist and also for autistic clients.

Background

To begin with some context, I have been working in my own private practice in Singapore for about four years since I graduated from my master's course in art therapy in 2019. Prior to this, I spent 10 years in various careers, each ending in burnout after a few years. Looking back, with my current knowledge of my neurology, it is no wonder that each of those careers ended the way they did.

Like many others who became art therapists, it was my interest in both art and social services that led me to pursue my postgraduate degree in art therapy. In the course of training, my peers and I became familiar with the concept of the wounded healer and how most of us subconsciously found our ways to this profession to heal our own wounds while journeying with others to heal theirs. Even when I graduated, I still did not know much about autism beyond the stereotype, and it was only two years later, in 2021, that I finally received recognition of my autism.

How then did I come to learn of being autistic? I have always felt out of place in groups and never felt like I truly belonged to any clique. When I returned to school as a mature student for my postgraduate studies, it felt like being a teenager again. Even my skin condition resurfaced, due to the emotional stress of having to process my traumas in the course of study. Little did I know that it was also the insidious stress of being a minority, due to my neurodivergence. I did fairly well academically and was a student leader, but felt the undercurrents of constantly being unkindly judged, although I reckon it was not obvious to others; only to me.

In April 2020, just a few months into the COVID-19 pandemic and less than a year since I began my private practice, I drew a cartoon, 'Blue Alien'. I was

'Blue Alien' (ink and watercolour) © Chan Shu Yin, 2020

just beginning my career as an art therapist and the pandemic threw my life into disarray. As a solo freelancer, jobs were being cancelled or suspended with no certainty when they would continue but we still had to pay business costs, such as rental payments, and it was a financially and emotionally trying time. My autistic traits seemed to amplify during this period and I became hyper aware of how different and isolated I felt. However, I still did not know I was autistic when I drew this cartoon.

I had been drawing as long as I could remember; it has been my one constant passion in life. I had worked for more than three years as a 2D visual effects artist in film. Training to be an art therapist had taught me how to use art journalling for self-care. It completely transformed my artistic practice, which was previously focused mostly on the aesthetic product. Becoming an art therapist enabled me to let go of perfection when creating and to enjoy the process. I no longer focused on making only beautiful things as a reflection of my self-worth, and it was with this lens and attitude that I was able to freely create these artworks. Through art journalling, I also uncovered more layers of myself, gaining deeper self-awareness. This was how I slowly and gradually uncovered my autistic self, as it emerged from my drawings.

What I learned from art therapy also enriched my work as an illustrator. It helped me not only to find my own artistic voice and style but also to believe in it. One of the themes I have constantly struggled with is whether to follow my own artistic style or conform to industry standards. I had previously been told my artwork was not commercially sellable, but later realised that I did not lack artistic skill; the challenge was finding collaborators who appreciated my work who would enable me to get published. Partnering with like-minded collaborators has been important in my work as an art therapist as well.

Learning how to let go of perfection enabled me to bring my personal ideas to fruition. This led to me finally having my work published in a children's book and getting commissions. From replicating reality and achieving visual seamlessness as a visual effects artist, I shifted to finding my own voice as an illustrator. This came from embracing the art therapy ethos to focus on the process, express my authentic self and let go of being perfect. It also taught me to trust my own intuition and abilities and to see value in my own artwork – which was easier said than done.

In 2020, about the same time that I drew 'Blue Alien', a good friend was diagnosed as autistic, and it was only then that I started to read and learn more about autism from actual autists, instead of just medical sources. What I learned gradually seemed to make sense as I connected the experiences of other autists with my own memories of struggles. I also found that a significant proportion of clients who sought me out were autistic or had ADHD. As I witnessed them in therapy, I learned more about their personalities and was pleasantly surprised to find that I often resonated with and related to them. As I was learning about them, I was learning about myself too. On a seemingly serendipitous journey, I finally received recognition of my own autism in March 2021, much to my joy and relief. It has been an enriching time since, learning to appreciate myself and my clients more, making better connections and being with a community of neurokin.

'Exhibit' (ink on paper) © Chan Shu Yin, 2021

Prior to discovering my neurology, I had thought that my sensitivity and my struggles were due to my traumas. As there has not been widespread knowledge in Singapore of autistics with relatively low-support needs, like me, no one had ever mentioned the possibility of me being autistic. The extensive personal therapy mandated by the art therapy course had helped me process a lot of my past traumatic experiences, but mostly it seemed to be about me and that I needed to work through my own issues of being overly sensitive. Systemic issues were not acknowledged, and to me it always felt like there was something missing. With hindsight, this lack of knowledge or acknowledgement of systemic issues, in part due to being undiagnosed, led to a form of unintentional gaslighting. It seemed like the onus was on me to stop overthinking and stop being over-sensitive, when in fact others had been prejudiced towards me due to my autistic traits.

Working as an art therapist post-diagnosis

While it is my view that being an art therapist has been a good fit for myself as an autistic person, I would like to acknowledge my privilege in having the resources to pursue education and also to run my own private practice. As freelancing does not provide as much predictability in income as a full-time job, it certainly helps to have fewer financial obligations to reduce the stress of needing to earn more.

It has been shown that autistic people are often unemployed or underemployed, work fewer hours and earn less than neurotypical people and peers with other disabilities (Chiang et al., 2013). Autistic people also struggle to be heard, are frequently unable to choose their career trajectories and tend to be directed by others towards work and goals they don't enjoy or want. Being able to direct one's career is an advantage of being self-employed, and I know of several autists who freelance or run their own business. Being a freelance art therapist enables me to plan my schedule so I can take better care of myself and meet my own needs, which is often not feasible if you are in full-time employment.

What I find rewarding about art therapy are the interactions I have with my clients. Although it is a professional and therapeutic relationship, getting to know my clients at a deeper level and building rapport is very satisfying for me. The joy I get out of these interactions is something that one may not get from most friendships. Discovering that I am autistic has also brought about a shift in my friendships, as personal growth led to me realising what I would like from my friends and how to go about forming more fulfilling relationships. Certainly, therapeutic relationships and friendships are very different, and navigating the boundaries and terms of each continues to be an ongoing process.

Self-determination

How does art therapy enable us to create our own path? In art therapy, the client wields the brush, moulds the clay, holds the pen. Although making art is preverbal, it is this that makes it effective in bottom-up processing – a mode that many autists prefer. When making art, we do not have to know what the finished product will be. We simply have to make a mark or an action, and continue doing it until the piece is done. Through this, we create what we want to, using our bodies and our senses; the reflection and cognitive processing comes later. When we do it often enough, and with the support of the art therapist, we get the sense that we are able to find a way without knowing. It nurtures a sense of being comfortable with uncertainty and also trusting in ourselves and our innate resources and insights. As we autists live in a society not designed for us, our own ways of being may not be externally affirmed, leading to a lack of self-esteem and self-belief. Through art therapy, we can not only discover our authentic self, but we can also build it. This can also be transferred to the career of being an art therapist.

'Exploring New Territories' (ink on paper) © Chan ShuYin, 2021

As postgraduate students, art therapy trainees come from various walks of life. Some are from a psychology or social sciences background; others may be from art backgrounds. There are also people making a mid-career switch from other backgrounds. During art therapy training, students are encouraged to be independent learners. When I was studying, we could specify our choice of client population for our clinical placement, although the actual placement depended on availability of a suitable setting. The role of art therapist in Singapore is currently less established and institutionalised than other roles, such as psychologists or social workers, although the profession is gaining visibility and art therapists are now more common than ever. Trainees and graduates can bring art therapy to a wide variety of new settings. While few full-time positions exist, art therapists who freelance have the benefit of more autonomy as they do not have to navigate the social hierarchies associated with full-time employment in one setting.

In sessions

While many forms of social interaction outside the therapy room may be under- or over-stimulating for me, in the therapy room I operate in a different mode. My senses are focused entirely on the space and what is happening in it and revolve around the client. I am attuned to the client's posture, facial expressions and what is being said and done. Influenced by my training in somatic experiencing, I am also alert to the client's states of activation, which signal to me how their nervous system is responding and cue me into what I might say or do next. There is a rough script to follow, and an overall flow that I am looking for, as I guide the client through what they might have to process, with pauses for them to ground themselves and pendulate – to approach the traumatic experience or memory in such a way as not to be triggered or overwhelmed. Neuro-developmental art therapy (Chapman, 2002, 2003) underpins my work.

Although my first and main psychotherapy training was in art therapy, I often use somatic experiencing techniques to help guide the client to process what they have expressed through the art-making. While observing the client, I am simultaneously observing my own body's reactions and they give me a clue to what the client might be experiencing. Hence, therapy work is a full embodied experience for myself and the client. We use the SIBAM model by Peter Levine (2010), exploring Sensation, Image, Behaviour, Affect and Meaning, to help the client in bottom-up processing and to feel more integrated. More top-down forms of therapy work for some people, but not for everyone; this way of working helps the client feel regulated and integrated without having to find a cognitive resolution to the issue. Often, learning to regulate through co-regulation and in turn developing the resources to sit with one's emotions and discomfort are what the client needs, more than more cognitive processing. According to Price (2022), many autistic people prefer bottom-up processing over more cognitive top-down processing. Art therapy works on bottom-up processing.

The stereotype that autistic people have no empathy couldn't be farther from the truth. I often feel highly empathetic and can feel the client's emotions viscerally in my own body. Perhaps keen observation of details, good pattern-recognition skills and the ability to look past social hierarchies allow me to see the person for who they are, beneath their social mask.

It has been shown that the biggest predictor of success in therapy is the client's perception of the quality of the therapeutic relationship (Horvath,

2001). Neurodivergent clients seem to gravitate to my private practice, and sometimes clients who stay with me for longer also end up discovering their own neurodivergence. Sometimes a client will end up not being a good fit, but this usually reveals itself early on in the therapy. If this happens, it may activate my rejection sensitivity and prompt feelings of abandonment, which are common experiences for many autistics. It helps to remind myself that I do not have to be a good fit for everyone, and not to take it personally.

Managing challenges

Being an art therapist definitely has its challenges, and focusing only on the positives would not provide a fair and holistic view. First, working in mental health settings would require many autistics to manage energy, sensory and emotional overwhelm. Although allistics have to do this too, autistics are hypersensitive and so need to focus on this more and ensure they have a caseload that they can manage. Some art therapists balance their therapy work with other less demanding work, such as art commissions or other part-time work. Personally, taking on illustration jobs alongside with my therapy work provides a good balance between working in isolation and interacting with others. Doing illustration work sparks my creativity and gets me in a flow state, while recharging my social battery. Therapy work helps me feel a sense of deep connectedness and satisfaction from uplifting others' wellbeing. As therapeutic work requires my full presence and action in the session, I make sure I allocate sufficient time afterwards to rest and rejuvenate.

'Earthing' (ink on paper) © Chan Shu Yin, 2021

Different kinds of therapy work, such as individual and group therapy, also require different sets of skills, with the latter demanding more logistical planning and facilitation. Knowing which kinds of work you prefer is helpful when planning your work schedule. It's also important to schedule in buffer time between sessions, and to allow mental space for unexpected changes. I found adopting an attitude of letting go of what I cannot control and focusing on what I can helped me cope with uncertainty. Receiving training in somatic experiencing has also helped me regulate my emotions, pay attention to my bodily sensations and hold better boundaries.

Boundaries are important for all therapists to observe, but even more so for autistic therapists, due to our sensitivity and our impartiality towards social hierarchies. Similarly, reflecting on the transference with clients, their caregivers, colleagues and other collaborators can be helpful for understanding the relational dynamics in our interactions.

When working with clients of the same neurotype, autistic therapists or therapists with ADHD often resonate strongly with the struggles and joys of clients. To allistic peers, this might come across as projective identification, and may be frowned upon. Just as with allistics, autistic therapists can benefit from our own personal therapy to ensure we are working on our own issues and do not become enmeshed with the client. Neurodivergent therapists have to carefully navigate the fine line and intersections between being a mental health practitioner and a neuro-kin with lived experience. At times, it may be hard for neurotypical practitioners to fully grasp or accept how much insight into our clients' experiences may come from having similar lived experience. Other professionals may even discount the inherent value of lived experience, and instead defer to outdated medical definitions and perspectives of autism. This is an area that many neurodivergent therapists continue to grapple with. Revealing our own neurotype to our peers could even be unsafe if there is lack of understanding. Interactions with other peers in the course of work can also be strained due to differences in communication and ways of working. As an autistic therapist, I have to constantly remind myself not to take things personally, that any friction with peers could simply be due to differences in neurotype, and that no one is to blame for these challenges.

I cannot overstate the value of having understanding and supportive collaborators and supervisors, especially for autistic art therapists. For freelancers, there is the freedom and flexibility to focus on collaborating more with other like-minded people. How much the art therapist's work is valued largely depends on the supervisor, since art therapy is not yet an established modality in many settings. At times, the art therapist's work may be less valued than verbal forms of therapy, such as counselling, especially when there is an in-house counsellor within the organisation or service, or when institutional dynamics are at play. However, in other settings, the non-verbal aspect of art therapy may be more valued, such as when working with autistic clients, children, or stroke survivors. Freelancing can feel lonely at times, and it can be helpful to channel our socialising or networking efforts towards like-minded neurodivergent people who share similar interests. This could be explained by Milton's double empathy theory (2012) that people of similar neurology understand each other better. This is not to say that an autistic therapist can only work well with autistic clients. While a number of my clients are autistic or have ADHD, a large number are not and do not. Perhaps having lived in a majority neuronormative society, having had to learn its ways to accommodate to others and learning about psychology have helped. Also, the social rules and hierarchies in a clinical setting differ from those in a social setting.

Planning your career path so your client groups and work suit your own areas of interest, personality and ways of working is helpful. At times, this happens in an organic manner, just as people of a certain disposition tend to be drawn to certain kinds of work and with likeminded people. It is also not surprising that such people might share similar neurotypes. Autistic therapists may be drawn to work with autistic clients, or clients with relationship trauma, due to our own experience with complex trauma from belonging to a minority neurotype.

It is, I think, important that autistic therapists do not compare their career and achievements with those of their allistic peers and peers in other mental health professions. It is essential to honour our own ways of working and not measure our self-worth by the number of hours we work and how much we earn. While being financially sustainable is definitely something we want to work towards, we also need to recognise that our brains may be driven by our special interests. Honouring our needs to build our work around our interests would enable us to sustain our career in the longer run and not burn out from boredom or fatigue. It would be ideal if we could find ways to weave play into our work, and art therapy offers many opportunities to do so. Honouring our energy levels also means recognising that our interest and vitality modulates organically in peaks and troughs. Allowing for periods of rest and play following a period of hyperfocus could be more suitable for us than following a rigid 9-to-6 regime. Some autistic therapists will work best when following a routine; some prefer to have some room for spontaneity. It may take some time and experimenting to figure out what works well for you.

Last, I believe it helps to have interests that are completely unrelated to the work. This allows for a sense of play and enjoyment untouched by capitalistic pressures to earn a living and make money. Knitting is a structured, repetitive activity and a socially-accepted stim that helps me destress from the emotional demands of psychotherapy. Knitting offers a complete contrast from the uncertainty of freelancing, and creating a garment from scratch also nurtures a sense that I am doing something useful in my downtime.

'Self-care' (ink on paper) © Chan Shu Yin, 2021

I discovered my autistic identity through my journey of becoming an art therapist. I continue developing my work with clients through my own lived experience, learning more about myself and what works for both me and my clients through a reciprocal feedback loop. I am not simply 'helping' or 'healing' my clients; I am also helped and healed by them and the energy they bring to the sessions. I am a work in progress and so is my work, and at the end of the day, as clichéd as it may be, the work is about learning to 'trust the process', as we do when making art (McNiff, 1998).

As Callum Stephen writes (2022):

> Despite the fact that society likes to categorise autistic people as out-of-the-box thinkers, many of us have expressed that in some situations we don't even consider anything connected to the box. The box isn't in our line of vision and we are not inside or outside of it. How can we be, if we are tied up with masking, sensory overload and the challenges of being a minority? When it comes to opportunities, I can tell that it does not occur to a lot of us to seek them out.

'The Box' (ink on paper) © Chan ShuYin, 2022

References

Chapman, L. (2002). A neuro-developmental approach to treating post-traumatic stress disorder and symptoms. In *Proceedings of the 33rd Annual Conference of the American Art Therapy Association* (p. 106). American Art Therapy Association.

Chapman, L. (2003). Neuro-developmental art therapy: Treating acute and chronic post-traumatic stress disorder and symptoms. In *Proceedings of the 34th Annual Conference of the American Art Therapy Association*. American Art Therapy Association.

Chiang, H.M., Cheung, Y.K., Li, H. & Tsai, L. (2013). Factors associated with participation in employment for high school leavers with autism. *Journal of Autism & Developmental Disorders, 43*, 1832–1842. https://doi.org/10.1007/s10803-012-1734-2

Horvath, A.O. (2001). The alliance. *Psychotherapy: Theory, research, practice, training, 38*(4), 365–372.

Levine, P.A. (2010). *In an unspoken voice: How the body releases trauma and restores goodness*. North Atlantic Books.

McNiff, S. (1998). *Trust the process: An artist's guide to letting go*. Shambhala.

Milton, D.E.M. (2012). On the ontological status of autism: The 'double empathy problem'. *Disability & Society, 27*(6), 883–887.

Price, D. (2022). *Unmasking autism: Discovering the new faces of neurodiversity*. Penguin Random House.

Stephen, C. (2022, March 23). *Autism and opportunities*. Instagram. https://www.instagram.com/autistic_callum_

SECTION B

To be that self which one truly is

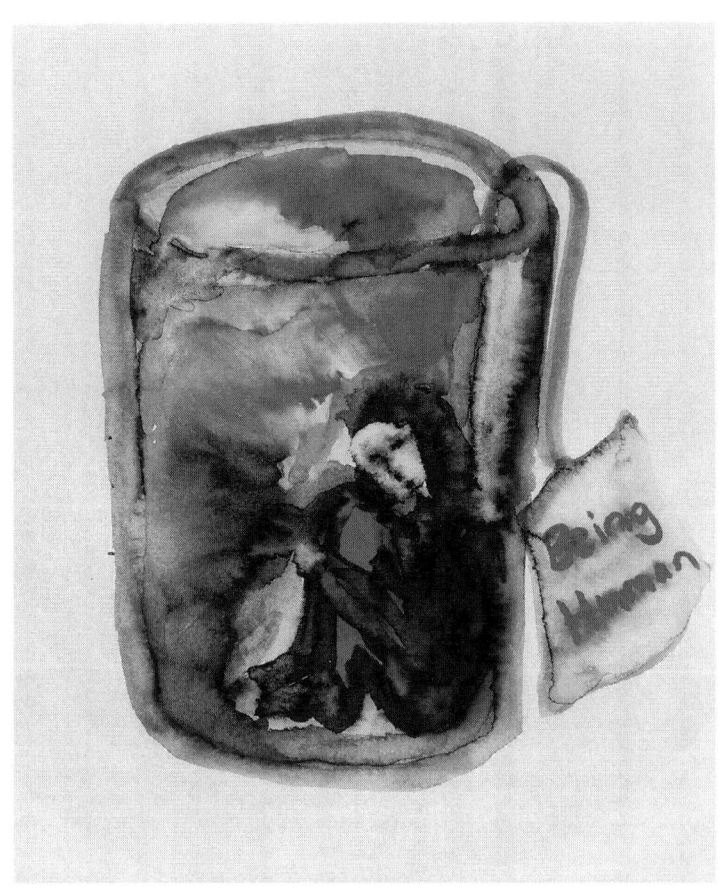

'Burnout' (watercolour on paper – greyscale image from colour)
© Elinor Rowlands

Introduction

As Carl Rogers (1961) said:

> The best way I can state this aim of life, as I see it coming to light in my relationship with my clients, is to use the words of Søren Kierkegaard – 'to be that self which one truly is'. (p.166)

If we are to create the environment in which our clients can move towards becoming the self they truly are, surely we have to do that work first.

That is an ambitious project for any human being, but especially for people who have, since their earliest memories, been given the message that they are somehow unacceptable. Leo Ricketts (Chapter 8) sums it up as: 'Don't be you.' As he reminds us, the essential element in therapy is not the modality but the quality of relationship. And a high-quality therapeutic relationship requires us to be who we are: to be congruent, to grow past those negative messages we have received.

In Natalie Furdek's words (Chapter 7), to be a 'good counsellor':

> I needed to have congruence in my own life and mind... congruence is the degree to which a person's behaviour is consistent with their inner self. In other words, it is the extent to which a person is able to be genuine, authentic and true to themselves in their interactions with others. Because I did not know my neurotype, there was absolutely no way for me to be congruent. I was a masked mess, my outsides rarely matching my insides.

Silvia Liu (Chapter 10) describes how, throughout the first part of her life and career, she felt her true self was rejected – and, indeed, she rejected it herself. She learned and used techniques to help others 'mask themselves to neurotypical standards, so as to make them more acceptable in society', and did the same for herself. For a long time, she trusted the research that said these techniques worked. Except, she says, that they don't. What works is radical acceptance: of others and of oneself. Only if we have the courage (and the vulnerability) to be ourselves can we show our clients that they can do the same. When a person has grown up with the message that they somehow have to be other than they are, that the self they truly are is somehow broken or undesirable, it is extraordinarily powerful to meet a therapist who is like them, and happy to be so. Instead of responding with mystification or disapproval, the therapist just says 'Yes'.

But that radical acceptance is not always easy, because there are genuinely things in us that remain difficult to live with, that remain hard to disclose and that perhaps make being a therapist difficult. It might be the meltdowns that come from overwhelm that Debbie Luck describes (Chapter 11); the effects of developmental trauma reported by Wendy Reiersen (Chapter 9); the incremental effects of belonging to more than one minority (Sharon Xie, Chapter 12), or even the clash between the autistic sense of justice and what can seem to us like a disregarding or dismissing of our core values. Writing about the autistic need for justice that she identifies in herself, Shirley Moore (Chapter 14) says:

> The more I do this kind of work and the more I recognise neurodivergence in the people I come across in these difficult situations, the more interested I am in the links between autism, moral injury, grievances and whistleblowing.

So how much of our own experience should we disclose? The criterion must always be what will be to the advantage of the client, and that is not always easy to judge.

But if our intention is to provide an environment of safety and trust for our clients to become the selves they truly are, then we, as therapists, must model that. Our main client group is one that has learned that their self must be hidden and has learned not to trust. In my own Chapter 13, I argue that boundaried self-disclosure, rather than being something to avoid, becomes one of the most important channels for that safety and trust.

Max Marnau

Reference

Rogers, C. (1961). *On becoming a person*. Houghton Mifflin.

Chapter 7

Finding congruence

Natalie Furdek

I lived for almost 50 years before I knew I was autistic. This chapter isn't meant to discuss all that this entailed, but it is meant to show how a career in counselling might unfold under those circumstances, and how it can flourish once a person knows their neurotype.

I was always fascinated with psychology and how the mind works. It's true that many autistic people look to television and other characters for examples of how to carry themselves, and my primary archetypes in early adulthood were the forensic psychologists on television shows. I never joined the United States Federal Bureau of Investigations as a 'profiler', but I did eventually obtain a master's level education, and in 2002 became a professional counsellor, licensed for independent practice in the State of Texas.

Early career and struggles with in-person service delivery

I was 31 years old and a single mother (with good support, I must admit, including that of my son's father) by the time I was fully licensed. My first job was at a well-funded, non-profit community counselling centre that was part a large hospital system. I had a nice office, great colleagues and a caseload of people who really needed help, could not afford it, and did not have to pay a dime for it. It was a utopian environment, as far as I was concerned.

And yet, three years later, I had become so unhappy that I resigned to take another position in the county's criminal justice system. I told my manager that I was seeking more experience in programme management, but my internal goal was to move away from direct service provision. For two decades, I looked back at this decision as the worst career move of my life. Now, I look back and can understand why I felt I had to leave.

The main reason I was so uncomfortable was the sessions themselves. I enjoyed the clients and loved the interdisciplinary teamwork. But I found sitting in the actual sessions with clients very difficult. Holding my feet and hands still was a constant preoccupation, and I just generally felt 'trapped' for those 50 minutes, even with my 'favourite' clients. At the time, I didn't have a framework for understanding that difficulty, and I created a narrative in my head that said I simply wasn't built for direct service provision and was 'no good' at it.

The final straw came when the centre hired a person I knew from my childhood as its receptionist. She was not a problematic figure at all in my earlier life, but she came to be very demanding and parental with me at work. It was infuriating to me each time she gave me 'an order' or approached me with tasks. I became an angrier person around the office and began looking for another job as a result.

From my vantage point now, I can see my autisticness playing out clearly. I describe myself now as basically 'allergic' to people being too close to me, and I relate to the demand avoidance that is common in autistics. In the medical model, it is known as 'pathological demand avoidance', or PDA, but I prefer the phrase 'persistent drive for autonomy' (Wilding, 2020).

However, there is a deeper truth I have faced in recent years about this. As a client-centred therapist (still to this day, in fact), in order for me to have been a 'good counsellor' at the time, I needed to have congruence in my own life and mind. According to Carl Rogers, a pioneer of client-centred therapy, congruence is the degree to which a person's behaviour is consistent with their inner self (1951). In other words, it is the extent to which a person is able to be genuine, authentic and true to themselves in their interactions with others. Because I did not know my neurotype, there was absolutely no way for me to be congruent. I was a masked mess, my outsides rarely matching my insides.

Disengagement from therapy practice

For the next two decades, I pursued other career paths: programme management, assessment and referral services, and finally, for 14 years, behavioural health policy work with the State of Texas. I was designated the state's 'subject matter expert' for several topic areas, ranging from women with substance abuse problems to infant mortality.

Often, in all these environments, someone would ask me why I didn't offer therapy. Every time, my answer was some variation of, 'I'm not a very good counsellor'.

Of course, my autism was with me in those jobs as well. I lost one job because I told a carelessly bad joke. In my policy work for the state, I was routinely called into my manager's office because someone had been again offended by my words or *tone*. I abruptly walked away from a 14-year career with the state because of my well-formed sense of justice and fairness, after reporting unethical behaviour (as required by state law, due to my position) and getting no response. My career 'path' looks rather similar to that of a tornado.

Luckily, during those two decades, I had also maintained my professional counsellor licensure requirements. So, in early 2019, in a true 'I-don't-know-I'm-autistic' meltdown, I gave a mere two weeks' notice and cashed out my retirement account. I decided to use the money to rent office space and establish a therapy caseload. It's important to note that, at this stage, I still thought I was a terrible counsellor. I also still had no idea I was autistic, although I knew there was 'definitely something wrong with me'.

Post-Covid-19 online counselling

In another reality, my departure from employment with the State of Texas might have earned the title of 'the worst career move of my life', because I truly did not have a very good plan, in hindsight. I would have returned to the very circumstances I was in at the start of my career: working at close quarters with clients and masking my need to be in motion, especially when talking to another person.

As I was starting my practice, Covid-19 had not yet come to bear on our society, but it would, just a few months later. As I searched for a good place for an office and investigated indemnity insurance, I found several online counselling sites. My work at the state had conditioned me to believe online services were sub-par. We would rarely fund anything other than in-person services.

I began working online anyway, and soon I was making a little bit of money. Referrals were a trickle because online counselling wasn't the viral success it is today. But for the first time I felt comfortable during sessions!

A few months later, the Covid-19 pandemic changed our world by driving many of us online for our social and business needs as we tried to avoid the virus. Suddenly, online counselling was popular! Immediately, I was working full-time and making more than enough to support myself and thrive financially. I was riddled with anxiety, though – what I would do when the pandemic was over and things 'went back to normal'?

I was anxious about that mainly because of how much I came to love providing counselling online. I was in the comfort of my own home, with my pets, appropriately dressed from the waist up but still in my pyjama bottoms and slippers. I could load the dishwasher between sessions. It didn't matter what my legs or hands were doing, as long as I kept them off screen. I could look at the person's face and eyes and they could look back, but the laser-like burn of eye-to-eye contact wasn't there.

A good number of my clients preferred (and this hasn't changed post-Covid) audio sessions, which are my favourite as well. Audio means I can pace, let my face relax, sneak a snack, pet my dog and cats, or watch the birds outside, all while being present with the client – and they likely do the same. Autistic communication relies less on non-verbal clues in conversation; autistic people can communicate with each other just as well as non-autistic people can communicate with their peers (Crompton, et al., 2020). Audio sessions can help some clients unmask more fully, which helps us both focus on the conversation at hand.

But while I finally felt the comfort of achieving true autonomy within the domain of supporting myself, I was not yet any closer to true congruence with myself. I wasn't aware of the underlying reasons all these changes were so helpful.

Finding autism

I had been in therapy periodically for my whole adult life. Starting from my teenage years, I often returned to therapy to work on depression and anxiety, each time hoping to get to the root of my troubles. I worked through my traumas, worked through them again, and then again. I worked on my beliefs about myself and my worth, again and again. But I was never able to answer that core question driving the anxiety and depression: 'What is the matter with me?'

Ironically, there was a moment when a therapist offered me the truth and I could not accept the gift: did I think I might be autistic? This was more than 20 years ago, before the American Psychiatric Association expanded its diagnostic criteria for autism in *DSM-5* (APA, 2013) (which essentially added more comprehensive sets of symptoms and allowed more people to be identified). My internal response to the question was to dismiss it out of hand, based on what I knew about autism at the time. I remember being offended and deliberately dismissive. I think it's critical to note that, at the time, there was no language available to therapists (especially to those of us in places like Texas) about neurodiversity; no way to explain to someone that autism isn't a 'bad thing to have'.

I reflect on this a lot – would things have turned out differently for me had I listened to that therapist? Would I have found communities of autistic people who had embraced themselves, as we can find now? How long would it have taken me to find the neurodiversity movement and the healing perspective we have today?

Those questions don't have answers, of course. But as I worked online during the pandemic, and my caseload matured, I found myself with a 'certain kind of client' quite often. They were usually women or transgender people, depressed and anxious, lots of relationship and employment troubles, all generally making the same accusations of themselves that I did of myself: 'Something is wrong with me.' I worked well with these clients; rapport seemed to come very easily.

Several months before my 50th birthday in 2021, two clients joined my caseload. Both were women with formal autism diagnoses. As I listened to these two clients, I noticed immediately that they were just like many of my other clients. Mortified that I might have a caseload of autistic people and not know it, I immediately began learning. I consulted with other professionals and took a certification course that presented autism as a pathology. I began having discussions with some of my other clients and conducting screenings to check if they needed to be referred for assessment for autism. Some went on to be formally diagnosed; many others ended up self-diagnosing, for various reasons.

In doing the screenings, I found myself in the scores too. Regardless of the tool I used, I was scoring very high, and eventually I began the process of pursuing my own formal diagnosis.

In my 'autism-is-pathology' training, there was a moment – only 37 seconds, actually – where neurodiversity concepts were mentioned. The trainer presented something so profound for me that I recorded those 37 seconds and began playing them to my clients. We were invited to consider that autism is a normal manifestation of the human genome, that we are not broken and do not need fixing. These concepts were immediately meaningful to me, and I wanted to know more.

I read two books – *Neurotribes* by Steve Silberman (2015) and *Neuroqueer Heresies* by Nick Walker (2021). I read several more, but these two shaped me and corrected my understanding of autism and its history. *Neurotribes* explained to me how in the world we, as a society, could have been so clueless for so long about autism. *Neuroqueer Heresies* gave me the permission, courage and empowerment I needed to speak out against the pathology model – and the proper language and vocabulary with which to do it.

Still, I had one doubt left to conquer: How can an autistic person (who also has alexithymia, mind you) be a 'good counsellor'? Is that possible or was I deceiving myself (and my clients)? I needed to dispel more myths in my mind.

After joining the Autistic Counsellors and Psychotherapists Facebook group (the crew writing this book), I had access to people who could answer questions like 'What's with autistic theory of mind and empathy?' with responses like 'Read about the double empathy problem' (Milton, 2012). Highbrow stuff, but straightening out each autistic myth, one after another, was healing, not just for me but for my clients as well.

My future feels good now

There are early studies (Kaku et al., 2021; Johnsson et al., 2019) from the time of the pandemic that are starting to show that online services for autistic people are well received. There's very little good research on autistic adults, but we do know that historically we have not been highly engaged in therapy (Crane et al., 2019; Brede et al., 2022). I believe and hope that further research covering the past few years will show this is starting to change. I believe the fact that I had a caseload of autistic people before I even knew what autism really was shows that the online method improves access.

Online services are great for me as an autistic counsellor, but clients benefit greatly as well. We can be home with our pets and other comforts; we avoid traffic and other logistical barriers; travel problems don't mean we miss sessions… the list of advantages goes on and on.

I think another reason why more autistic people are and will be accessing therapy is that online working means it is much easier to find autistic therapists. And that makes a huge difference to people's ability to engage. My career shows that, even before we know a client (or therapist) is autistic, there's a rapport that's just easier to establish. And once we do know? Wow, that's when the fun can start, and we can really begin to heal depressive and anxious beliefs. It's not always easy work, though, of course.

Because of the exhaustion associated with masking when working with neurotypical clients, I now market to and accept neurodivergent clients exclusively, as of late 2022. When I'm working with autistic and ADHD clients, I feel energised and enriched by our therapy and our ability to use our common 'dialect'.

There's a common saying that often makes the rounds on social media: 'Build a life that doesn't hurt.' This is my mantra since discovering autism. I've since taken a lot of other steps in the other domains of my life to stop hurting. But being able to achieve this in the domain of work has been something I never thought possible.

My work environment does not hurt. Doing therapy with my clients does not hurt. For the first time, work is sustainable. I haven't done 'retirement maths' (as in, how-many-more-years-do-I-have-to-do-this maths) in several years. But more importantly, I know what congruence feels like – in therapy sessions and outside of them as well. I 'found myself' and 'know myself' and 'have self-compassion' and actually understand what those words mean and feel like now. And I get to help clients do that for themselves as well.

References

American Psychiatric Association. (2013). *Diagnostic and statistical manual of mental disorders* (5th ed.) (DSM-5). APA.

Brede, J., Cage, E., Trott, J. & Palmer, L. (February 2022). 'We have to try to find a way, a clinical bridge' – autistic adults' experience of accessing and receiving support for mental health difficulties: A systematic review and thematic meta-synthesis. *Clinical Psychology Review, 93*, 102131. doi: 10.1016/j.cpr.2022.102131

Crane, L., Adams, F., Harper, G., Welch, J. & Pellicano, E. (2019). 'Something needs to change': Mental health experiences of young autistic adults in England. *Autism, 23*(2), 477–493. https://doi.org/10.1177/1362361318757048

Crompton, C.J., Ropar, D., Evans-Williams, C.V.M., Flynn, E.G. & Fletcher-Watson, S. (2020). Autistic peer-to-peer information transfer is highly effective. *Autism, 24*(7), 1704–1712.

Johnsson, G., Kerslake, R. & Crook, S. (2019). Delivering allied health services to regional and remote participants on the autism spectrum via videoconferencing technology: Lessons learned. *Rural and Remote Health, 19*, 5358. https://doi.org/10.22605/RRH5358

Kaku, S.M., Chandran, S., Roopa, N., Choudhary, A., Ramesh, J., Somashekariah, S., Kuduvalli, S., Rao, V.S. & Mysore, A. (2021). Coping with autism during lockdown period of the COVID-19 pandemic: A cross-sectional survey. *Indian Journal of Psychiatry, 63*(6), 568–574. https://doi.org/10.4103/indianjpsychiatry.indianjpsychiatry_344_21

Milton, D. (2012). On the ontological status of autism: The 'double empathy problem'. *Disability and Society, 27*(6), 883–887.

Rogers, C.R. (1951). *On becoming a person: A therapist's view of psychotherapy*. Houghton Mifflin.

Silberman, S. (2015). *Neurotribes: The legacy of autism and the future of neurodiversity*. Avery.

Walker, N. (2021). *Neuroqueer heresies: Notes on the neurodiversity paradigm, autistic empowerment, and postnormal possibilities*. Autonomous Press.

Wilding, T. (2020, April 4). *Changing the name PDA*. [Blog.] Tomlin Wilding. http://tomlinwilding.com/changing-the-name-pda/

Chapter 8

Don't be you

Leo Ricketts

The clues were always there. My Facebook page just reminded me of a status I posted 12 years ago, when a friend arranged a surprise day out for me and her husband: 'Leo is nervous. I don't mind surprises at all. So long as I know what they are, when they're going to happen and how much I'll like it.'

So, if you don't mind, I'll begin by quoting myself. On my website, it says:

> The relational approach emphasises the relationship between client and therapist as central to the therapeutic work and focuses on connectedness to others. I believe that, in order for a person to be emotionally healthy, they must maintain fulfilling and satisfying relationships with those around them. My client and I work together to forge a strong, uplifting and secure relationship that can serve as a model for future relationships the client will strive to develop. (Ricketts, n.d.)

I wrote that when I launched my private practice in 2015. I was completing my training in relational transactional analysis, and I wanted people to understand the importance I place on relationships in my work. When I meet a client for the first time, there are two things I always tell them about how I work.

First, the aim of therapy isn't happiness. The aim is to spend as much time as possible being okay. Happiness is an occasional side effect of being mostly okay. Second, when we work together, we form and develop a relationship. It's an intimate relationship because we will talk about intimate things, and hopefully build warmth and trust so we can be okay (see? There it is already) talking comfortably and honestly about our deepest feelings and darkest thoughts. That relationship is not a side effect of our work; it's the principal therapeutic tool.

An autistic relational therapist?

In 2015, I had no relationship with the words neurodiverse, neurotypical and executive function, and only a broad and shallow understanding of ADHD, dyslexia, dyspraxia and the other neurodivergent ways of being. I knew a little bit more about obsessive compulsive disorder (OCD) as I was convinced (correctly) that I'd lived with that since being a small child.

I also had a better understanding of what being autistic meant. I always 'got' autistic people when I met them or heard them talk on the radio or saw TV documentaries about them.

Them. I thought 'them' because, even though I related so much to those people, I held stereotypes about autists that ruled me out for that particular label. Every online test I did placed me much closer to autistic than 'typical', but outside of a likely diagnosis: I'm sociable; I can form and maintain relationships; I can make and hold eye contact.

As my practice developed, I worked more with neurodivergent people in general, and autistic people in particular. Not only did I click with them in a way that seemed meaningful, but I also became increasingly sure that I *was* one of them. I didn't just understand and empathise with their experiences of the world; I shared their experiences. I spoke to my partner – also a therapist – and she echoed and supported my self-diagnosis.

In 2022, I worked with a client going through a psychological assessment for dyspraxia. Their experience of their psychologist sounded so warm and positive that I contacted him myself and began my own assessment to confirm what I now knew – that I was autistic.

Not only was that strongly confirmed, but I also received an unexpected bonus prize: I'm also ADHD. That wasn't on my radar. This very common combination is sometimes written as AuDHD, and that's how I describe my way of being, although in this chapter I use the terms AuDHD, autist and autistic about myself, as it is my autistic experience that has so far dominated my life. ADHD makes sense to me, but I'm still trying it for size and wearing it in.

It's fascinating to me that, in my own life, friends and family have all been surprised by the news that I'm autistic, but precisely no one has been taken aback by the ADHD bit. That, apparently, has always been visible. Not to me. Perhaps because I was so aware of my autistic self, I got really good at disguising it so I might fit in better. I wasn't thinking about hyperactivity or inattentiveness, so I didn't know that I should try and hide it.

Confirmation bias?

I got my Shiny Piece of Paper – my diagnosis – six months ago (at the time of writing). Since then, the proportion of neurodivergent clients in my practice has shot up to 85%. The thing is, only about half of that increase is down to new clients seeking out an autistic therapist. The rest is made up of existing clients exploring their own neurodivergence, some of whom have been working with me for several years.

What's going on? Integrity, accuracy and objectivity are three gifts my autistic brain has insisted I focus on. For a while, I was concerned that my new label meant I was subconsciously passing on to my clients the idea of possible neurodivergence. Was I leading some of my clients down a neurodivergent path, just because I was somehow fired up about my own AuDHD self?

I was fastidious about not talking about neurodiversity in therapy sessions unless my client explicitly brought it up first. But there it was. Seemingly all of a sudden, a bunch of my clients suddenly told me that they'd been thinking about whether they were autistic or dyspraxic or ADHD, often for some years.

I talked about this with my own therapist and with my supervisor, both of whom I've worked with for almost 10 years. They both told me the same thing, and it's changed how I see my practice and my identity as an autistic therapist. These clients have stayed with me because of the relationships we have built together; the strength and depth of those relationships will be down to how we relate to each other, at least at a subconscious level, and how we relate to each other is all about the neurodivergence we share. The 'neurodivergent click' is real.

I decided to come out as an AuDHD therapist.

Man up

We get the clients we need. Or deserve. This is a cliché you hear throughout training, and it keeps happening, seemingly all by itself. In my practice, I have always seen a lot of people who identify themselves as queer. That may be around sexuality, gender, relationship models, neurotype or any combination of those. If I have to nail some labels on myself, I'm a cisgender male, heterosexual and married to a woman. Superficially at least, the word queer is not one that people would apply to me.

Why then do my therapeutic relationships with clients who identify as queer develop as quickly and deeply as those with my autistic clients, and feel as easy and comfortable? This came to make more sense to me when I was considering how public to be about my autism. The phrase I heard people using to describe revealing their autistic self was 'coming out'. This connection to queerness feels natural and comfortable.

Growing up as an autistic kid but not knowing it meant that I felt different – really different – in ways I didn't understand. Some of the differences were clearly visible to other kids and I was often ridiculed and bullied for them. I felt that I didn't fit in with most others. They all seemed to feel comfortable in their own skin and in the world, and I felt comfortable in neither.

Where I could see differences, I spent huge amounts of energy in trying to make them invisible. I learned to make the right faces, be funny, and defer to bullies so they'd like me and not hurt me. I learned never to let on that nothing made sense to me.

One thing above all jarred. There were certain things I was supposed to do, say and think because I was a boy. I should be competitive and argumentative. I should enjoy ridicule, physical toughness and even violence. I should be ruder than girls, preferably dismissive of them, and be able to respond with aggression if challenged. Not only could I do none of these things; they simply made zero sense to me. What had any of that got to do with whether I stood or sat to pee?

Add to this my lack of physical presence. As a 'grown man', I am five-foot-three inches tall. As a kid, I was exceptionally short and looked several years younger than I was. I had long hair and was regularly asked whether I was a boy or a girl.

For 55 years, I held all of these differences, puzzles and discomforts without being able to name them or have any context for them. You might understand then why finally having solid answers and contexts for those experiences and feelings was so powerful, and why, in expressing my difference and it becoming a visible core of my identity – personally and as a therapist – the words 'coming out' have felt right.

Neuroqueer

I am beginning to explore the word neuroqueer. There are a number of different definitions floating about, and these will probably coalesce in time. Or they will expand and spawn subsets. Who knows? As I understand it today, the word describes the experience of one's neurodivergence – in my case, being AuDHD – and expressing it in ways that challenge accepted norms around sexuality, gender and neuronormativity. All of this resonates with me and with my practice.

Gender dysphoria – feeling like the body you were born with is at odds with your gender identity – isn't something I experience. I'm 'okay' (there it is again) with my biological sex, and I don't especially mind the label 'man', but to be honest, it seems increasingly meaningless to me. Holding tightly to my AuDHD identity is like squeezing a long-lost teddy bear suddenly returned after decades of separation. There is an intense feeling of familiarity, home and newness all rolled into one.

That feeling has allowed me to let go of the last remnants of expectation attached to Being a Man. Rather than feeling unbearably confused about what that means, I am now delighted not to have a clue and not to care.

A bunch of my autistic clients feel the same. The relief of not having to try to fit in, whether it be about how we express or don't express emotions, to act up to our gender, or to have relationships and sex the way 'everyone else' does, is intense and joyful.

The next time someone tells me to 'man up', I will comfortably and cheerfully tell them to fuck right off.

Ch-ch-ch-changes

Has my AuDHD identity changed how I practise? That's hard for me to say. More than half my current clients have been working with me since long before the diagnosis and my disclosure of my neurodivergence. No one yet has ended their therapy because of it. My own experience is that how I work relationally has been dialled up several notches.

When preparing this chapter, I asked one of those clients if she would answer some questions for me about what she'd noticed had changed – if anything – in our work these past few months. I've changed her name here, and I asked her to choose that name. She'd like me to refer to her as Beatrice. Beatrice is a woman in her 30s. She was diagnosed dyslexic as a child and is currently exploring the possibility that she may also be ADHD. Here are some of the things she said:

> My own diagnosis [dyslexia] became a focus again after you disclosed your diagnosis, and I'm probably more aware now of the wider implications of a neurodivergent diagnosis, in the sense of feeling 'Other', and it's made me ruminate on that more.
>
> Bringing some of your own experience to the conversation, in such a way that allows for further exploration of certain points, is useful, and it benefits the atmosphere it creates. It creates a more conversational tone, as opposed to something more clinical.
>
> I've had suspicions lately that I may also have some traits of ADHD in women, and I think that knowing that you pursued a formal psychological evaluation, maybe at some point I might want to do that and take it a bit more seriously than 'I wonder if...'
>
> Does the neurodivergent 'click' exist? I think it exists at a subconscious level, but when it becomes apparent explicitly, it reinforces

the relationship. Even before your diagnosis, the sense that you get the clients you need made sense. I wonder whether, even then, there was some 'click' or experience we shared of having been neurodivergent in society, and that meant that our connection was already there, without us having named it.

If our work has changed since your disclosure, then it's been very comfortable and doesn't feel like a different therapeutic relationship now. There's a more animated, positive quality to what you're saying that may not have been there before.

Talking about my own dyslexia has had a bearing on how I understand myself in terms of my confidence, relationships etc. I am open about my neurodivergence in practical terms – explaining that my spelling is poor – but I would never get into the emotional ramifications of those things anywhere else. Having a conversation where you bring something similar to my experience creates a space where my experiences are okay and my responses to them are okay.

Thank you, Beatrice.

Sames

As a therapist, it's important to keep yourself out of your client's experience as much as possible. It's so tempting to share a similar experience to one your client is relating, especially if their feelings about it resonate with your own. But to do so shifts the focus away from the client to you and can set up expectations that your client must interest you or tell stories that relate to you, or even end up in competition with your own narrative. We all know people who do that in our own lives. As one of my clients describes it: 'If you've been to Tenerife, she's been to Elevenerife.'

More often, though, I notice that this doesn't apply in the same way when I'm talking to autistic clients. Another difference I've noticed in my work recently is that I talk more. Until recently, the conversational rhythm of therapy sessions was quite consistent. I would say very little for the first two-thirds of a session. In the final third, I would gradually come in with reflections, themes and summaries. Now it's a lot more two-handed throughout. I reckon this is me discovering my own congruence – what's going on on the outside more closely matches what's going on on the inside.

Congruence is a goal of therapy for our clients, so it's right that I can model that. With autistic clients in particular, I feel freer to share 'same' stories. When I do, I always check it out with them afterwards. 'Was it okay that I told you that?' So far, so good. Usually, they reply that it made them feel like I understood them, that they had permission to tell me more, and that they weren't alone in their experiences. My favourite description of this dynamic comes from Janae Elisabeth (2020), blogging as Trauma Geek. Every autist I've shown it to loves it:

> Whenever we gather groups of neurodivergent people together, the idea that we can't socialize well begins to seem rather silly. We certainly don't socialize like neurotypicals do, but we have our own set of social rules as well as consequences for breaking them.
>
> We don't do small talk. We enjoy parallel play and shared activities that don't require continual conversation. When we talk, it gets deep quickly. We discuss what's real, our struggles, fears, desires, obsessions. We appreciate a good infodump, and there's no such thing as oversharing. We swap SAME stories – sharing a time when we felt similarly in our own life, not as a competition, but to reflect how well we are listening to each other. (para.32)

Learning

As of today, I've been practising as a therapist for 3,016 days. (Of course I'm sure, I'm autistic.) Conversely, I've been practising as an autistic therapist for only 178 days. What am I learning so far?

Unlike the autistic stereotype, I can indeed make and hold eye contact; it's a big part of my job. However, I now realise that this doesn't come naturally. I have actually developed a bunch of automatic techniques and spend lots of energy keeping this up. If my concentration wanes, my gaze falls away.

Unlike the autistic stereotype, I can indeed form and maintain relationships. It's a big part of my job. However, this comes from the need to constantly scan for patterns in order to fit in, which means that I don't make assumptions about people and therefore show a great deal more curiosity, empathy and understanding.

When I work with neurodivergent people, I am more congruent, and we connect more deeply more quickly. It takes no effort to be with them, and this is a revelation. Most work drains my battery, but neurodivergent clients charge my battery. I come out of those sessions with more energy than I went in with. This is because I speak neurotypical fluently but neurodivergent is my native tongue.

My radar for neurodivergence, especially of AuDHD, is pretty good. Of course, I don't diagnose people, but my hunches have a near-perfect success rate so far. There are certain things people say that make my neurodivergent whiskers twitch:

- I never seemed to fit in.
- I always feel like an alien.
- I just didn't understand other people, they all seemed to 'get it' but I never could.
- Why am I always tired? Everyone else seems to have loads of energy.

Similarly, there are common things clients say as they come to understand their neurodivergence:

- Now I know who I am.
- Now everything makes sense.
- Now I understand what masking is and when I'm doing it and when I'm unmasked.
- Now I 'get' the vehicle I'm driving.
- I need to reframe everything.

All the research I've seen about effective talking therapy includes the same finding: the most important factor isn't what kind of therapy is delivered; it isn't how closely the therapist follows their modality, and it isn't how well structured a treatment plan is. It's the quality of the relationship between client and therapist that has the greatest impact on outcome.

I'm finding that the more I allow myself to be myself, and the more I understand who that is, the richer my relationships with my clients become, and the more my clients can be okay with who they are.

References

Elisabeth, J. (2020, May 23). *Lost in translation: The social language theory of neurodivergence.* Medium. https://autietraumageek.medium.com/lost-in-translation-the-social-language-theory-of-neuro divergence-part-1-of-2-1963ba0073c5

Ricketts, L. (n.d.). *My approach.* https://leoricketts.com/my-approach/

Chapter 9

Trauma and the autistic therapist

Wendy Reiersen

I was once asked at a job interview about my specialisation in developmental disorders and developmental trauma. I was asked if I saw a lot of autistic people who had been traumatised. My reply was, 'Have you seen any who haven't?'

How could they not be?

It's a common misperception that autism is simply a reaction to childhood trauma, but correlation is not causation; our lives are more complex than that. When considering the many ways that being neurodivergent can lead to traumatic and complex stressors, it is not hard to see why they can frequently co-occur. Even simply looking at the diagnosis of autism is a reminder that how we inconvenience others is viewed as a pathological character flaw.

Being autistic increases the chances of experiencing developmental trauma as a child and decreases the chances of having the resources to cope with those experiences. Autistic adults may have learned to communicate in a manner that is more likely to be understood and accepted, but we still have challenges and can still be traumatised – the very act of masking or camouflaging has been recognised as a risk for mental and physical health problems, and even suicidality (Price, 2022; South et al., 2021). When our very foundations of social interaction are wrought with conflict, it is not hard to imagine how trauma could co-occur so frequently. Clients who work with me, whether autistic or not, report being able to unmask sooner because of my clear empathy with complex situations, especially regarding marginalisation and trauma. This allows them exceptional progress, compared with their previous therapy experiences.

Protective factors and resilience are important in this connection. Protective factors are the things that help a person cope successfully and so remain untraumatised (remember, trauma is something that exceeds one's ability to cope). They result in resilience – the ability to bounce back (Ackerman, 2019).

Being resilient doesn't mean that you are immune to trauma or that you can't be hurt. And it depends on both internal and external factors. Resilience comes from internal abilities to cope, such as the ability to communicate and to self-soothe, to make sense of things and so on, as well as the availability of whatever we need in order to cope, such as support and access to resources. Being able to communicate that you are hurt and to receive comfort increases resilience. So does being able to go to the doctor when you are sick or injured. So does having information that you need. A lot of resilience comes from our relationships and from having a community that we know accepts us and is there for us. Resilience can also be learned, if one has adequate support, such as in therapy or in the context of supportive relationships (Ackerman, 2019).

Autism is something you are born with and so, diagnosed or not, you are likely to have experienced traumatic experience. I was not diagnosed autistic until I was 42 years old and already a therapist. When I was a child, autism was not generally well understood, and most people didn't think that a girl might be autistic (Sarris, 2017). Autism continues to be underdiagnosed in females (Adams & May, 2022). Autism was a fascination for me from when I first heard of it, and a part of me always related to it, but I didn't know why, and back then I didn't have the conscious thought that I might be autistic myself. In fact, I was still misdiagnosing myself even after I had become a therapist.

I have spent my life trying to figure out 'how to get it right' and guessing at what I was supposed to be and how I was supposed to act.

As I grew up, I had a growing awareness of my father's general awkwardness. Sometimes someone would comment that I had his odd sense of humour. My dad was never diagnosed autistic, but everyone who knows him now considers it obvious. I had enough difficulty with being bullied and picked on by other kids, and instinctively I associated awkwardness with Dad's special interests in maths and science, and I didn't want to be like that.

So I gravitated to social sciences, and eventually to psychology.

By the time I started college, I would have chosen a major in psychology, and I knew that my motivation was to figure out why my family was so weird. At that point, as far as I knew, my family had almost completely avoided contact with the mental health system. We just didn't talk about emotions or mental health. Most things interpersonal or social had been resisted or avoided. I had been severely depressed continuously since elementary school, and I attributed it to the bullying back then. I had tried and tried through my teen years to tell somebody that I wasn't okay, but was shut down and given explanations about how I didn't know what I was talking about. I didn't know how to talk to my parents about not being okay emotionally. Protective factors, and so resilience, were in short supply.

In an undergraduate introductory psychology lecture, the professor told the class of about 900 students, 'If you have your own issues, we don't want you in this field.' I gave up and changed my major to communicative disorders. I thought that I could help non-verbal children to be able to communicate. I was interested in what it was like for the child who couldn't communicate, or the child who had trauma that stopped them from communicating, such as a child with selective mutism.

I applied for graduate school in speech pathology, and they turned me down because I was weird and they didn't understand me. They told me that I should consider getting a second bachelor's degree in engineering or something, but that I should definitely not work with children. How would I be able to correct their disordered speech when there was this weirdness about me that the faculty couldn't make sense of? I was devastated. I thought at first that I would appeal the decision or apply to other graduate schools and become a speech-language pathologist after all, but I fell back into depression, and I gave up. The result was that at that time I didn't even get my degree. I got married and started a goat dairy. My depression worsened and I hit a wall. Something had to change.

It took more than a decade for me to re-discover that my calling was in mental health and psychology. My own lack of ability to communicate in the generally expected way had made it difficult for me to make myself understood. At the same time, others with mental health challenges related to me and felt that I could understand and help them, although the gatekeepers to training and work in this field tried to stop me. It took several more years to get past the message that I received over and over again about needing to have perfect mental health before I could consider being a therapist. I had hit rock bottom with depression and had seriously contemplated suicide a few times.

How, from that extreme low point, as a still-undiagnosed autistic person with the developmental trauma that almost inevitably goes with that, did I come to acquire enough resilience to be able to be a protective factor, first to myself and then to my clients?

What was the process of acquiring it and how did it lead to my qualifying as a therapist and finally recognising my identity as an autistic – and traumatised – person?

It was at that point that I found a book in the library, *Undercurrents: A life beneath the surface*, by Martha Manning (1996). The author was a psychologist who suffered worsening depression that was treatment-resistant and wound up being hospitalised for ECT treatment. She wrote about being aware of her own symptoms while at the same time treating her clients and apparently still being able to help them, even though she was not able to pull herself out of her own depression without help. I was inspired that she could be a therapist while going through depression and thought that maybe there was a chance for me too. Another book that I found around that time was *Who You Were Meant to Be: A guide for finding or recovering your life's purpose*, by Lindsay C. Gibson (2002). This book is about changing careers as an adult and recognising what you want to do with your life, as opposed to what you might have been trying to do because someone else wanted you to do it. It was in books like these that I found a lot of the validation and encouragement that I was not able to get from interactions with people in my life. Books have always been an important resource for me.

The internet afforded me a place to grow social connections and find my voice in interacting in communities that shared my special interests. I became a moderator for an online community related to this field, which gave me some experience of working with others with mental health issues. I was active with that community all the way through graduate school and into establishing my career as a therapist, and I still have friends who I have never met but originally connected with that way.

When I decided to go back to school, the first thing I had to do was to finish my bachelor's degree. By that time, I was 30-something and had three children but was very isolated and as socially awkward as ever.

I learned most of my missing social and communication skills in graduate school and from learning therapy modalities to help my clients, independent study and online relationships and communities. Graduate school gave me a framework and the opportunity to develop skills and know what I needed to learn, and to get practice and feedback and credentials, but I probably learned more from independent study.

My first postgraduate internship was at a residential treatment centre, where I was hired to develop a dialectical behaviour therapy (DBT) programme for the teens attending the centre. I had been very interested in DBT even before graduate school, but my school didn't offer any courses on specific modalities like that. I learned DBT by reading the manuals (Linehan, 1993, 2015) and figuring out how to teach the skills from the worksheets and other information in the books. Learning DBT that way, as a therapist, was how I started to learn about how emotions work and how to communicate about emotions, as well as mindfulness, acceptance, interpersonal skills, communication, and distress tolerance skills.

Marsha Linehan developed DBT as a treatment for people diagnosed with borderline personality disorder (BPD). It is an evidence-based treatment that has also been found to be effective for mood disorders, anxiety, PTSD, addictions, and a number of other mental health conditions too. I explain DBT as essentially a system for teaching or learning the skills that people who are getting along pretty well in life and relationships probably have had access to, whether they were taught those skills or somehow figured them out intuitively – skills that those who struggle with life and relationships may never have had the chance to learn. These skills might have been a life changer (and protective factors) for me if I had been able to access them much earlier in life. I could see the potential benefit in having DBT skills as part of the curriculum in school, presented at an age-appropriate level, starting in elementary school.

At this point in my life, I had misdiagnosed myself with BPD. That is not surprising, although I knew that I did not exactly meet all of the criteria for this, as BPD is one of the most common misdiagnoses for autistic women (McQuaid et al., 2022). In addition, when I tried to talk to my then therapist about sensory processing symptoms or anything related to autism, she shut me down. She was reluctant to tell me what she thought my diagnosis might be, but did mention the possibility of PTSD. I dismissed that – at that time I didn't recognise any of my life experiences as trauma, as I had not experienced any 'Big T' traumatic events. Present-day me would easily diagnose me, as I was beginning my career, with complex PTSD (C-PTSD) – a diagnosis that is recognised in the latest edition of the International Classification of Diseases manual of mental disorders (World Health Organization, 2022), but not in any editions of the American Psychiatric Association's Diagnostic and Statistical Manual of Mental Disorders (APA, 2022) (DSM-5-TR) to date. C-PTSD is a diagnosis for the symptoms resulting from complex trauma, including developmental and relational trauma. And, indeed, autism – the combination of developmental disorder and developmental trauma discussed above.

Complex trauma is not any less severe than 'Big T' trauma; indeed, it is thought to have a more profound impact (Levin, 2010). Autistic people are at risk for both types of trauma, but especially for complex trauma (Lobregt-van Buuren et al., 2021; King & Desaulnier, 2011). In my opinion, most if not all people who are diagnosed with BPD have experienced complex trauma and would probably meet the criteria for C-PTSD. This is an important distinction because a diagnosis of a personality disorder such as BPD implies a flaw in the person with that diagnosis, while C-PTSD emphasises that the symptoms are in direct relation to the experience of trauma and are therefore understandable, and not an innate flaw in the person.

Even after completing graduate school, I had difficulties with jobs and working. I had had a few jobs as a young adult. I was a substitute teacher in a daycare/private school (that is how I discovered that I don't have the skills to manage larger groups of children). I have worked with people with disabilities and I have worked in nursing homes. After going back to school, I worked at several different residential treatment facilities for teenagers.

I have had some good experiences in jobs, including some co-workers and supervisors who were wonderful people and were very helpful. I have loved most of the clients and populations I have worked with. However, I have always found that my loyalty tends to go to the clients in any given setting, rather than to the employer. I have struggled to understand the needs and expectations of management, especially when I don't see those things as contributing to the welfare of the clients. I often find myself in a position where the demands of management exceed my capacity and energy levels, but I try anyway, even if it means that I don't have any time or energy left over for life outside of work. Then communication breaks down and resentment builds. From my personal experience, I would suggest that most autistic people would be able to work 20–30 hours per week, as opposed to the 40+ hours that are typically considered a full-time work schedule in the US. The problem is that working fewer hours may well mean not having an adequate income or adequate access to healthcare under the US insurance system, unless you have a partner or are otherwise supported by family or some form of alternative income. Since losing access to such essential components of survival can itself be traumatic, it is again not surprising that so many autistic people who struggle to work at the level necessary to be self-sustaining also experience trauma.

At the age of 42, I had completed my master's degree in clinical mental health counselling, fulfilled the required number of internship hours across three different work settings and was a fully licensed mental health counsellor. At times I had been overworked; at other times I had been unable to get enough work to live on. I had never held a job for more than two years. I had been divorced for a couple of years and was entirely on my own. After losing a job at a community counselling centre where the hours and workload far exceeded what I was able to do, I was almost ready to give up on my relatively new career. Then I applied for vocational rehabilitation (a US federal and state service for people with disabilities to find or maintain appropriate employment) in one last attempt to get enough support to get and keep a job. I was referred for therapy once again, this time to try eye movement desensitisation and reprocessing (EMDR) to address my cumulative trauma. EMDR can be a very effective treatment for identified trauma, but it did not work for me because I was not able to pinpoint specific traumatic events to work on.

This therapist happened to mention to me that on that day he had identified several people who were probably autistic, which he found unusual. I mentioned my suspicions that I might be autistic. After a few screening questions, he scheduled me for formal testing, and I received my diagnosis. He suggested reading about Asperger's syndrome (now included under the autism diagnosis), and in particular anything by Tony Attwood (see for example, Attwood, 2006). Reading about Asperger's/autism with the validation that this included me allowed me finally to make sense of my life. I am citing Attwood mainly because that was a starting point for me, but I would encourage reading a variety of authors about autism, and especially seeking out those who are autistic themselves. It also allowed me to start to find my tribe and to make connections with the growing neurodivergent community.

Trauma itself does not make a person better or stronger. However, trauma does often motivate us to find the resilience to grow in order to overcome it. Resilience is not automatic. Resilience, as mentioned before, comes from within and from without, and generally does require assistance and support. As therapists, it is vital that we work towards our own healing so that we can be a support to others.

As I've said, even the demands of academic training and full-time work may be traumatic when the situation becomes too much to cope with, the demands exceed our internal resources, and we lack the internal and external resources and supports necessary to cope.

As mentioned at the start of this chapter, therapy for autistic people has much in common with trauma therapy. Autism itself is not necessarily trauma, and trauma does not cause autism. However, autistic people seek therapy when they have been affected by trauma, and if they have never experienced trauma, they may not be in need of therapy.

What makes a particular therapeutic modality appropriate for clients with autism, or with trauma, for that matter? One key element is that it supports agency. The nature of trauma is that it deprives a person of choices that they have the right to be able to make. Overly structured or behavioural therapies, such as Applied Behaviour Analysis (ABA)[1], are often experienced as traumatising or re-traumatising, especially so-called therapies whose purpose is to coerce a person to conform to neurotypical standards.

---

1. ABA therapy is a behavioural therapy that uses a system of rewards and punishments to shape behaviour, or, in other words, to train children to conform to neurotypical expectations. More recent adaptations to ABA may include some attempt to teach about emotions or to observe some of a child's preferences, but the essential premise of ABA is conformity. One essential component of trauma-informed therapy is collaboration with the client. ABA specifically excludes the client as a member of the treatment team. (See also Silvia Liu's Chapter 10.)

What is agency? Agency is more than taking action or simply making a choice. It includes recognising our own role in how we respond to our internal and external experiences and experiencing ownership of our own role in those interactions (Heller & Kammer, 2022). We can support agency by offering people choices and asking for consent, as well as through exploring with curiosity. For example, we can invite discussion with a statement like 'I am curious about what thoughts or feelings you have about _____' or 'Would it be okay to explore this a little deeper?' Agency is also supported by inviting the client to be curious about their own responses to challenging circumstances, without blame or judgement, and maybe recognising how a response may have been necessary or helpful even if it didn't seem to be, at first glance.

Reinforcing agency is one of the four pillars in neuroaffective relational therapy (NARM). This is a modality that was developed by Laurence Heller specifically for developmental trauma (Heller & Kammer, 2022).

In my experience, many autistic clients prefer at least some structure and direction in therapy, which does not necessarily exclude supporting agency. Autistic clients may benefit from an organised, step-by-step presentation of relevant skills or psychoeducational material, with room for discussion and encouragement to consider whether the intervention is okay for them. This calls for giving clear instruction at times, in a non-directive way. I will often clarify with clients when something is offered but not required, and reinforce that clients are the best experts on themselves.

Although my preferred modality is the neuroaffective relational model (NARM), I frequently do draw from DBT, acceptance and commitment therapy (ACT) and other modalities when they offer something that is useful to the client. Another option is to suggest books and other resources for independent learning and allow clients to choose for themselves, with the invitation to discuss in session anything that they find interesting or would like to explore further.

Much of the trauma that autistic people experience is due to the invalidation of our lived experiences and our own emotions. Autistic people have and experience emotions every bit as much as anyone does, even if part of the diagnosis is difficulty understanding and communicating emotions. Complex trauma is typically the result of emotional abuse, neglect and invalidation. The first step towards healing and preventing this trauma is non-judgemental listening and validation of emotions. What autistic children or adults need is the same as everyone needs. It is to be understood and accepted, and to be able to understand ourselves and be empowered to be wholly ourselves.

References

Ackerman, C. (2019, July 9). *What is resilience and why is it important to bounce back?* PositivePsychology.com. https://positivepsychology.com/what-is-resilience/

Adams, C.A. & May, T. (2022, February 9). *Autism is still underdiagnosed in girls and women. That can compound the challenges they face.* The Conversation. https://theconversation.com/autism-is-still-underdiagnosed-in-girls-and-women-that-can-compound-the-challenges-they-face-176036

American Psychiatric Association. (2022). *Diagnostic and statistical manual of mental disorders* (5th ed. text revision) (DSM-5-TR). APA.

Attwood, T. (2006). *The complete guide to Asperger's syndrome.* Jessica Kingsley Publishers.

Gibson, L.C. (2002). *Who you were meant to be: A guide for finding or recovering your life's purpose.* New Horizon Press.

Heller, L. & Kammer, B. (2022). *The practical guide for healing developmental trauma.* North Atlantic Books.

King, R. & Desaulnier, C.L. (2011). Commentary: Complex post-traumatic stress disorder. Implications for individuals with autism spectrum disorders – part II. *Journal on Developmental Disabilities, 17*(1), 47–59.

Levin, A. (2010). 'Complex PTSD' may result when trauma is ongoing. *Psychiatric News, 45*(23), 32–32. https://doi.org/10.1176/pn.45.23.psychnews_45_23_040

Linehan, M. (1993). *Cognitive-behavioral treatment of borderline personality disorder.* Guilford Press.

Linehan, M. (2015). *DBT skills training manual* (2nd ed.). Guilford Press.

Lobregt-van Buuren, E., Hoekert, M. & Sizoo, B. (2021). Autism, adverse events, and trauma. In A.M. Grabrucker (Ed.), *Autism spectrum disorder* (pp.33–42). Exon Publications. https://www.ncbi.nlm.nih.gov/books/NBK573608/

Manning, M. (1996). *Undercurrents: A life beneath the surface.* HarperOne.

McQuaid, G., Strang, J. & Jack, A. (2022, March 21). *Borderline personality and late, missed, and mis-diagnosis in female autism: A review of the literature.* PsyArXiv Preprints. https://osf.io/preprints/psyarxiv/t37vj

Price, D. (2022). *Unmasking autism.* Harmony Books.

Sarris, M. (2017, July 25). *A lost generation: growing up with autism before the 'epidemic'.* [Blog.] Kennedy Krieger. www.kennedykrieger.org/stories/interactive-autism-network-ian/lost-generation-growing-up-autism-before-epidemic

South, M., Costa, A.P. & McMorris, C. (2021). Death by suicide among people with autism: Beyond Zebrafish. *JAMA Network Open, 4*(1), e2034018. https://doi.org/10.1001/jamanetworkopen.2020.34018

World Health Organization. (2022). *International classification of diseases* (11th rev.). *(ICD-11).* WHO.

Chapter 10

The journey from research knowledge to lived wisdom

Silvia Liu

'I self-identify as autistic,' I proclaimed excitedly to a couple of psychology professionals I met in Taiwan. My psychologist friend was there too, and they were conversing about his experiences in using applied behavioural analysis (ABA)[1] to treat autistic children two decades ago. I felt the urge to interject because I wanted instead to talk about the autistic experience, to centre on autistic voices, and to use the opportunity to educate.

I saw the two colleagues' expressions freeze in a moment of suspense, not quite knowing how to respond to what I had just said. There was a shiny, pregnant moment that could have turned into an important and possibly fulfilling discussion if they had responded with curiosity. I would have been able to show more of myself while educating more psychology professionals about autism. Win-win.

---

1. The autistic community and neurodiversity advocates have strongly denounced ABA for the harmful principles it is built on and its abusive practices. My favourite resource for opposing ABA is *The Great Big ABA Opposition Resource List* on the Stop ABA, Support Autistics blog (n.d.). Moreover, two major studies conducted by the US Department of Defense over a nationwide sample (more than 6,000 in sample size for each study) have demonstrated the ineffectiveness of ABA for treating autism (Donovan, 2020; Stewart, 2019). In these studies, 76% of children and young people who received ABA showed little to no change over 12 months of ABA while 9% showed worsened symptoms as measured by ABA therapists (Stewart, 2019), and the number of ABA hours given showed no statistically significant correlation with outcome measures, and symptoms worsened over time in older children (Donovan, 2020). The European Council of Autistic People's position statement (EUCAP, 2024) offers a helpful summary of the critiques of ABA and related behavioural 'therapies'.

But then my friend cut through that moment with a casual, 'Yeah, I don't get it.' [Pause] 'Just kidding.' [Laughs].

This is a friend I had disclosed to and spent some time educating about the problem of ABA and the predominant behavioural lens in psychology. This is a friend I have spoken to about how I identify strongly with the autistic experience, that it does not seem obvious because of how well I mask, and how my subjective experience does not at all match what he observes on the outside.

I was stunned.

In the next moment, the two colleagues excused their own ignorance about autism quickly and awkwardly before moving on, with no acknowledgement of what had just happened. My heart dropped. And my friend never got to learn how disappointing and hurtful his statement was.

* * * * * * *

With 42 years of experience under my belt, I mask well enough to know when to let a thread go instead of continuing to tug on it. As an Asian autistic therapist, I am collectivistic and value the need of the group over the need of the individual. I have had years of conformist training on how to behave in a manner that puts people at ease, not only as an Asian person but also in clinical psychology during graduate school. In addition, years of the trauma of my true, unmasked self being rejected have greatly influenced my decisions on how to navigate any given social moment. In the above example, my need to be fully seen and my need to dive into my special interests (autism, people, psychological systems) were easily lost as I switched into my programming to smooth over the social tension in the moment.

The impact of losing whole interactions to masking is both cumulative and compounded over time. In economic terms, we suffer a huge opportunity cost of lost meaningfulness. Our loss is experienced as a grave sense of grief around being invisible to others and our distinct status of being marginalised. It matters not that I appear to be sociable and fit into society. I am left with an unrelenting sense of being othered wherever I go. And I have gone places – from Indonesia to Singapore to Canada to the US to Taiwan – with the wound of never belonging, never being seen and never being accepted fully as I am.

The irony is, I used to run social skills groups for children and adolescents to help them learn how best to do exactly this – masking themselves to neurotypical standards, so as to make them more acceptable in society. I wanted so badly to help others feel accepted, without realising that I myself learned and executed these neurotypical behaviours without ever feeling loved for who I am. What else could I do but believe in scientific research? Research shows that social skills programmes like the Program for the Education and Enrichment of

Relational Skills (PEERS) from the University of California, Los Angeles (UCLA) are helpful in increasing prosocial behaviours (e.g. Moody & Laugeson, 2020; Zheng et al., 2021). These programmes work. And I love that these evidence-based practices (EBPs) have step-by-step instructions that help us implement change in the lives of those who need it. My autistic brain loves manuals; the more detailed the better. Spell it out, because beginners need specific instructions to do it right and the more experienced need reminders to stay consistent in their service provision. In EBP speak, this is about fidelity to the model.

I gravitated to all things manualised. ABA was often proclaimed as the 'gold standard' early intervention for autistic children (e.g. Medavarapu et al., 2019). So, I became a behavioural interventionist out of college, lured by the promise of a scientific and effective modality, and I used ABA to help autistic children learn and grow. Later, I dove into cognitive-behavioural therapy (CBT) because it is consistently touted as an effective therapy for psychological problems. In my doctorate programme, I expanded my repertoire, learning dialectical behaviour therapy (DBT – an evidence-based treatment for borderline personality disorder) and parent-child interaction therapy (PCIT – an evidence-based treatment for disruptive behaviours in children). I worked hard to be certified as a PCIT therapist and within-agency trainer and completed a 300-page doctoral dissertation on PCIT, for which I earned distinctions.

All of these manualised treatment modalities have behaviourism in common. Therefore, I am steeped in the tradition of behaviourism. In fact, it was comforting for me to believe that human behaviours can be reduced to programming. Then, perhaps, I could programme myself to be happy and fulfilled.

I had a great life, you see – a loving marriage, two lovely kids, and the highest education level in my family. I grew up safe and sheltered, loved by my grandmother and two hard-working parents, who provided more than I could ever want or need. I was given opportunities afforded by my father's entrepreneur lifestyle that many of my peers did not get. I had incredible luck to meet my husband when I was 19 turning 20, so that I did not need to struggle in my 20s to find stable, life-altering love. At no point in my life did I ever have any reason to be unhappy. And yet, depression came to be my companion early in childhood and continued to rear its head whenever it pleased.

The big question is 'Why?' It's my favourite question for everything. But it was a question I could never answer for myself.

Why would I suffer from depression when everything went smoothly in my life? Yet, in my late teens, the weight of depression was so heavy that I turned it into hatred and shame towards myself. I felt more worthless than scum. It made no logical sense. Unfortunately, the therapist that my father took me to was not helpful at all. She was not only incredibly incompetent in the Asian culture and overly passive; I actually felt traumatised by how much she did *not* understand me. I left that one session thinking that I must be so broken that people did not get me. But I was sick of being broken in a way I could not comprehend. I wanted to get better.

My only option was to rely on myself, because I knew myself better than others knew me. So, it came to pass that CBT helped me to continue living. To be specific, it was a CBT self-help book, thankfully easily accessible for a young adult. CBT taught me how to break down my thoughts, behaviours and feelings into a logical system that I can analyse, and to use specific interventions to move towards my goals. I capitalised on my natural strengths of persistence and a can-do attitude to forge forward in changing my beliefs and my behaviours. I religiously caught my distorted thoughts and painstakingly pushed back against them, because of course I could not bring myself to believe a more temperate, less vile narrative of myself. I did not allow myself to entertain the belief that I could have merits, especially because I had not demonstrated any redeeming acts of value. I forced myself to do painful things. Some were social; others targeted situations I feared.

I was fearful of making phone calls to strangers (for example, to order pizza); it was so overwhelming with all the decision points, difficulties in communicating, and not knowing what to say. Thus, when I saw that I could volunteer for Vancouver Crisis Center and get trained in how to talk to suicidal people, I jumped at the opportunity. I figured that, if I can learn to respond in serious situations, I would be able to make a casual call more easily. Each time the crisis line rang, my gut churned and I gritted my teeth as that illogical fear hit me like a brick wall. I picked up every time. It was years before my planned exposure was completed, and I was relatively desensitised to picking up the phone. I continued to have trouble making personal calls, but I knew how to ride that wave when I needed to force a call out of myself. It was 15–20 years after graduating from Vancouver Crisis Center that I learned how to make calls without missing a beat, but it was that first wave of exposure that helped me function well enough for the next leg of my journey.

I was also fearful of presenting to strangers because, well, who wouldn't be? So, you've probably guessed it by now, I forced myself to volunteer for the Vancouver Red Cross Center Abuse Prevention programme, where I presented about child abuse and intimate partner violence to whatever school students I was assigned to. I was wracked with anxiety every time, but apparently people could not tell.

CBT works. I was rehabilitated. My anxiety was managed, my depression diminished, and I could tell myself, 'I can do things when I put my mind to it.'

This pattern continued. Why wouldn't it? Why mess with something that works?

I built my self-esteem around my ability to persevere past my own fears and resistance. I learned to love interventions that are proven to work. Of course, CBT worked. The behavioural interventions fixed my programming and the cognitive interventions were logical and stepwise. They are essentially a fulcrum of change. When I worked in ABA, of course that worked too. Children in ABA learn to give the responses they are trained to give. When I learned PCIT, of course that worked as well. Children put in time-out until they learn to comply. I loved how everything made sense. These interventions work.

Except they don't

I was still sad. And I was not sure why. When I had my first child, I used PCIT with him, and he cried inconsolably in time-out. As a new mom, I could tell that he didn't have a way to calm himself. I gave up sleep training after he puked because he cried violently for too long. I gave up PCIT with him after I realised that my child needed something very different from the clear and firm limits that PCIT offered. He needed co-regulation. He needed co-sleeping. He needed shared, relational togetherness until his system matured enough for him to do it himself. Once that happened, he didn't need to be taught limits the way that I was told he needed to be taught.

I was still sad. I continued to doubt myself and believe in self-deprecating narratives at every opportunity. Something was missing. I lay in bed, burnt out. The completion of my doctoral dissertation was six to seven years delayed. My lifelong perseverance ran out.

I just wanted a break from having to try so hard all the time. Life sucked. It didn't matter what I had accomplished academically or as a psychology student/therapist trainee. These things probably don't even count at the end of the day. It certainly didn't matter the number of babies I birthed, because I was somehow always going to be a terrible mom, one way or another. My firstborn needed a lot of support developmentally and, despite knowing his needs on an intellectual level, I was unable to undo the Asian mom standards and programming in me for several years. I was chronically stressed throughout my graduate school programme and could not understand why I seemed to have more trouble with everything than my cohort peers. I was more self-aware than most and was exposed to more disparate cultural situations than many, yet this had not helped me navigate a very confusing world. I considered myself well-versed in CBT skills, including third wave CBT (ACT, DBT), but I never felt my humanity was completely anchored in my practice as a budding therapist. Something was certainly missing.

Then the floodgates broke.

I meandered into Facebook communities that educated me on the neurodiversity movement (Jaarsma & Welin, 2012). Namely, I dove into the wisdom of lived experiences in the Neurodiversity-Affirming Therapist Facebook group, which started my journey into understanding my own neurodivergence. Many of the neurodiversity-affirming therapists were neurodivergent, which included autism, ADHD and other brain differences resulting from trauma and mental illnesses. They taught me what it truly means to be strength-based and to see a person as a whole, instead of pathologising their behaviours. They dismantled biases and assumptions I held about how a person should be in this world. They introduced me to books and articles that educated me in concrete ways to be affirming of differences, which fitted with the values I have always held.

Growing up, I knew I was different, often never fitting into what seemed to be 'normal' social things. My whole goal of childhood was to belong and blend into the background somewhere. But, as skilled as I became, I never felt like I succeeded.

I suddenly felt at home when I started hearing the lived experiences of autistic people. It was a strange phenomenon after so many years of feeling like a square peg in a round hole. But more than that, it was strange to consider myself as possibly autistic when I was considered by many to be sociable. This did not fit what I learned about autism in the textbooks. It did not fit what looked like autism in the autistic boys I worked with. It would certainly be unthinkable to self-identify as autistic in the Asian context, because of the extremely negative stigma attached to autism in Asia. It is unspoken, but in Asia, where status and ability to earn money is top priority, basically autistic = unable to function = no worth/value. Moreover, it would be strange to *choose* to put a stigmatised label on myself when there are many people who seem more socially awkward and withdrawn among Asian immigrants than I appear to be.

And yet, I fit. A surprisingly snug fit.

The lived experiences of other autistic women fitted me so well, down to my hypermobility and gastrointestinal issues, my internal dialogue and intense need for exposition, my idealistic values and needs, my masking and apparent sociability, the subsequent consequences of burnout and depression, and the subtle social difficulties (at times too expressive, not understanding how I offended others, and so on) that I've experienced throughout my life. I resonated so much with autistic people from different backgrounds and cultures that I felt a creeping sense of relief and kinship as I considered this identity for myself. When I put on the lens of autism, my constant fear of being misunderstood, my penchant for direct communication, my prevalent sensory needs, and my deep connection with Very Grand Emotions (Vance, 2019) all made sense. I suddenly belonged.

I slowly learned to undo my ableist ideas about my child, myself and others. This allowed me to accept how my child and I could never be like the rest of the world. I learned the strengths of my autistic brain, the saving grace of my special interests (or Intense Pervasive Interests, as coined by The Awetist (2022)), and the necessity of my unique neurotype in the grand scale of things. I started to love myself in ways that I could not access in the past. I spread the love by helping other neurodivergent people learn about their own unique neurotype and how best to work with their strengths and challenges. I started to hear from my clients that the support I give for learning about themselves as they are, modelling radical acceptance and undoing ableist societal structures, is life-changing and immensely helpful for them, just as it was for me. I followed the recommendations in the Facebook groups to try out brainspotting (Grand, 2013), an offshoot and evolution from EMDR (Shapiro & Brown, 2019), and experienced quantum shifts in my ability to be the kind of mom I wanted to be to my child.

I think back to the autistic children I worked with during my ABA days. The intervention 'worked' in the limited way that it was designed to work (i.e. teaching certain behaviours). But did it also convey the idea that autistic people are somehow broken and needed to be fixed? Moreover, did it fail to teach the more important message that the autistic child is valued as they are, that their ways are lovely instead of strange, that their neurotype is necessary instead of flawed, that their needs are respected instead of ignored, and that their interests are delightful instead of abnormal? Because *I am not broken.*

Did my love of CBT and other manualised treatments help me love myself deeply as a person and acknowledge all my efforts as a therapist? It clearly didn't.

And why would I feel so comfortable with the free-flowing brainspotting modality when I hated the openness and presumptuousness of psychodynamic interpretations?

It is because I, an autistic Asian person straddling multiple cultures, have as much right to self-determination as any other person.

Do not make interpretations of me. Let me tell my own story.

Let me tell you how I know I am autistic, even though you'll find that I navigate social interactions well enough, with my special interest being people. Let me tell you how I scored low on the Empathy Quotient test (Baron-Cohen & Wheelwright, 2004), but that I am really quite an empathic[2] and good therapist

---

2. Autistic people are incredibly empathic because of our hyperconnected brains (García Dominguez et al., 2013; Supekar et al., 2013) and sensitive nervous systems (Pardo et al., 2005).

because I lived and cultivated the wisdom from four decades of healing. Let me give you evidence of how the psychology 101 textbooks you've read are wrong about autism– things I had to learn from a Facebook group after I was done with the courses of a well-respected doctorate programme. Let me tell you how I regret all the one-dimensional behaviourism I participated in and how much I truly love the tingle of my autistic brain.

Let me speak for myself. And if you're a friend, then celebrate with me my coming into this identity.

References

The Awetist. (2022, December 24). *Reframe.* Facebook. www.facebook.com/photo/?fbid=118202844472813&set=a.112257348400696

Baron-Cohen, S. & Wheelwright, S. (2004). The Empathy Quotient: An investigation of adults with Asperger syndrome or high functioning autism, and normal sex differences. *Journal of Autism and Developmental Disorders, 34*(2), 163–175.

Donovan, M.P. (2020). *The Department of Defense Comprehensive Autism Care Demonstration: Annual Report 2020.* Report to the Committees on Armed Services of the Senate and House of Representatives. Department of Defense. https://altteaching.org/wp-content/uploads/2020/10/Annual-Report-on-Autism-Care-June-2020.pdf?x78693

EUCAP (2024, April 2). *Position statement on the use of Applied Behavior Analysis and related behavioral methods in the context of treatment, therapy, habilitation or education for autistic people.* https://eucap.eu/2024/04/02/aba-statement

García Domínguez, L., Stieben, J., Pérez Velázquez, J.L. & Shanker, S. (2013). The imaginary part of coherency in autism: Differences in cortical functional connectivity in preschool children. *PloS One, 8*(10), e75941. https://doi.org/10.1371/journal.pone.0075941

Grand, D. (2013). *Brainspotting: The revolutionary new therapy for rapid and effective change.* Sounds True Inc.

Jaarsma, P. & Welin, S. (2012). Autism as a natural human variation: Reflections on the claims of the neurodiversity movement. *Health Care Analysis, 20*(1), 20–30.

Medavarapu, S., Marella, L.L., Sangem, A. & Kairam, R. (2019). Where is the evidence? A narrative literature review of the treatment modalities for autism spectrum disorders. *Cureus, 11*(1), e3901. https://doi.org/10.7759/cureus.3901

Moody, C.T. & Laugeson, E.A. (2020). Social skills training in autism spectrum disorder across the lifespan. *Child and Adolescent Psychiatric Clinics of North America, 29*(2), 359–371.

Pardo, C.A., Vargas, D.L. & Zimmerman, A.W. (2005). Immunity, neuroglia and neuroinflammation in autism. *International Review of Psychiatry, 17*(6), 485–495.

Shapiro, R. & Brown, L.S. (2019). Eye movement desensitization and reprocessing therapy and related treatments for trauma: An innovative, integrative trauma treatment. *Practice Innovations, 4*(3), 139–155.

Stewart, J. (2019). *The Department of Defense Comprehensive Autism Care Demonstration Quarterly Report to Congress.* Department of Defense. www.altteaching.org/wp-content/uploads/2019/11/TRICARE-Autism-Report.pdf?x78693.

Stop ABA, Support Autistics. (n.d.). *The great big ABA opposition resource list.* https://stopabasupportautistics.home.blog/2019/08/11/the-great-big-aba-opposition-resource-list/

Supekar, K., Uddin, L.Q., Khouzam, A., Phillips, J., Gaillard, W.D., Kenworthy, L.E., Yerys, B.E., Vaidya, C.J. & Menon, V. (2013). Brain hyperconnectivity in children with autism and its links to social deficits. *Cell Reports, 5*(3), 738–747. https://doi.org/10.1016/j.celrep.2013.10.001

Vance, T. (2019, March 23). *Very Grand Emotions: How autistics and neurotypicals experience emotions differently.* NeuroClastic. https://neuroclastic.com/very-grand-emotions

Zheng, S., Kim, H., Salzman, E., Ankenman, K. & Bent, S. (2021). Improving social knowledge and skills among adolescents with autism: Systematic review and meta-analysis of UCLA PEERS® for adolescents. *Journal of Autism and Developmental Disorders, 51*(12), 4488–4503.

Chapter 11

Befriending the beast: A therapist and her meltdowns

Debbie Luck

As a very young child, I was remarkably calm and peaceful, known for always being happy and content. I had a (mostly) silent wisdom about me, quietly observing the world through giant blue eyes, sucking my thumb as I ran my blankie through my fingers like rosary beads, as if I were soundlessly praying and connecting to a higher power, gently self-rocking in a semi-meditative state.

I chose not to speak, hiding the fact that I could, which suited me well as I had no desire to interact with anyone other than my immediate family, and they understood my non-verbal commands: pointing and making sounds when I had a want or a need, leaving me be when I hid my face, cuddling me when I climbed onto their laps. I had everything that I needed in my safe little world.

If the environment around me ever did seem overly busy or loud, I would take refuge under the stairs and focus all my attention on the sensations in my mouth as I devoured salt and vinegar crisps, bag after bag, inhaling their sharp scent as if it were my life force. If my body felt it needed to move, I would hide in the bathroom, pretending to brush my teeth while I spun round and round, lost in my imagination.

If I experienced brief feelings of unsafety, I could rewatch one of my favourite videos or read a book, taking refuge in the memorised dialogue, knowing that it would instantly soothe me – a feeling of being *home*.

I instinctively knew how to shut out the external world and manage the energy inside my body, and, as I had a preternatural sovereign presence for my age, those around me let me be. I was independent and perfectly content if everything remained in its correct little order.

And then it happened: I was thrust into the world of education. I had been so excited about my first day of school, believing it would be just like my favourite book and TV show, *Anne of Green Gables* (Sullivan, 1985). Just like Anne, I loved to read, and I couldn't wait to be a part of this exciting new world, to learn and to make new friends.

Only the school I arrived at was nothing like Green Gables. It could not have been further from the idyllic, one-roomed 'whitewashed building, low in the eaves and wide in the windows' that I'd held for so long in my imagination (Montgomery, 1981).

Here, I was not seen as calm, happy or wise, but instead as lazy, clumsy and the weird child with a wildness that must be tamed. My thumb was wrenched from my mouth and blankies were only for babies at home time. All day I thought of them, discarded on the shelf beneath my pushchair. It made my heart and stomach physically hurt. The other children called me names; even the teachers seemed to find me irritating, and I had no idea why.

The large, cold corridors smelt strange and unfamiliar – an overpowering blend of urine, sweat and pencil sharpenings. Under the spell of the harsh fluorescent-tube lighting, the place seemed overwhelmingly exposed, with no nooks or safe places to which to retreat and hide. There were all these strange rules, such as you could only drink after you had eaten, and, as I couldn't eat without water, I spent lunchtimes hungry and agitated. Here, nothing quite made sense.

To integrate, I revealed that I could speak, and that, far from being absent, my vocabulary was very advanced for a child my age, as were my reading skills and ability to learn from the world around me. But my enthusiasm for knowledge and understanding only agitated my peers and teachers further. I would ask relentless questions, trying to understand this new world, desperately trying to be a part of it, but they interpreted this as an act of rebellion and troublemaking – a way to undermine the authority of those in charge and, worse, as an attempt to divert the teachers' centre of attention away from my classmates to me.

I was labelled gifted in maths and English, and yet I could not spell, cut a straight line, understand distances or tie my shoes. My clumsy heavy-footedness earned me the nickname 'Calamity', as I ricocheted off the small wooden desks whenever I had to leave my chair. I would fall over a lot and get shouted at for walking strangely and not using all the parts of my feet. My failure at these seemingly easy and normal tasks only added evidence to their case that I was simply an attention-seeking, lazy child who wanted others to serve her.

Their solution was to isolate me, and I spent hours sitting at a desk facing the wall at the front of the classroom, trying to draw straight lines or cut out straight-lined triangles and perfect circles. Over and over, I was made to repeat these tasks, tears rolling down my cheeks, each time failing to be the version of me they needed me to be, even though I genuinely tried as hard as I could.

I can't recall the exact day of the week, or even the year, but I remember that, without my stims (those repetitive movements to soothe me – my thumb, blanket, spinning), something built up inside – like a boiler with too much pressure trying to force expanded hot air through pipes that were too constricted – resulting in… epic meltdown.

Of course, no one called it a meltdown back then. Although each school report stated that I had social issues and lacked certain skill sets, because I was seen as gifted and no one knew a lot about autism in girls, that meltdown, and all subsequent meltdowns, were interpreted as tantrums – a way to manipulate those around me to get my way.

So, what is a meltdown and how does it differ from a tantrum?

Tantrums in young children are commonplace because generally children of this age have not yet gained the emotional vocabulary and developed the meta-cognition skills, the process of 'thinking about thinking' (Chick, 2013), to understand and express their feelings, wants and desires. They are caught in the tug and pull of striving to become fully independent, sovereign beings, while still reliant on and heavily attached to their caregivers.

A tantrum is often caused because a child feels a want is being denied, even if that want is as simple as needing attention or rest. Therefore, tantrums have a purpose, an end game: the child wants a resolution, and they will use their tantrum as a manipulative tool to get their needs and desires met.

Meltdowns, while looking like tantrums, are quite different. A meltdown is simply a reaction to being intensely overwhelmed and overstimulated to the point where the body and mind cannot process and absorb any further information (Nannery & Nannery, 2021). Stimulation can arise externally from the outside world and internally from thoughts, feelings, perceptions and bodily sensations. As many autistic people struggle with interoception (sensing internal signals from the body), it can be extremely difficult to identify when overstimulation is occurring (Poissant, 2023).

A meltdown is not a behaviour that can be controlled or unlearned, and generally it cannot be prevented once it has begun, as it needs to run its course. A meltdown has no goal other than to release the built-up energy from the body, and in this way it ensures our survival.

Meltdowns can vary in how they manifest for the individual, in their degrees of intensity and duration, and on the situation and stimulations present. They can be loud and appear violent, and include screaming, ranting, shouting, hitting, smashing and self-harm, or they can be akin to a type of shutdown: the person may withdraw, go mute, and become unable to connect, process and communicate with the world around them.

Even now, I remember all too clearly the deep shame of that first public meltdown. I was making a card for Mother's Day, but I couldn't colour within the lines or cut and fold the card so that the edges were straight. The teacher bent over me, her face too close to mine, loudly pointing out my mistakes. The smell of her breath, laced with coffee and cigarettes, was overpowering, and I instinctively covered my nose. She grew angry and her voice became louder as the other children began to laugh. I knew the card, like me, wasn't good enough, but the more I tried, the worse it became. The frustration built as the noise of the room swirled in a crescendo. Feeling the piercing heat of all eyes on me, the intensity of the smells, the harsh lighting, the noise of so many voices... I lost control.

I never wanted to hurt anyone else; I think maybe I wanted to destroy myself and anything I had created, so I tore up the card and, as my brain surged with overload, I wildly hit my fists against my head and ranted until words became only a string of incoherent insults aimed at myself: 'Useless, bad, stupid', then howls, and finally, just whimpers.

When I regained some semblance of balance, I was horrified at who I had become. Spiritually left naked and exposed, I was rendered mute. The silence was deafening, as the other kids sat shocked in stillness, assuming the insults had been aimed at the teacher. I could see the disgust in her eyes, which was too much for me to bear on top of my own shame. I wanted the ground to swallow me up. I wanted to die.

From that day onwards, my meltdowns became a dirty little secret, a thing I tried to push deep down and bury. In abject fear, I did everything I could to become what others needed me to be, hoping that, if I could be perfect 99% of the time, I might be forgiven if the beast returned, instead of being permanently rejected. The pressure was immense, and I spent a lot of time alone, trying to hide my failings and punishing myself.

I would spend weeks to months locking myself away, burnt out and too afraid to show up in the world. In public, I learned to wear the mask that others needed to see, even though it exhausted me to the point of physical pain. I found ways to get by, mimicking and mirroring the 'acceptable' behaviour of those around me, although I often interpreted that behaviour incorrectly, or took it to extremes, so even then I failed. And, of course, I would do anything to please people, which led me down its own dark path.

The older I grew, the more factors there were to aggravate the meltdowns: hormonal changes, new societal rules and expectations (many of which did not make sense to me and yet everyone else seemed to just understand), and, of course, the ever-changing landscape of schools, university, workplaces and people.

It didn't matter how kind, loving and gentle I was, or how hard I tried. Even when I developed a deep connection with someone, the moment they witnessed or even heard second-hand about one of my meltdowns, I would be shunned and treated as if I was some awful violent person, even though the only person my meltdowns ever hurt was me.

And so, is it any wonder I developed such deep shame, believing I was bad, evil, broken, tormented by a raging paranoia that I would be exposed and then cast out for good? The older I became, the deeper this shame grew.

In my mid-20s, when my son died shortly after birth due to a series of hospital mistakes, I was utterly convinced this was punishment for the evil that lived inside me. People like me did not deserve a family; we deserved to live in this world alone.

Following my son's death, in his honour, for the next 15 years I dedicated myself to absolution, trying to find an answer – a way to eradicate this dark unholiness that lived inside of me, a way to slay the beast. I trained as a therapist, a meditation teacher, an energy healer, a shadow worker, and more besides. My life became solely about healing and using any knowledge I gained to help people. But in my own battle, still the beast would not leave. I could feel her in there, breathing, waiting to destroy. I hated her with a searing passion.

For so many of us with autism, adult meltdowns are the shadow that we have to hide in order to be accepted into society. We experience not only the meltdown itself but the aftermath – those devastating moments as we come back into our being and realise the destruction we have caused. We may have to navigate physical injury, marks, scratches, bruises and tender patches where we've banged our fists against our head one too many times. We have to face our emotional distress, shame, embarrassment and fear as we scan our environment, desperately assessing who may have seen or heard, and what the consequences might be. It can be a wholly isolating experience.

For me, having qualified as a therapist and still encountering the beast, I faced an even deeper level of shame and isolation, afraid to speak my truth for fear of being judged and labelled incompetent, a fraud or, worse, unsafe for my clients.

Deb Dana asserts, 'The ability to self-regulate is built on ongoing experiences of co-regulation. Through co-regulation we connect with others and create a sense of safety' (2020, p.3). In other words, when our own nervous system feels as if it is spiralling, we need to be in the presence of someone who can remain calm, grounded and relaxed, and share their regulated state with us. Consequently, she says, 'connection is a wired-in biological necessity; isolation, or even the perception of social separateness, leads to a compromised ability to regulate' (2020, p.27).

How do we, as autistic beings who never experienced co-regulation for our meltdowns as children, experience it now as an adult, when we hide that part of ourselves from the world? How do we experience this necessary connection when our beasts serve to keep other people at bay and keep us isolated? How do we learn to trust when, as children, our meltdowns were seen as tantrums – something to punish? And how do we learn to regulate when there is so little open dialogue and therefore so little understanding of and training around adult meltdowns?

These issues are compounded further when we come to understand that, unlike tantrums, anxiety or stress, which may all be eased with standard regulation techniques and tools, meltdowns can be extremely difficult to regulate because of their uniquely individualised nature and the specific needs of the individual, and because, when in meltdown, the body itself becomes a hazard, and the agent of that body is no longer in the driver's seat. The beast has taken control of the wheel.

Consequently, the self-regulation and mindful practices that we have been taught in our therapy training can, at times, be more aggravating. Would you want to ground yourself in your body when your body has become the enemy? Could you be mindful in the here and now when the here and now is attacking and overwhelming you from every angle, externally and internally? Would you want to take slow diaphragmatic breaths when each one of those inhales has the potential to anchor you into a present moment where you will become acutely aware that every inch of your body is crawling with sensory overload, and you're overstimulated to the point of physical pain? Would you be able to name five things that you can see when your brain cannot take in any more information because it is in a temporary state of cognitive impairment and your inability to process only adds further to your frustration and despair?

Therefore, it is imperative that any regulation technique used with an autistic person (and, arguably, any person), needs to be bespoke and tailored specifically for the individual, because if not, it has the potential to cause harm and create further unsafety within an already burdened system.

I have come to understand that, if we want to build robust therapeutic practices that address adult meltdowns, we have to stop locking the beast away in the shadows and instead be willing to get to know and learn from it, and to do this we must extend the same loving compassion and empathy to our beast as we would to anyone in distress.

Most importantly, we must be willing to share our experiences of adult meltdowns and create an open dialogue, free from shame and fear of judgement. As Yalom (2002) suggests:

> We therapists should be open to all our own dark, ignoble parts, and there are times when sharing them will enable [others] to stop flagellating themselves. (p.219)

I have spent much time befriending my beast, learning to observe her emergence with curiosity as opposed to judgement, finding ways to understand her non-verbal language, and inviting her to be my guide as I voyage through my unique autistic ecosystem.

I have learned to observe my neuroception – that part of my brain that operates outside of awareness, constantly scanning for signs of threats or safety (Porges, 2004). I have closely surveyed how this part of me classifies what is felt to be too much (hypersensitivity) or too little (hyposensitivity), what is interpreted as safe and soothing, and how all classifications and parameters may alter depending on context and situation.

Consequently, I have learned how and when my system summons the beast, and slowly I have come to appreciate her function and purpose. She is not trying to harm me; she never was; she is simply trying to ensure my survival by creating space.

We humans are taught that, if we encounter a wild animal, we should keep our distance and, if necessary, freeze and remain still. When I become overstimulated, the external world becomes too much, and everything becomes a threat. That's when the beast's energy appears, merging with my own, her wildness sending a signal to the world to back away and give me space. She is an invisible barrier, preventing any further energy or stimulation from entering my system.

Isn't this what we as therapists do? We create a safe environment that offers our clients a space away from the noise, influence, and impact of the outside world.

Secondarily, the beast's overwhelming kinetic energy renders all my internal systems temporarily exhausted. Ever so briefly, there is no thought, emotion or sensation as my entire system prepares to reset, which in turn creates an internal space where I can reconnect with my true essence.

Over time, on the very tail end of a meltdown, I have come to witness that fleeting moment of silent calm – a moment of pure being, devoid of all internal noise. It is akin to a sigh of relief as the tension leaves the body and mind. It is a deeply beautiful, almost sacred juncture, just before the system restarts and the mind leaps back into action, re-flooding the system with regrets, shame, what-if predictions and fears.

As therapists, irrespective of our modality, when we offer acceptance and empathy to all of our client's parts, behaviours and experiences, even the darkest shadows, it dissolves, if only for that moment, the noise from their internal dialogue and narratives. This, in turn, creates space for them to reconnect to their authentic nature; a space where they can safely explore their inner world and past experiences without fear of judgement or rejection; a space to safely experience co-regulation (Rogers, 1961).

Although the beast's methods may be wildly different, I would argue she and I have chosen the same work. Further still, we share the same work ethic. When the beast emerges, her primary focus is my safety, as she helps me remove the threats and energies that are causing my system distress and keeping me dysregulated. She has a job to do; her role is clear, and in those moments, I am her sole priority. This is exactly how I view my work with clients, and perhaps this is why I have never had a meltdown during or before a session. Like my beast, I know my role and take that role very seriously.

I am no longer afraid of the beast, my body or my behaviour during a meltdown, as I now view it as a simple biological process trying to ensure its organism's survival. I now understand that the problem is not the beast but how I and others have responded to her. Much as we therapists offer our clients space away from the world for a contained amount of time (usually an hour), the beast does the same and only stays while she is needed. It is me who has chosen to keep myself in isolation by attaching to the shame narrative that I was taught as a child. And that same narrative was written by people with little to no understanding of autism.

In accepting my beast, I have learned to accept myself on an entirely new level. I am a competent and effective therapist who experiences adult meltdowns, and I am okay with that. In fact, I'm proud of it, because these experiences have made me a deeply compassionate and knowledgeable therapist.

This is where the true healing lives because, by removing the shame, self-loathing and embarrassment, instead of being flooded with dense, heavy emotions, and fear-evoking predictions when my system reboots post-meltdown, I can extend that moment of calm and connection to my inner being.

From this state, I can take account of and address any damage that I may have caused to myself, my environment and my relationships. I can take ownership of my actions and behaviour and listen to the impact my meltdowns may have had from an open, non-defensive state. And I can gently educate those around me and explain how my words and actions are simply a tool to create a space for my system to reboot without external interference.

I have learned to trust my beast and, as a direct result of this relationship, I can easily remain grounded and unfazed when in the presence of other beasts. I understand how each beast serves a purpose and, as I 'speak' the language of the beast fluently, I can communicate with them in a non-threatening way. Most importantly, I understand how to give a beast the space they require while still remaining present, and this, in turn, creates a safe space for co-regulation.

In my experience, when a beast feels truly understood, compassionately accepted and valued for showing themselves, they come to understand that there is no threat present and allow themselves to soften a little more readily, gently stepping aside to let Self regain control of the wheel (Schwartz, 2021).

When we can create the same space for our beasts as we do for our clients, taking time to understand their frame of reference and communication style, over time they will share with us the blueprint of our unique autistic ecosystems and self-care needs. If we are really willing to listen, the beast will teach us how to stand in this world as a sovereign autistic being, free from shame and armed with valuable healing knowledge. Finally, after 43 years, I've come to see my beast as the mentor and protector she is, and although at times it's a wild ride, there is no one else on this earth I'd rather have beside me.

References

Chick, N. (2013). *Metacognition*. Vanderbilt University Center for Teaching. https://cft.vanderbilt.edu/guides-sub-pages/metacognition/

Dana, D. (2020). *Polyvagal exercises for safety and connection: 50 client-centered practices*. W.W. Norton & Co.

Montgomery, L.M. (1981). *Anne of Green Gables*. Seal Books.

Nannery, S. & Nannery, L. (2021, May 31). What is the difference between a meltdown and a tantrum? *Psychology Today*. www.psychologytoday.com/gb/blog/what-say-next/202105/what-is-the-difference-between-meltdown-and-tantrum

Poissant, S. (2023). *Interoception, autism and the importance of body awareness*. The Rainbow Clinic. https://rainbowclinic.com.au/interoception-autism-and-the-importance-of-body-awareness/

Porges, S. (2004). Neuroception: A subconscious system for detecting threats and safety. *Zero to Three, 24*(5), 19–24.

Rogers, C. (1961). *On becoming a person*. Houghton Mifflin.

Schwartz, R.C. (2021). *No bad parts: Healing trauma and restoring wholeness with the internal family systems model*. Sounds True Adult.

Sullivan, K. (Director). (1985, December 1). *Anne of Green Gables*. TV series. CBC.

Yalom, I.D. (2002). *The gift of therapy*. HarperCollins Publishers.

Chapter 12

Asian American autistic alien

Sharon Xie

My name is Sharon Xie, and I am a psychologist in Washington, USA. I work with families, young adults, and children of all ages in their journeys of self-discovery and agency. Long before I discovered that I was autistic, I knew as an immigrant what it felt like to be perceived as different, to be an outsider and, at times, to be deeply lonely. Spurred on by those experiences, I felt that, as a psychologist, I would be in a unique position to help others bridge the gap in their understandings of one another and build much-needed connection and compassion. When I defied the 'better judgement' of my elders to pursue my degrees in this field, little did I know that I would one day loudly broadcast my differences to the world by writing my own chapter in a book by autistic therapists.

My identity as an Asian American autistic alien is an indelible part of who I am and what I bring to the table in my work as a psychologist. It is the reason why I tell my young neurodivergent clients that they are the experts on themselves and help them create the space they need to explore who they are and discover what works for them. I have found that I cannot truthfully and wholeheartedly advocate for my clients in their awareness, acceptance or even celebration of their differences if I cannot do the same for myself. This chapter is as much for me and the younger Sharon, desperate to find her community, as it is for those who are still searching to find theirs.

Resident alien

I learned from a young age that I was 'different' from others, but the specifics of why I felt that way only came into focus for me over the past couple of years.

The primary explanation I had for my differences for most of my life was also my most visible difference – the difference that I couldn't hide even if I tried, that everyone recognised and reflected back to me: I am Chinese, a minority in the US. I also felt like a minority within a minority; my immigrant experience didn't quite match that of my parents' generation, but nor did it match my brother's, who was born in the US several years after we immigrated. I am a '1.5 generation immigrant', born in China but raised in the US. My identity felt like it had been forged between the push and pull of two vastly different cultures and ideals.

My younger self bristled reflexively at being labelled a 'resident alien' by the US government, and I yearned to be recognised and accepted as a citizen. Had I been more savvy about American pop culture in my youth, I might have recognised a kindred spirit in the half-human, half-Vulcan Spock from the TV series *Star Trek*. Instead, I despaired that I would be the perpetually awkward foreigner, both in the US and in China, and I frequently wondered if I belonged anywhere.

Introduction to 'face'

Like Spock, I gathered enough data over time to note some interesting differences in Chinese and American sociological constructs. For instance, there's a Chinese sociological construct called 'face' – 面子 (*miàn zi*) – a concept akin to honour, dignity, respectability or pride. Much time, energy and emotional labour is devoted to cultivating it, managing it, saving it, or helping others save theirs so that everyone can maintain 'face' together. Since Chinese culture often downplays the concept of the individual in favour of the family or the group, one must also go to great lengths to protect 'face' for the greater good of the community. Even lies rebranded as the truth are welcomed and encouraged, as they spare everyone uncomfortable loss of 'face'.

I am convinced that this concern for 'face' in my own upbringing was further compounded by the fact that my parents grew up under the shadow of the Cultural Revolution and belong to the generation most terrorised by the Tiananmen Square massacre. From one generation to the next, we have been primed for conformity and compliance, because to step visibly out of line is to risk death.

Being able to mask differences, camouflage and blend in with the norm has been essential for our survival, and as an autistic psychologist, I often pause to consider the sociocultural context of my clients' motivations and experiences.

Different

I recall becoming conscious of the fact that I was 'different' on the first day of first grade. I had already lived in the US for a couple of months but, until that day, I had spent most of my time cocooned within environments steeped in Chinese language, culture and traditions. One particular moment of that day stands out.

It was lunchtime. 'Why, in a country of relative abundance, are we sitting on the ground to eat?' I wondered. I had grown up in a world where one strived to dine a healthy distance away from the ground, which was often too dusty or littered to be considered an appropriate place for eating. There was something both freeing and unsettling in the realisation that social rules could be changed willy-nilly.

The only two words I knew to say that day were, 'No English', so I tried smiling apologetically at anyone who looked my way. As I mimicked the actions and affect of the children around me, I also tried my best to hide my discomfort, sat in the overly bright Southern California sun, on a prickly patch of lawn that was somehow still spongy and wet. In my experience, Chinese people avoided the sun to keep from tanning, but clearly the rules were different here.

And what about all the ants? Why are we putting ourselves and our lunches so close to them on this horridly swampy grass? I looked around in wonder that everyone appeared so at ease, collecting wet grass stains on their bottoms and risking contaminating their lunches. My mind eventually drifted to pondering what a foreign place I was in, and how much I would have to learn and change in order to blend in and belong.

My parents had worked hard for my opportunity to grow up in the US. In my six-year-old heart, I was determined to do this right, and I wasn't about to lose 'face' by giving away the fact that I was a clueless foreigner.

Learning to camouflage

In school, I established a reputation of being relatively shy and quiet. I was not so in actuality, but I thought that being my boisterous and opinionated self was not allowed. I tried to smile often, to show that I was friendly and approachable. I studied how others behaved and talked, and I paid close attention to what others might be thinking of me. I was also paralysed with fear of saying or doing anything that would bring too much attention to myself. I didn't feel like I had much in common with the other children, and the times that I recall being the centre of attention were times of embarrassment or rejection. I was certain this all had to do with the fact that I was an immigrant who hadn't yet learned enough about American culture.

I learned enough to gradually blend into the background of most classroom settings and excelled at camouflaging what I thought and felt, to the point that I hardly knew what I thought and how I felt. Still, lurking beneath the surface were the feelings of inadequacy, deficiency and foreignness that I had had on the first day of first grade. They followed me everywhere I went, showing up at unexpected times and moments long after I thought I had mastered the language and 'acculturated' to American life. My identity as an immigrant, coupled with a personal history of traumatic childhood events, served as justification for any misunderstandings or disconnection I felt between me and my peers.

In Chinese culture, the topic of mental health is taboo and stigmatised, so that all neurodivergences can be lumped under one term – 神经病 (*shén jīng bìng*) – synonymous with being crazy/psychotic/mentally sick. Autism is called 自闭症 (*zì bì zhèng*) – literally, 'self-closed disease', meaning 'one who is imprisoned within themselves'. There is also a strong fear in Chinese culture that being surrounded by such people all day can only lead you becoming 'crazy' yourself.

This stigmatising and pathologising ideology, infused with Confucian beliefs of social hierarchy within an authoritarian state, demands that you must hide your inconvenient truths and differences by walking the narrowest heteronormative and neuronormative path. In a traditional Chinese cultural upbringing, we are expected and encouraged to uphold an acceptable, desirable 'face' that we present to the world, even if it is far from the reality of our personal lives and inner selves. You can shout and cry in private, but in public you have to hide that anguish behind a smile and a reputable appearance.

The many shutdowns I had in my early years evolved into private meltdowns in my pre-teen and teenage years. If my parents had believed in therapy and could have afforded it, I would have been diagnosed with depression and anxiety, or even perhaps 'oppositional-defiant disorder'. Instead, we all settled on the explanation that I was obstinate, egocentric, illogical, angry, sullen, explosive, difficult, rude and clearly capable of doing better if it were not for my stubborn defiance. We were also masters at saving 'face', and as such, I was encouraged to build my outward identity as an intellectually gifted and generally competent student, who eventually made it to grad school, got her PhD, and opened a clinic.

Still, I was also the child who became situationally mute ('Oh, she's just being shy right now'); who now, as an adult, stumbled over or completely lost her words in high-stress situations ('Well, English is my second language, after all'). I was the child who observed others and wondered how they all just *got* each other; who, as an adult, began rehearsing scenarios and scripts before events and gatherings and scrutinising every interaction afterwards. I was the student who spent the occasional recess hiding in the bathroom to avoid potential social stressors and rejection, and who now strategically retreated to the bathroom during parties to get away from sensory overwhelm.

Those truths were better off hidden and tucked away, so invisible to everyone else that they even became invisible to me. Even worse, my graduate training further reinforced the message that, if I just worked harder and practised more at behaving normally – eating well, sleeping well, taking deep breaths and meditating more often – I, too, could be rid of my anxiety and meltdowns.

Self-transformation

It didn't occur to me that I could be autistic until I was 35. My formal training in psychology didn't give me the antidote I needed for the problematic and ableist views of mental health I had inherited from my Chinese upbringing. Rather, it subtly reinforced the stigma and pathology as valid. Depressed, anxious, personality-disordered people need intensive cognitive restructuring and behaviour change. People 'on the spectrum' need ABA; they need to have their behaviours controlled, their impulses punished and their bodies regulated. My formal education repeated the same message: assimilate, save face, stay masked, blend in and step back in line. Even as I floundered more than I could ever admit, I clung desperately to two of my favourite mottos from my mentors: 'Fake it 'til you make it,' and 'Follow the path of least resistance'.

My observable behaviours – graduation, licensure, running a practice, exercising, sleeping, socialising, and other outward measures of success – masked from everyone the reality of my own neurodivergences. It was incredibly confusing and impossible within this narrow view of wellness to reconcile my observable behaviours with the undesirable behaviours that made their way out during my meltdowns. Trained in a pathologising, behaviour-focused framework throughout my life and formal education, I believed that, despite my many capabilities and accomplishments, I was also quite broken and prone to moral failures.

Flying under the radar and hiding the uncomfortable truth that I was struggling with two different realities was my path of least resistance – until it wasn't. My strategy of blending in, saving face and masking my differences finally fell apart when I became a working parent. I could not raise my child with empathy, validation and compassion if I did not first do the difficult work of treating myself with the same consideration and care.

And if CBT and DBT didn't 'work' for me as promised, then what hope did I have of truly helping my clients? What if I couldn't strong-arm my way out of anxiety and depression just by eating and sleeping better or socialising and exercising more? It felt hypocritical and unethical – deeply abhorrent, even – not to believe in what I preached.

Ultimately, I found that I could not model awareness, acceptance, confidence and validation simply by going through the motions and feigning it; I had to live it. By the time I received my clinical diagnoses of autism, ADHD, OCD and PTSD in 2022, at the age of 36, I had already begun refocusing my worldview through a neurodiversity-affirming lens. This self-transformation in turn transformed my work, helping me to hold space for my neurodivergent clients in a way that allowed them to find their own truths within neuronormative cultures and systems.

Autistic psychologist

After processing the revelation of my autistic identity for several days, my mother called me with a familiar note of concern in her voice: had I spent too much time and been unduly influenced by the neurodivergent people in my life? Did my dear friend Catherine's autistic identity rub off on me because we've been close friends for more than 25 years? Would potential clients be put off by the notion of working with an autistic therapist?

I offered instead an alternate perspective: therapists cannot provide clients with informed choices or informed care if we do not understand neurodivergence. Living my own neurodivergence as an Asian American autistic individual is what makes me so well-equipped to work with my neurodivergent clients. If I hadn't been a master of disguise, and eventually recognised myself as such, I would not be able to help my clients recognise when they themselves engage in masking or camouflaging to their own detriment. If I hadn't come to recognise my own internalised ableism and the systems under which I inherited it, I would not be able to help my clients recognise those systems for themselves.

Now, rather than labelling ourselves as 'lacking or deficient in social skills', my clients and I discuss the 'double empathy problem' (Milton, 2012). Rather than labelling a meltdown as the result of being 'irrational and having poor self-control', we talk about sensory differences, spoon theory (Miserandino, 2010) and the humanistic and social models of disability. We recognise problematic narratives about desirable versus undesirable neurodivergences, and that every one of us is much more complex and multifaceted than those narrow lenses could ever capture. Any modality of therapy has the potential be insufficient, negligent and cruel if we do not understand and approach our clients within a neurodiversity-affirming framework.

There is always room to grow, and I hope to continue to learn as a neurodiversity-affirming therapist well beyond the end of this chapter. Ironically, the fearful warning that I would 'become one of them' was ultimately quite prophetic: by systematically ruling out the fallacies that I had been told about myself, I finally stumbled upon my own autistic identity. As Spock once said, quoting Arthur Conan Doyle's fictional (and arguably autistic) detective Sherlock Holmes (Conan Doyle, 1890, p.93), 'When you eliminate the impossible, whatever remains, however improbable, must be the truth.'

References

Conan Doyle, A. (1890). *The sign of the four.* Spencer Blackett.

Milton, D.E.M. (2012). On the ontological status of autism: The 'double empathy problem'. *Disability and Society, 27*(6), 883–887.

Miserandino, C. (2010). *The spoon theory.* Butyoudon'tlooksick.com. https://butyoudontlooksick.com/articles/written-by-christine/the-spoon-theory/

Chapter 13

Working in one's own community: Self-disclosure and being 'that self which one truly is'

Max Marnau

Self-disclosure is a very sensitive area in counselling training and in the profession's ethical frameworks. There is no doubt that boundary violations and exploitative dual relationships are unacceptable and, indeed, prohibited, but need that mean that boundary crossings must also be so? As Ofer Zur explains (2018):

> One of the biggest concerns with boundaries is the myth of the '*slippery slope*.' The term 'slippery slope' refers to the idea that failure to adhere to rigid risk management-urban-analytic standards will undeniably lead to harm, exploitation and sexual relationships. (para.14, italics in original)

After discussion, he concludes that:

> Despite the persistent popularity of the term among ethicists and risk management experts, the 'slippery slope' is a baseless and illogical construct. (para.15)

He adds that the concept, which would ban all self-disclosure for fear of what it might lead to, is 'especially dangerous when it comes to rural mental health practices' (para.16). In my view, it's not just dangerous but impossible to abide by such a stricture without damaging the community and the therapeutic relationship itself.

And it may be quite simply impossible to abide by, in a community where everyone knows everyone, where there is only one GP surgery, one music venue, one greengrocer, one church, and where there is very little middle ground between being thoroughly known and withdrawing entirely from society.

* * * *

When a therapist works in the community they live in – figuratively or literally – then, as Schank and colleagues argue (2010), 'acts of everyday living are self-disclosures' (p.503). This is certainly true when the community is geographical, especially if it is non-urban. The Scottish Borders, where I live and work, is relatively sparsely populated and it was inevitable that I would meet my clients while shopping in the supermarket, at music gigs, in the café and maybe even in the GP or dentist's waiting room. In the days of working only in person, in my first meeting with a new client, I had a script that ran approximately: 'The Scottish Borders is like a village. It is inevitable that we will meet now and then. I won't acknowledge you, but if you choose to acknowledge me, I will respond.'

That never presented a problem. A couple of clients discovered that I like Red Leicester cheese and a few discovered that I like traditional music. Occasionally I had to prevent my face from betraying anything when a client criticised a friend, or vice versa. Sometimes a client would acknowledge me, and I would respond; sometimes they would not. And that was all.

Before the Covid pandemic and the move to telehealth that it necessitated, my community, and so my caseload, was limited to the Scottish Borders. It was varied as to age, gender and presenting issue, and perhaps 90% non-autistic.

As an inhabitant of the Scottish Borders, I could not avoid those acts of everyday living that amounted to self-disclosure; with the move to telehealth, I was presented with a choice.

My practice could – and did – now extend throughout the UK and occasionally beyond. Would I take the opportunity to become anonymous, one head and shoulders on a screen among the world's billions, or would I choose to join another small community, a community in which I would both live and work, and by the very fact of my allegiance to it, become potentially even more visible and 'disclosed' than I was when my caseload was confined to my fellow Borderers?

That community is the autistic community, in which I already silently lived, but in which I had not, up until then, had the opportunity to work.

I have described the rationale and the process of that choice in detail elsewhere (Marnau, 2021, pp.26–29). Here I will just say that, within months, I was living and working in the online autistic community, my caseload was 80% autistic, and I was fully 'out' as autistic and navigating (at first, on a wing and a prayer) that sensitive area of self-disclosure.

The change came when I was asked by a charity to offer brief online therapy to autistic women in Scotland, simply on the grounds that I am autistic, female and live in Scotland. From almost all of those women, I heard a similar story: childhood and youth undiagnosed, labelled as stupid, lazy, difficult, picky, arrogant, weird, misbehaving, thoughtless, misfit; given a variety of diagnoses, none of which quite seemed to fit; then a late autism diagnosis, presented in terms of deficiency, disorder, pathology, incapacity. And then – the final indignity – being assigned a therapist who did not understand autistic people; indeed, who did not see the need to do so, the aim of therapy being to help the client cease to be weird, a misfit … all those words: to give up, in short, all hope of becoming 'that self which one truly is' (Rogers, 1961, p.163), the self that they had struggled to mask or camouflage all their lives, and had maybe glimpsed during the diagnostic process.

I could not in all conscience refuse to stand in solidarity with those women – and later men as well – who were my community, my tribe (that word resonates for me as a person of Jewish origin), my neurokin.

I had already had a small amount of experience of working in a community in which I lived, figuratively speaking. Not a geographical community, but a community of kinship or shared experience to which I myself belonged: survivors of spiritual abuse. This is a fairly rare specialism, and most people who write or offer support in the area are themselves survivors. It is taken as the norm that understanding comes from lived experience and not from theoretical study. And maybe that is why these clients were not interested in my own experience. They expected me to be a fellow survivor, even if I had not clearly stated it in my profile. They did not expect me to disclose my experiences, and I very rarely felt that it would be therapeutically useful for me to do so.

Whereas in the case of autism, the situation is radically different. Until very recently (and to a surprising extent still), autistic people have been the object of research and discussion by non-autistic people. We were the 'done to', the research subjects, not the 'doers', the researchers. The experts were experts by study, experts in theory – and too often very far from experts, in fact.

A search for therapists who work with autism in the Counselling Directory in 2022 (www.counselling-directory.org.uk) produced 4,689 results. Adding Asperger syndrome increased that to 6,389. Of those, how many stated in their profile that they were autistic? A small handful. Very few of them even listed any training in autism. This is not a criticism, simply an observation and an indication of how difficult it can be to find a therapist who properly understands our neurotype, let alone one who shares it. 'Autistic (or neurodivergent) therapist' is not a searchable term.

If being an expert by experience is not the norm, unlike in the field of spiritual abuse, then providing autistic therapists for autistic people requires that we 'out' ourselves publicly. And, as I suggest, this raises certain issues and requires us to address and maybe rethink this highly sensitive area, whose boundaries are presented in most therapy training as uncrossable.

Before I came out as autistic, if a client sought counselling with me for a particular issue, they would have had no idea whether or not I had myself experienced that issue (although in the case of spiritual abuse they could make a good guess). And, apart from confirming that guess if asked, I can't remember an occasion when I told them – or even considered telling them. A shared painful experience – an assault, maybe, or lived experience of depression – is the sort of thing that would normally be 'not for the counselling room', or not without an exceptional reason, a great deal of reflection and, probably, discussion with your supervisor.

I am a person-centred therapist. Carl Rogers, the founder of my modality, listed 'congruence' among his 'necessary and sufficient conditions for therapeutic personality change' (Rogers, 1957, pp.95–103). In Rogers' own words, congruence is, if I understand it correctly, the therapist being 'that self which he truly is' in the counselling room. It does not mean telling a client everything that comes to mind, but for an autistic therapist, it would seem to include not camouflaging or masking. If I do not have the self-esteem and courage to be the self that I truly am, how can I expect it of my client?

I have found elements of feminist theory of therapy enlightening in realigning my ethical approach. For example, the Feminist Therapy Institute code of ethics states (1996/1999):

> A feminist therapist discloses information to the client that facilitates the therapeutic process…The therapist is responsible for using self-disclosure only with purpose and discretion and in the interest of the client. (p.4)

According to Mahalik and colleagues (2000):

> feminist therapists were more likely… to support the use of self-disclosure to promote a more egalitarian relationship with the client and to provide better opportunities for the client to choose a therapist to serve as a role model. (p.194)

This rationale 'to promote a more egalitarian relationship with the client and to provide better opportunities for the client to choose a therapist as a role model' applies in the case of autistic–autistic therapy. The two may appear contradictory: either the relationship is equal, or the therapist is a role model (and therefore 'superior'). However, in the context of therapy provided both by and for a minority or oppressed group, the contradiction disappears.

For a group of people who have been consistently treated as less – less capable, less worthy, less reliable – and have consistently had their freedoms curtailed, their authentic selves denied, their experience and understanding negated and their very being described in terms of deficiency (here you might list women, autistic people, people of colour, members of the LGBTQIA++ community, and so on), having a therapist who openly shares the very characteristic that is at the root of the client's trauma and sense of worthlessness can be revolutionary.

It is hard to believe in unconditional positive regard when nothing of the kind has ever been offered to you. So, to look at one's therapist after describing an experience that nobody has ever understood or accepted, and to see that not only do they understand the experience but they share it, can be life-changing: not only understood but mirrored.

An important element in autistic–autistic self-disclosure is what is known in autistic circles as 'sameing'. It has often been noted that autistic people show empathy by offering a similar experience of our own. This is sometimes misunderstood as 'making it all about us', and a therapist who uses sameing must use it with great care. But an autistic client who knows their therapist is also autistic will, consciously or not, expect it, and perceive its absence as incongruent.

Paradoxically, the more important self-disclosure is, the more important boundaries become. I can think of no occasions where it would be therapeutically significant – either negatively or positively – for a client to know that I like Red Leicester cheese. My taste in music might or might not create a superficial bond, and for that reason I would think twice before intentionally communicating it, although the language of music, of singing, of playing, of listening, can be very useful and illuminating. But… acts of everyday living are self-disclosures.

Self-disclosure is not an either/or and can be seen as a continuum. As Mahalik and colleagues observe (2000):

> The use of self-disclosure should be recast from the dichotomy of whether to self-disclose or not to a continuum of degrees of self-disclosure… seeing self-disclosure on a continuum serves to highlight the dangers of underdisclosing and overdisclosing because to date most of the literature focuses on the latter while ignoring the former. (p.190)

If 'revealing the therapist's self is inevitable when clients observe a therapist's age, gender, ethnicity, race, and physical challenges in addition to how a therapist decorates his or her office, dresses, sets fees, chooses settings in which to practice' (Mahalik et al., 2000, p.190), then my way of being, my autistic way of being, also reveals my self – my autistic self: my modes of expression; my apparently slow processing (it's worth noting here that autists probably do not process slowly; we are simply having to process far more than neurotypicals do (Beardon, 2021, p.55)). I am quite open about this; I may say, for example, 'Give me a minute to process that.' My tendency is to close my eyes and/or play with fidget toys when I am really concentrating. Like many autistic people, my tones of voice are not always conventional, and my questions do not always sound like questions – more like statements. After a lifetime of being misunderstood, I often now say, 'That was a question' or, 'This will be a question – with a question mark after it' and I may even sometimes sketch that question mark in the air. I could list many similar things. All that has proved very beneficial in 'giving permission' to my autistic clients to do their equivalent.

This is the very opposite of the masking and camouflaging that autistic people use as we struggle to fit in, to 'pass' in a society that is designed neither by nor for us. This is almost universal in those autists who are able to do it: indeed, 'high-masking' is increasingly used by autists as a substitute for the misleading term 'high-functioning'.

We hide our autistic selves and mimic neurotypicals, either from real life or from films or television. We force ourselves to engage in social and other activities that neurotypicals appear either to enjoy or to tolerate but that fill our sensory and cognitive capacity to overflowing and overwhelming. We succeed some of the time, but at a high cost: masking is recognised as a risk factor for anxiety, depression and suicidality. Cassidy and colleagues' study of autistic adults (2018) found that 'Camouflaging significantly predicted suicidality... after controlling for age, sex, presence of at least one developmental condition, depression, anxiety, employment, and satisfaction with living arrangements'.

And, maybe worst of all, it is at the cost of the self that we truly are and reinforces the message that that self is fundamentally unacceptable.

It was only recently, when I revisited spiritual abuse and the characteristics of the cult, that I noticed a striking similarity between the experience of being autistic in a non-autistic environment and the experience of being in a cult – namely, the adoption of a pseudo-personality or pseudo-identity. Autistic people mask or camouflage in order to fit in neurotypical society; in a cult, a person learns to be the kind of person the cult requires. For example, Singer (2003) explains:

> As part of the intense influence and change process in many cults, people take on a new social identity… when the group refer to this new identity, they speak of members who are transformed, reborn, enlightened, empowered, re-birthed, or cleared. The group-approved behavior is

reinforced and reinterpreted as demonstrating the emergence of the 'new person'. (pp.77–78)

Members are expected to display this new social identity. The similarity between this and certain coercive 'therapies' aimed at making autistic children appear non-autistic is stark.

As a survivor of spiritual abuse, I know from experience the deep effect of thought reform within a cult, and the creation of a cult pseudo-personality. I know how hard it is to access the person one was before, how eternally triggering the words belonging to the cult's loaded language or cult jargon lexicon can be. Steve Hassan comments, 'Cult jargon will often elicit the cult identity' (Hassan, 2012, p.101). I know in a way that no theoretician can ever know how dangerous it can feel simply to be my self.

As a late-diagnosed autist, I know from experience the deep effect of struggling to conform to what is apparently the only acceptable way to be, and the creation of the mask. I know how hard it is to access the person within who is not acceptable and who is my self, how eternally triggering the words of criticism, deficiency, pathology and dismissal can be. I know in a way that no theoretician can know how dangerous it can feel simply to be my self.

Just as returning to the outside world after time in a cult 'should' simply mean that we have understood the untruth of the messages and can proceed with our lives, so a diagnosis of autism 'should' simply mean that we understand why we have felt alien and misunderstood all our lives, and why we find so very difficult the things that 'everyone else' accomplishes with ease. And we 'should' simply be able to slip into our new autistic identity and cast aside the irrelevant demand to fit in.

But it's not as simple as that. In both cases, in a cult and in our lives as autists in a non-autistic society, the very worst thing we can do is be our selves. As suggested above, the effects of both mirror the effects of trauma.

And, indeed, since trauma is the experience of threat to life, limb or freedom, a cult survivor and a late-diagnosed autist are both suffering from trauma properly so called, and are likely to show signs of post-traumatic stress disorder.

Thought reform, reprogramming of the personality, enforced masking – these do not ultimately work, or not without causing immense damage to the system. Gillie Jenkinson (2008) describes the pseudo-personality as an introject:

> material – a way of acting, feeling, evaluating – which you have taken into your system of behavior but which you have not assimilated in such fashion as to make it a genuine part of your organism – your self. (pp.214–219)

Fritz Perls (Perls et al., 1951) compares an introject to unwholesome food:

> Physical food properly digested and assimilated becomes part of the organism; but food which 'rests heavy on the stomach' is an introject. You are aware of it and want to throw it up. If you do so, you get it 'out of the system'. Suppose, instead, you suppress your discomfort, nausea, and tendency to spew it forth. Then you 'keep it down' and either succeed, finally, in painfully digesting it or else it poisons you. (p.189)

And this is where the autistic therapist comes in. We know, just as the survivor of spiritual abuse knows, the poisoning effect of the introject. We know the invisible trauma of having your self rejected as unacceptable over years, and maybe decades. Most of us high-masking autists have been told (probably multiple times) 'You don't look autistic.' No. We probably also don't look traumatised, or at least our lives don't look as if they contain trauma. And so we find ourselves diagnosed with generalised anxiety disorder, depression, personality disorders and even psychosis.

So, when autistic clients come to us with these presenting issues and diagnoses that have been foisted upon them, we need to let them question what they have been told, to dig underneath the diagnoses, for the first time perhaps to take the time to describe what it is like to be them. It will almost certainly be the first time that they have seen a 'mental health professional' nod and acknowledge their experience as normal, unsurprising, even obvious.

A common trajectory for my clients is to present with (for example) generalised anxiety disorder and depression, or symptoms of PTSD, 'for no apparent reason'. They come hoping to learn how to 'manage' all this. In the process of our work, they start to disentangle (I am quoting one of my clients, with their permission) 'what is the autism, which is just how I am made, and what is the effect of living in a society which makes no allowance for that'. Recognising and accepting 'how I am made' gives me permission to reshape my life, as far as I can, to fit my self, rather than bending that self out of shape to fit the demands and expectations of a non-autistic society. And it also gives capacity and permission to recognise the invisible trauma of:

- constant misunderstanding ('It must be my fault')
- almost universal negative judgement ('They must be right')
- being unable to tolerate what everyone else seems to find pleasant, or at least tolerable ('I must be picky, a drama queen, over-sensitive, making a fuss')
- being unable to understand or achieve what everyone else seems to find easy ('I must be stupid or lazy or both')

- damaging therapies aimed at changing behaviour without any regard for the experience behind the behaviour.

The result can be, and often is, transformational. 'You mean my responses are entirely understandable, that trying to live according to this non-autistic society is genuinely anxiety-provoking, genuinely depressing, genuinely traumatising?' Yes. And I know it from experience.

If, as therapists, we refuse to show ourselves, if we refuse to engage as one autist with another, one survivor with another, we are reinforcing all the damage, all the 'othering' that has been inflicted on our clients by the cult or the non-autistic society.

A caveat here. As mentioned above, the more important self-disclosure is, the more important boundaries become. I have found that holding boundaries, bracketing and constant self-questioning ('For whom am I asking this question, or saying this thing?') are of paramount importance. Self-disclosure is:

> most helpful to clients when it (is) a conscious decision on the part of the therapist in which the therapist (has) an explicit clinical rationale based on an assessment of the client's needs… Thus, clinicians who are aware of how they arrive at a clinical decision are in a better position to exercise power ethically and responsibly by making self-disclosure a helpful part of the clinical treatment rather than something done impulsively. (Mahalik et al., 2000, p.196–197)

I have made the choice, for example, to withdraw entirely from the social element of the autistic community, except with my peers on Facebook, in the Autistic Counsellors and Psychotherapists group. I have thus chosen not to put myself in a position in which I might unintentionally or even unknowingly self-disclose to a client or potential client. That is a personal choice and not necessarily the only acceptable one.

In his book *The Gift of Therapy*, Irvin Yalom titled one of his chapters 'Blank Screen? Forget it! Be real!' (Yalom, 2001, pp.75–82).

With all the caveats, there are times when a client needs anything but a blank screen. They need a human being, and they need a human being who inhabits the same world as they do, literally or figuratively. They need someone who knows from experience that there is no work or affordable housing available in their small town and that the town council is still 90% male and 100% white, or that almost every communication seems to end in misunderstanding and the lights and the noise in almost every venue are unbearable. After believing all their life that they are alone on the journey, they need to know that there are fellow travellers (Yalom, 2001, pp.6–10), and that one of them is there, listening.

Therapists don't come to work to address our own problems. We do that elsewhere. And it is essential that the client knows that deeply. But for a client to know that their therapist has faced similar struggles and has found a way to be the self that they truly are, despite – or in the midst of – those troubles, gives hope. And without hope, what use is the best therapy?

References

Beardon, L. (2021). *Avoiding anxiety in autistic adults*. Sheldon Press.

Cassidy, S., Bradley, L., Shaw, R. & Baron-Cohen, S. (2018). Risk markers for suicidality in autistic adults. *Molecular Autism, 9,* 42. https://doi.org/10.1186/s13229-018-0226-4

Feminist Therapy Institute. (1996; revised 1999). Feminist Therapy Institute code of Ethics. *Women & Therapy, 19,* 79–91. www.apa.org/pubs/books/supplemental/Supervision-Essentials-Feminist-Psychotherapy-Model-Supervision/Appendix_D.pdf

Hassan, S. (2012). *Freedom of mind: Helping loved ones leave controlling people, cults, and beliefs.* Freedom of Mind Press.

Jenkinson, G. (2008) An investigation into cult pseudo-personality: What is it and how does it form? *Cultic Studies Review, 7*(3), 199–224.

Mahalik, J.R., Van Ormer, E.A. & Simi, N.L. (2000). Ethical issues in using self-disclosure in feminist therapy. In M.M. Brabeck (Ed.), *Practicing feminist ethics in psychology* (pp.189–201). American Psychological Association.

Marnau, M. (2021). Coming out as an autistic therapist. *Therapy Today, 32*(1), 26–29.

Perls, F., Hefferline, R. & Goodman, P. (1951). *Gestalt therapy: Excitement and growth in the human personality*. Souvenir Press.

Rogers, C.R. (1957). The necessary and sufficient conditions of therapeutic personality change. *Journal of Consulting Psychology, 21*(2), 95–103.

Rogers, C.R. (1961). *On becoming a person*. Houghton Mifflin.

Schank, J.A, Helbok, C.M., Haldeman, D.C. & Gallardo, M.E. (2010). Challenges and benefits of ethical small-community practice. *Professional Psychology: Research and Practice, 41*(6), 502–510. https://doi.org/10.1037/a0021689

Singer, M.T. (2003). *Cults in our midst*. Jossey-Bass.

Yalom, I. (2001) *The gift of therapy*. Piatkus.

Zur, O. (2018). *Therapeutic boundaries and dual relationships in rural practice: Ethical, clinical and standard of care considerations*. Zur Institute. www.zurinstitute.com/online/rural14

Chapter 14

The autistic sense of justice and moral injury: Battling the system and blowing the whistle

Shirley Moore

Like many counsellors and psychotherapists, I began my training journey as a mature student and, in common with many autistic adults, I have explored a number of different careers. Some were more successful than others. I have undergraduate and postgraduate degrees in engineering, and I worked as a doctor in the NHS for 10 years after completing my medical degree, latterly specialising in anaesthesia and intensive care.

My autism diagnosis came during a period of what I now recognise as autistic burnout, while on long-term sick leave from the NHS. For me, at that time and in my work and home environment, being autistic and working as a doctor proved to be mutually exclusive. I was one of the first doctors to write publicly about being autistic (Moore et al., 2020), and now community networks of autistic doctors can be found online, much like the network of autistic counsellors that led to this book. In common with other autistic doctors' experiences (Doherty et al., 2021), I got on well with patients but struggled in relationships with my colleagues and managers. The lack of time I had to spend with patients was one of the many stressful aspects for me of working as a junior doctor, and when it all became too much, I dreamed of alternative careers where I could make a difference to people's lives, have some control over my work and focus on one thing at a time – ideally somewhere I could see daylight during the working day. I had been on sick leave for more than a year and was facing imminent dismissal when my counselling journey began. A chance encounter with a psychotherapy student led to a discussion about counselling training. That evening, I discovered there was a counselling skills course starting at my local college, and I enrolled.

As a recently diagnosed autistic woman, I began the training with the familiar butterflies in my stomach, but also with an unusual feeling of optimism. I was 42 and, being a Douglas Adams fan, I felt particularly tickled that this number is the answer to 'the great Question of Life, the Universe and Everything' (Adams, 1979). Perhaps I was finally on the right path in life and the world would start to make sense.

I had always been a 'good' student. Although battling executive functioning challenges, I always met deadlines (though often with minutes to spare), did well academically and followed 'the rules' (at least, the rules that made sense to me). I was shy, hated conflict and disliked attracting attention. I would rather struggle for hours trying to work things out for myself than ask a question and alert the tutors to my 'stupidity'. I was competent but not confident. I slid under the radar, which was exactly where I wanted to be – the 'model' undiagnosed autistic woman, walking the tightrope of life unaided by a balancing pole, terrified of falling and failing.

I thoroughly enjoyed my counselling certificate course. I disclosed my autisticness early on, and was met with curiosity and kindness. I felt safe to ask questions. I even allowed some of my unfiltered thought processes into discussions and was able to laugh about how they might appear weird to others, whose thoughts often appeared equally weird to me. I was the only openly autistic student, but it didn't feel like a typical neurotypical space. I never felt the need for adjustments or accommodations, and I completed my course excited for the next stage.

Three years later, I was suspended from my person-centred diploma course and facing the threat of legal action; I had several complaints in progress and had made whistleblowing disclosures; I was hurt, traumatised and completely focused on holding the institution to account. I could not relax; I wasn't sleeping; I was full of embitterment and my relationships were suffering.

Of course, I did eventually qualify as a counsellor, and I am delighted to be able to contribute to this book evidencing the valuable contribution autistic therapists bring to the field. I now work in private practice, using a predominantly person-centred approach and, although I don't work exclusively with autistic clients, they make up the majority of my caseload. While some of my training experiences were very challenging, they have proved helpful in scaffolding my therapeutic work. Alongside my counselling work, I volunteer for the Psychotherapy and Counselling Union, supporting people through complaints processes, and I also sit as an independent panel member on resolution and fitness-to-practise panels. Many of the people I work with, either in my counselling 'room' or in more formal regulatory or quasi-regulatory environments, are hurt, embittered and dealing with moral injury. They are not uncommonly involved in grievance or whistleblowing processes or have been through them, with serious and long-lasting effects on their mental health. The more I do this kind of work and the more I recognise neurodivergence in the people I come across in these difficult situations, the more interested I am in the links between autism, moral injury, grievances and whistleblowing.

Moral injury, described as a 'soul wound' by Jonathan Shay (2012), who is credited with bringing the term into modern use, is a relatively new concept. Like post-traumatic stress disorder (PTSD), it originated in the military. Unlike PTSD, however, moral injury is not considered a mental illness and there are no diagnostic criteria, although it can certainly lead to the development of mental health problems. Litz and colleagues (2009) offer a working definition of 'potentially morally injurious experiences':

> Perpetrating, failing to prevent, bearing witness to, or learning about acts that transgress deeply held moral beliefs and expectations. (p.700)

They suggest that this is not limited to witnessing or participating in cruel or inhumane actions; it includes more subtle acts that transgress a moral code, and also failing to prevent immoral acts of others. Moral injury can lead to profound guilt and shame and may underlie or result from whistleblowing action.

Whistleblowing is the reporting of certain types of wrongdoing in the public interest. Protect, a charity supporting whistleblowers in the UK,[1] defines whistleblowing as:

> a worker raising a concern with someone in authority – internally and/or externally (e.g. to regulators, MPs, the media) – about wrongdoing, risk or malpractice that affects others.

The difference between a whistleblowing declaration and a grievance or complaint is that whistleblowing is done in the public interest, whereas complaints or grievances involve issues that directly affect the individual raising them. Organisations and those working for them (whether remunerated or not) will have varying rights, responsibilities and protection, and in some situations there will be very little support for those raising concerns, or indeed those dealing with them.

---

1. https://protect-advice.org.uk

There can be serious consequences for whistleblowers (Lim et al., 2017), who may risk their reputation, career, livelihood and relationships, and, as I discovered as a student whistleblower, protections are often far more limited than people might expect. Furthermore, few whistleblowers are financially compensated for reprisals to their altruistic actions. Even apologies are rare.

For many, life can feel as if it will never be the same again. Even those who raise concerns internally or lodge a personal grievance can experience negative actions. In addition to the factors that led them to complain in the first place, they can encounter issues such as alienation from colleagues, bullying, harassment and even referral to disciplinary processes, the stress of which may lead to physical or mental health problems. They can experience harm from moral injury – not just from learning about or participating in acts that transgress a moral code but from the failure of the very codes that are in place to encourage the reporting of such acts and to protect those that do.

It is widely, but mostly anecdotally, recognised that autistic people are more likely than neurotypicals to raise grievances or 'blow the whistle'. Attwood (2008, p.130) suggested that 'many "whistle-blowers" have Asperger's syndrome', and McCowan and colleagues (2022) note that autistic doctors, as a group, 'have a tendency to speak out and strive for social justice – for example, unsafe patient care or staff mistreatment', and that this may lead to protected disclosures outside their place of work. There have been calls for empirical research to investigate the link between autism and whistleblowing (Lewis & Evans, 2021).

There is some overlap between autistic characteristics and the symptom profiles of certain personality disorders, and so there is potential for misdiagnosis (May et al., 2021). Until relatively recently there was a belief that autistic people were likely to have low IQ and severe communication deficits. This may be why personality disorders, rather than autism, have historically been associated with complaints. The Offender Assessment System's personality disorder screening tool (Anna et al., 2015) suggests that 'making frequent written complaints' may indicate a personality disorder. Although there is a right to complain, and recognised processes and procedures to follow, negative assumptions may be made about the motivations and character of those who do so.

In my work as a counsellor and doctor and in roles of helping with systemic accountability, I have observed the suggestion of a personality disorder (by non-specialists) to cast doubt on the reliability of the complainant. In my own experience, the fact that I had 'declared additional support needs (autism spectrum disorder)' was disclosed to an external regulator – an infringement of my information rights. I see no reason for this other than to distract from my complaints, which were ultimately upheld. So why might autistic people be more likely to make a formal complaint or to blow the whistle than non-autistic people? Why is whistleblowing and raising concerns often pathologised, and does being autistic predispose someone to more negative consequences for doing so?

In general, autistic people have a deeply ingrained sense of honesty and fairness. This is not a trait unique to autism. It seems, however, that autistic people are less likely than non-autistic people to be able to over-ride this sense for personal gain, and more likely to experience increased concern about the moral cost of ill-gotten gains (Hu et al., 2021), perhaps making them more susceptible to moral injury. I suggest we might also find it very difficult to over-ride our sense of honesty and fairness to avoid personal loss or harm. Lewis and Evans (2021) suggest that autistic people may rigidly believe that there will or should be consequences if something bad happens and that proven wrongdoing will be rectified, denying the existence of organisational and other barriers that may prevent this. They also suggest that autistic people may not notice, or indeed care about, the social cues that might indicate reprisals are likely.

When I think about my own whistleblowing experience on a counselling course, I was certainly driven by a sense of honesty and doing what was right. I was primarily concerned for clients, believing they should have confidence that a recognised qualification indicated certain academic achievements and professional standards. I was willing to sacrifice my place on the course to follow through with my concerns, and it very nearly came to that. I believed that I had proven wrongdoing and there should be consequences. I was naïve in not appreciating the organisational and political barriers to holding the organisation publicly accountable. The course no longer runs, and I am confident that I meet UK standards to practise ethically as a counsellor. Yet I still sit with a sense of unease that I am misrepresenting my qualification. The moral injury I experienced by accepting a certificate that I believed was unjustified still affects me. I ignored the social cues that I was alienating myself from fellow students, who would have preferred me not to 'kick holes in a sinking ship'. The driving sense of fairness for me over-rode the unhappiness of my colleagues.

So autistic people might be more likely to raise and persist with complaints when non-autistic people might choose to ignore it, or simply not care, but what about the pathologising of their complainant behaviour? Is autism just a convenient synonym for being mentally unstable and so unreliable and not credible? Hu and colleagues (2021) investigated morality and personal gain, comparing autistic spectrum disorder (ASD) cohorts with 'healthy' [sic] control subjects. They pathologise atypical moral behaviours in autistic individuals as driven by a specific 'dysfunction' of the right temporoparietal junction. The study found that autistic individuals are more inflexible when following a moral rule. Furthermore, they found that, when an immoral action occurred that benefited them, autistic people 'experience an increased concern about their ill-gotten gains and the moral cost'. On first consideration, it is incredible to me that integrity and altruism can be considered dysfunctional and undesirable, yet when I think of the many clients I see who are experiencing moral injury and severe mental distress linked to these very qualities, perhaps it is not so surprising to see this framed in a medical model.

I believe there is more to the pathologising of complaints than an inflexibility in moral standards. Complaining is a form of communication – at its simplest, it is letting another person know that someone is feeling displeased, angry, frustrated or hurt. It can connect people if the complainant is heard; it can make them feel better, understood and validated, but it can also lead to relationship breakdown and the escalation of the complaint or the submission of further complaints: 'If you don't listen to me, I will find someone who will listen and will make you listen.' One of the defining characteristics of autism is a difference in communication. This is already pathologised as a deficit in the diagnostic manuals, so it is perhaps no surprise that the addition of an expression of dissatisfaction to an already atypical communication style could lead to communication breakdowns and be attributed to the complainant's autism. Autistic people are often accused of being blunt and can be confused and frustrated by people 'sugar-coating' what they say, preferring direct communication. An autistic complainant may therefore appear to neurotypicals to be critical and unkind. Even providing simple feedback can be difficult. My own experience of submitting multiple complaints and whistleblowing escalated from an informal expression of my dissatisfaction with aspects of my counselling course, where I had not felt heard. Had the course team been more receptive to my input, the escalation could have been prevented and issues resolved much more easily for both parties.

Anna and colleagues (2015) present 'Robert', who is 'prone to developing grievances against professionals by writing long, acerbic and litigious complaints'. In my experience, autistic people often write lengthy, detailed, tangential and blunt complaints that can be challenging, not to mention time-consuming, to read. I have engaged in personal communication with neurotypical therapists looking for advice on how to get a client to stay on track, not understanding that this is their process, albeit a process that can be challenging when therapy is time-limited. Like short-term therapy, grievance procedures are also limited by time and there are usually strict timescales for making and managing complaints, so it is easy to see how a lengthy complaint might be pathologised.

Many autistic people have highly focused and intense interests that they pursue to a degree that many neurotypicals cannot comprehend and may pathologise as 'obsessions'. What if a complaint becomes a focused interest? Persistent or vexatious complaint policies often consider complainant behaviour to be unreasonable when reports are too long, contacts are too frequent, repetitive complaints are made repeatedly with minor differences, and complaints are pursued through multiple channels. It is easy to see how an autistic person might unintentionally fall foul of such a policy despite the best intentions. All complainants want to be heard. For my own complaint about my course, being heard made a huge difference and could have benefitted everyone had it happened earlier in my efforts to improve the situation. I finally felt heard after validation of my concerns from external parties and a formal written apology. As a counsellor, I can help my clients identify their objectives, what they need to be heard, how a positive outcome would look, and how other outcomes might feel. Autistic complainants may not feel heard until they can be sure that someone understands all the details and nuances about how a situation arose, what happened and why it is wrong. Neurotypicals responding to complaints may not be able to demonstrate this to the satisfaction of the complainant but will often believe they have done so. This is an example of the 'double empathy problem' (Milton, 2012) – people who experience the world very differently from one another tend to have difficulty empathising effectively with one another.

Acts of proven wrongdoing in a grievance or whistleblowing case can lead to sanctions and result in financial, professional and personal consequences for the individual or organisational respondent. There are some who will go to great lengths to avoid this, who are more concerned about protecting their own interests and reputation than avoiding harm to the complainant. DARVO, which stands for Deny, Attack, and Reverse Victim and Offender, was first introduced as a concept by Jennifer Freyd (1997), who originally applied it to the area of sexual assault. Attacking a complainant can involve questioning their motivation and mental health by pathologising or villainising them. Those with a known or suspected mental health label are clearly even more vulnerable to this. Respondents sometimes suggest they have been harmed by the complaint, due to stress, forced neglect of other duties or threat to status or reputation. Regardless of whether criticism is justified or not, it can bring up intense emotional discomfort at the challenge of the self-concept, which is often enough to shut down any form of reflection. Instead, DARVO is activated in self (concept)-defence. Everyone is the hero in their own story.

Our own autistic behaviours can cause harm to ourselves too. Pursuing perceived justice, when taken to extremes, can impact on a person's work, income and personal life. 'Let it go', 'Forget about it', 'Put it behind you' and 'Move on with your life' are phrases often uttered by well-meaning friends, family members and even some therapists. As a therapist with firsthand experience of sitting on the other side of the table, having felt the impossibility of those things,

I can come alongside my clients and help them decipher and articulate what their needs are and how others may support them in their process.

Getting stuck on this can result in damaged relationships, less endurance for masking and loss of ability to focus on other important parts of life, such as self-care, routines, interests and employment. As life falls out of balance, the 'window of tolerance' – the metaphorical space where 'various intensities of emotional arousal can be processed without disrupting the functioning of the system' (Siegel, 1999) – shrinks to a tiny porthole. You could say the autistic person becomes more obviously (stereotypically) autistic and so more vulnerable to ableism, stigma and deteriorating mental health. This is, of course, an example of 'burnout', a place where I 'meet' many of my clients. Being autistic and having been through similar experiences, I can offer my clients a safe and supportive space to find the path forward that can best help them. Sadly, not all autistic clients who need such support have access to it. Those who lack appropriate support can face a particularly challenging road. It is my aim to help as many people as effectively as possible, which is what led me to becoming involved in systemic advocacy.

When the desired outcome to a raised concern is not met, it can be poisonous, pervasive and soul-destroying. Linden (Linden & Arnold, 2020) discusses embitterment as a response to injustice, humiliation and breach of trust with a persistent desire to reverse what has happened, reinstate justice and get even. Linden suggests the label 'posttraumatic embitterment disorder' for these symptoms (2003), although this has not been widely adopted. As a person-centred psychotherapist, I am much less interested in diagnostic categories and criteria than I was when a medical doctor. However, it is easy to imagine how the autistic mind, with its sense of fairness and justice, could be predisposed to such symptoms. Indeed, I recognise embitterment in some of my clients, who believe they have been failed by 'the system'. In a cruel twist, intrusive thoughts and emotional arousal experienced in response to an unjust event can be the very factors that prevent an autistic person (already predisposed to intense, repetitive and looping processing) from engaging or persisting with therapy strategies that may help achieve a sense of resolution, especially in the absence of desired formal outcomes of complaint procedures.

Embitterment can be very hard to resolve. In practice, I have observed a few things that can help a client move forward, but there are no quick fixes. The first is satisfactory resolution. Resolution restores faith in the system. Justice is achieved. The second is distraction. Distraction can take many forms, some more beneficial than others. My distraction was aerial gymnastics. When hanging upside down, high in the air, it is difficult to ruminate on anything other than the correct wrapping of the silks or *corde lisse*, and desperately hanging on. Not letting go is particularly advantageous in this situation. This was my mindfulness. I have experienced few autistic clients who embrace traditional mindfulness. Being able to focus intensely on something (other than the all-consuming issue) can give the brain a rest. Time and distance can also be healing, but the quantities needed of both are likely to be significant.

Whether the people I come across in my regulatory and therapeutic work are going through active grievance or disciplinary or whistleblowing procedures and burning out; whether they have gone through formal processes but are still trying to cope with negative consequences or moral injury from doing so; whether they are embittered from events that they have no hope of resolving in the way that would satisfy them; whether their concerns are 'objectively' reasonable in others' minds, they are all hurting and vulnerable to prolonged mental distress.

While I can validate my client's feelings and allow them to explore their behaviours, I can't resolve the complaints process for them or achieve justice for them. Yet I can believe my client's experience, validate how they feel about it, and share their frustration and dismay at their situation. I find peeling the anger onion can be helpful. What are the feelings underlying the rage at the injustice experienced? Some therapists may look at exploring blame – whether on self or others. This can be damaging, especially where there is inadequate rapport. Blame neither resolves past events nor prevents future recurrences. So, we talk about strategies, expectations and perceptions of responsibilities. This can be a breakthrough. One can improve oneself and one can also take steps to avoid repeating history, such as by focusing on protective factors that can help someone avoid revisiting the people, places or situations that are perceived as likely to cause further harm.

As I develop as an autistic therapist and meet clients who have (like me) blown the whistle or who are considering raising a grievance, I have to be mindful that my own personal sense of injustice is not triggered, or if it is, at least I recognise it. I have gained a lot of knowledge and experience fighting 'the system', but as a counsellor, my role is not to advocate for my clients. I can truly empathise with feelings of unfairness and embitterment and the all-consuming pursuit of justice, but I cannot validate their concerns or allocate any blame. I often find that clients want external reinforcement that they are 'right', but that is not for me to say.

Since my diploma days when I first blew the whistle, I have strived to produce meaningful change within professional therapy institutions – for example, in research ethics and data protection. What I have learned from my clients and my experiences in college has helped me to achieve change and continue to do my best to help my clients, both directly and systemically. I hope those involved in complaints processes learn to recognise the characteristic communication styles and underlying altruistic motives of autistic complainants in order to better support them through the process, and that they help all involved to come to a satisfactory resolution. I hope others join me in valuing autistic complainants for their transparency, accountability and good governance.

References

Adams, D. (1979). *The hitchhiker's guide to the galaxy*. Pan Books.

Anna, M., Logan, C., Bull, C., Nicklin, E., Craissati, J., Shaw, J., Tew, J., Garvey, K., Turner, K., Chauhan, M., Joseph, N., Minoudis, P., O'Rourke, R., Simons, S. & Chuan, S. (2015). *Working with offenders with personality disorder: A practitioner's guide* (2nd ed.). NHS England. www.england.nhs.uk/commissioning/wp-content/uploads/sites/12/2015/10/work-offndrs-persnlty-disorder-oct15.pdf

Attwood, T. (2008). *The complete guide to Asperger's syndrome*. Jessica Kingsley.

Doherty, M., Johnson, M. & Buckley, C. (2021). Supporting autistic doctors in primary care: Challenging the myths and misconceptions. *British Journal of General Practice, 71*(708), 294-295. https://pubmed.ncbi.nlm.nih.gov/34319879/

Freyd, J.J. (1997). Violations of power, adaptive blindness, and betrayal trauma theory. *Feminism & Psychology, 7*, 22-32. https://dynamic.uoregon.edu/jjf/articles/freyd97r.pdf

Hu, Y., Pereira, A.M., Gao, X., Campos, B.M., Derrington, E., Corgnet, B., Zhou, X., Cendes, F. & Dreher, J.-C. (2021). Right temporoparietal junction underlies avoidance of moral transgression in autism spectrum disorder. *The Journal of Neuroscience: The official journal of the Society for Neuroscience, 41*(8), 1699-1715. https://pubmed.ncbi.nlm.nih.gov/33158960/

Lewis, D.B. & Evans, H. (2021, April 19). *Autistic employees as whistleblowers: Are employers ignoring potentially valuable assets?* Discussion paper. Middlesex University. https://repository.mdx.ac.uk/item/89564

Lim, C.R., Zhang, M.W.B., Hussain, S.F. & Ho, R.C.M. (2017). The consequences of whistleblowing. *Journal of Patient Safety, 17*(6), e497-e502. https://doi.org/10.1097/pts.0000000000000396

Linden, M. (2003). Posttraumatic embitterment disorder. *Psychotherapy & Psychosomatics, 72*(4), 195-202. doi:10.1159/000070783

Linden, M. & Arnold, C. (2020). Embitterment and posttraumatic embitterment disorder (PTED): An old, frequent, and still underrecognized problem. *Psychotherapy and Psychosomatics, 90*(2):73-80. doi: 10.1159/000511468.

Litz, B.T., Stein, N., Delaney, E., Lebowitz, L., Nash, W. P., Silva, C. & Maguen, S. (2009). Moral injury and moral repair in war veterans: A preliminary model and intervention strategy. *Clinical Psychology Review, 29*(8), 695-706. https://doi.org/10.1016/j.cpr.2009.07.003

May, T., Pilkington, P.D., Younan, R. & Williams, K. (2021). Overlap of autism spectrum disorder and borderline personality disorder: A systematic review and meta-analysis. *Autism Research, 14*(12), 2688–2710. https://doi.org/10.1002/aur.2619

McCowan, S., Shaw, S.C.K., Doherty, M., Grosjean, B., Blank, P. & Kinnear, M. (2022). A full CIRCLE: Inclusion of autistic doctors in the Royal College of Psychiatrists' values and Equality Action Plan. *The British Journal of Psychiatry, 221*(1), 371–373. https://doi.org/10.1192/bjp.2022.14

Milton, D. (2012). On the ontological status of autism: The 'double empathy problem'. *Disability and Society, 27*(6), 883–887.

Moore, S., Kinnear, M. & Freeman, L. (2020). Autistic doctors: Overlooked assets to medicine. *The Lancet Psychiatry, 7*(4), 306–307. https://www.thelancet.com/journals/lanpsy/article/PIIS2215-0366(20)30087-0/fulltext

Shay, J. (2012). Moral injury. *Intertexts, 16*(1), 57–66. https://doi.org/10.1353/itx.2012.0000

Siegel, D.J. (1999). *The developing mind: How relationships and the brain interact to shape who we are* (2nd ed.). Guilford Press.

SECTION C

Autistic therapists for autistic people

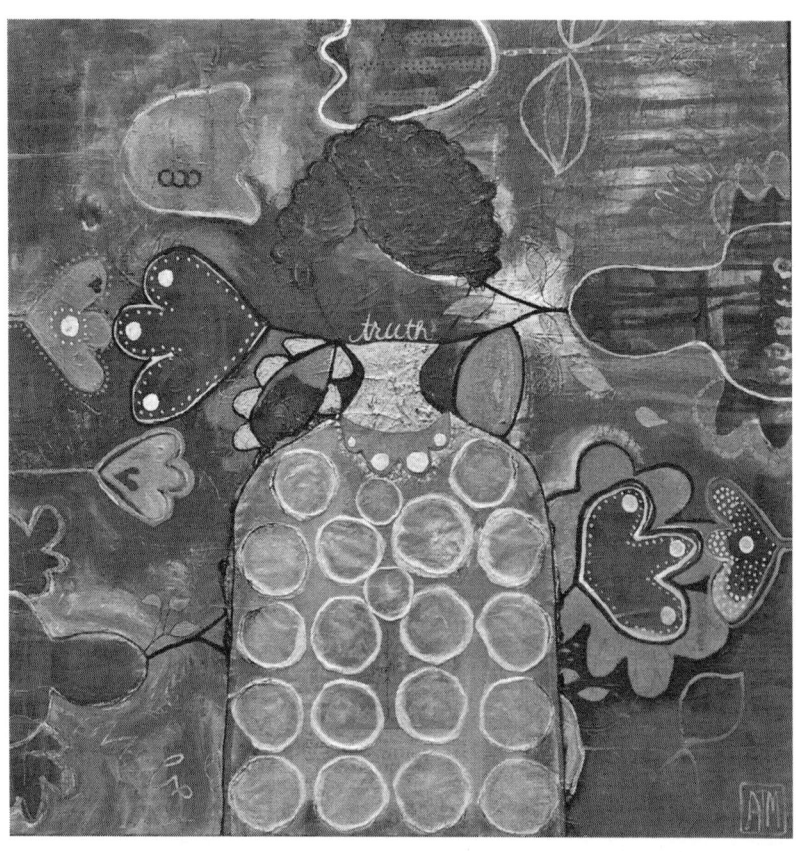

'Maybe If I Say It' (mixed media – greyscale repro from colour)
© River Marino

Introduction

If autism is, as Katherine Balthazor (Chapter 15) suggests, a language and a culture, then it is unsurprising that there is a different quality to autistic-to-autistic therapy. We all work with allistic clients, and if an allistic therapist is willing to enter into the autistic world and speak our language, then that can work too. But it is hard to achieve that ease that comes from a shared culture and language. Kathy Carter (Chapter 20) explains: 'My very autisticness is my strength, especially in working with other autistic people' – people she calls her neurokin.

The client and the therapist both need to be given, as Elinor Rowlands (Chapter 17) puts it, 'permission to exist', and to exist in their own autistic culture.

Wilma Wake (Chapter 19) brings this out very clearly when speaking about her client, 'Kathryn'. Both she and her client belong to that 'lost generation' of autistic women who have lived most of their lives without diagnosis, with all the struggles that this entails. In her work, Wilma's autism is front and centre. As she puts it:

> My therapy is not a bland listening to my client. It is an impassioned interactive journey together. We are fellow travellers on the same road, and we talk about the scenery along the way.

Finding one's tribe is an essential part of coming to know oneself. That shared experience is so important, and since autistic people have a very high incidence of co-occurring conditions, even chronic illness can become another source of strength in the therapeutic relationship. Rebecca Antrim (Chapter 21), looking back on her diagnosis of ME/CFS, says her acceptance of her situation changed not only her own life but her way of doing therapy:

> I know how it feels to feel like an 'offshoot of an offshoot' and to experience the mixed emotions of dealing with both a mental and physical diagnosis and the impacts that this can have… it has made me a more compassionate therapist with invaluable lived experience that I can use to help others with very specific needs.

We have called this section 'Autistic Therapists for Autistic People' but the supervisor–supervisee relationship is just as important as that between therapist and client. We have therefore included chapters from two supervisors in this section.

Amy Walters (Chapter 16) sets out to explain why her specific neurodivergence makes her a great supervisor: the supervisor she wished she had had. But the chapter is much more than that. Its deep insight into the autistic supervisor and the autistic supervisee provides an instruction manual for any supervisor in how to supervise – and for any supervisee in how to get the most out of one's supervision.

Romy Graichen (Chapter 18) explores the nature and importance of the often-used phrase 'neurodiversity-affirming'. She argues:

> The aim of good supervision is to help the practitioner to be more available for their clients, to hold and contain their material and facilitate change. I argue that neurotypically informed supervision does not support the neurodivergent supervisee to do this.

And we hear the voices of both Romy herself and her supervisees explaining why this is so.

All these chapters are about autistic therapists working with autistic people. But, paradoxically, these chapters perhaps offer the clearest descriptions for allistic people of how to enter into our language and culture. It is not so difficult after all.

Max Marnau

Chapter 15

Complex trauma, language and culture in autistic counselling

Katherine Balthazor

At times, counselling can feel like fighting the river – the forces and obstacles are simply so much bigger than you. Sometimes all you can do is teach folks how to hold onto the sides of the boat and try to enjoy the journey.

As an autistic person, bringing my genuine self to the profession has been an extraordinary asset in ways that can be surprising. For instance, in the above analogy, had you considered that the client could be using the same tools, yet still be trapped outside of the boat? Some of this chapter will directly discuss my own experiences of providing counselling and the concepts that have helped bring me insight along the way. Regarding a trauma trigger warning, trauma is discussed in general terms and in relation to complex trauma, but acute trauma events are not described in this chapter.

I have been a licensed professional counsellor and certified rehabilitation counsellor for about a decade, and I have a master's degree in rehabilitation psychology. My roles have often focused on helping individuals with any kind of disabilities to enter, re-enter or remain in the workforce. Rehabilitation counselling integrates mental health counselling with vocational rehabilitation. Clinically, I have worked and volunteered in many related settings, such as hospitals, clinics, schools, government and telework. Counselling was not my first career. Before counselling, I worked primarily in the animal field, in roles ranging from adoption counselling and caretaking to being an animal control agent. My work in the animal field directly guided the transition to counselling, as I found myself lacking in verbal communication skills, despite excellent non-verbal/non-speaking skills. I figured that, although I had learned from the animals how to be a mammal, my interactions with their owners had not been sufficient to teach me how to fit in with humans, so I might as well take formal college training in how to be human. Enter counsellor training, stage right.

While I was training as an applied behavioural analysis (ABA) therapist, a child changed my life forever. On my very first day, I noticed that one of the clients was remarkably similar to me when I was a child. I saw how misunderstood the child's language was. Due to my unique perspective, I approached the client differently to the way the other staff approached them. We were told to achieve therapy goals under observation. The same client worked with several trainees on the same day, one at a time. Although management initially objected to my less traditional approaches, they quickly saw results and even used my actions that day to improve trainings and outcomes. Here were our goals and what happened:

- Therapy goal: engage client.
  - As soon as the client entered the room, the client turned off the lights. Other trainees turned the lights on. Client meltdown.
  - Personally, I found the overhead lights painful and unnecessary. With the client's help, we found an alternative source of acceptable soft light and the client readily engaged. Goal achieved.

- Therapy goal: elicit spoken language.
  - Other trainees tried to command the client to speak. The client retreated to the opposite side of the room, trying to get away from them.
  - At the opposite side of the room, I began dancing with a toy basket on my head. The client wanted to dance too. I said a couple of words. The client mirrored me. Goal achieved.

The big difference in approach was that I listened to the client's full range of language, not just the language rooted in words. I tried to understand the culture the client brought to us and the patterns in the client's actions. Facing our communication with openness led us down a better road than the well-intended coercion the client otherwise faced. The client wanted to connect, play and grow. They did not want pain. The client spoke in silent language, in a world lacking the correct translators for our mutual language. I know how that feels.

When the client noticed that I was listening to their silent voice, engagement with me became so high that the client would not work with the other trainees.

I was told to leave the room and observe through a one-way mirror. For the client, this brought on severe separation anxiety, which was surprising to my colleagues, given the short duration of our interaction. And in that moment, I started to slowly realise why my own life was, and had always been, going so poorly. Behind the mirror, my heart broke for this child, realising the possible implications of this for this child's future, based on my own past. I was new and did not know what to do. However, I did realise that I had been that child, in different contexts. Misunderstood. Harmed by overly confident people who thought they were helping, even in the context of therapy itself. The truth of the matter is that there are not very many of us who take the time to interpret silent, non-written language. I have been told that many people perceive it as almost a sort of mind reading. It's not.

Let me say that again: it's not mind reading. If you study animal behaviour, you realise certain patterns are consistent and logical. A gaping baby bird longs for its mother to return with a meal. A scared cat puffs itself out to look bigger and more intimidating. Humans like to see ourselves as above the simple pathways of logic of the animal kingdom. In some ways, that is true. People can use language with elegance unknown to most species. Even so, most human behaviour does follow certain forms of logic, even if we do not fully understand in the moment. We are far more complex, and we often reject the simpler logic in life. This is why I got an advanced degree in order to feel human and, maybe, with luck, be able to feel less alien in this strange world.

Although I did not quite reach the realisation that I was autistic at the time of that training session, I started trying the sensory regulation skills I was learning and teaching my clients. They helped! And I decided to select rehabilitation counselling as my major, as it would teach me algorithms of interaction. I could learn how to talk to all people in a way that was acceptable and even desirable. Perhaps I could even become useful and feel valued. Therapies were helpful but never seemed to have been adapted to what I needed from them.

Often, as therapists, we teach explicit concepts but fail to explain implicit components. For instance, in dialectal behaviour therapy, there is a concept called 'wise mind'. Wise mind proposes that it is bad to be either too emotional or too logical; instead, it is best to attain a balance of both. As a patient, it was unclear to me why operating only within a logical mind is supposed to be bad. Computers can communicate highly effectively, entirely void of emotion, without issue. As a patient, I would sit in therapy thinking 'Make it make sense', but to no avail. Becoming a counsellor taught me what lurked beneath the surface of such statements. For example, emotion is a common experience among humans that tends to be a large driver of human behaviour, regardless of whether both parties express/feel the emotion. Failing to consider emotion can itself drive emotion-based responses. At the time, I used to wish my interactions with others were more like how computers conversed. Logically, that would feel less stressful. Thus, wise mind seemed counterproductive. However, when I dove more into the implicit rules of social interactions, especially with people who are not also autistic, the importance of wise mind became more sensible. I also developed a better understanding of how to teach it than just 'Here is a set of rules – follow them'. Because I did not start out with the same assumptions and neurotypical cultural norms, I am more likely to teach therapeutic concepts more wholly and explore with fewer misplaced assumptions.

As a patient, mental health treatment without implicit explanation often felt like a form of gaslighting, where everything bad was my fault for 'not following the process', even if I followed the process. I wanted to learn how to communicate more effectively with others and I also wanted to understand why I could not understand therapy. It seemed like learning to fully understand fears and frustrations would be a sensible way to decrease their impact.

Fast forward about a year and a major trauma later. My treatment team for years kept trying the same things over and over, but we felt stuck. Things got increasingly difficult as my traumas escalated, both in terms of acute (e.g. major events that threatened life or safety) and chronic traumas (e.g. constant stress related to being neurodivergent in a neurotypical world, social exclusions, and so on). However, I brought my experience with this child to my treatment team. After explaining that I had met an autistic child who strongly resembled me at that age, I asked, 'Am I autistic?'

Getting formally assessed as an adult (especially as a woman) was a long and rough road, but I was eventually formally diagnosed as autistic. Unfortunately, there are few providers willing to even assess autistic adults, and this was especially the case back then. Soon after I received my diagnosis, I realised that finding treatment resources for autistic adults is nearly impossible unless systems consider a person to be 'nursing home level of care'. Usually that means there are comorbid diagnoses such as intellectual disabilities, epilepsy and others. So, access to help has been difficult. Side note: occupational therapists are very good resources if you are newly diagnosed. I wish I had known that earlier in my life and career!

When I moved to government employment, my client list was always diverse, especially in terms of medical conditions. Over time, I realised that I found my autistic clients, in general, usually the easiest to work with in terms of communication, especially if the client came to sessions independently or if the only people in the room were also neurodivergent (such as autistic parents/guardians/spouses). By the end of most days on the job, overall, I would find myself exhausted. However, with some of my autistic clients, I would feel recharged. A friend explained to me that the Covid-19 pandemic taught her there are people who recharge one's battery and people who drain it. She is absolutely right. But why did I feel so drained after some folks but not others? It did not make much difference how straightforward a case was, the level of positive regard, or even whether a client was hostile versus kind/welcoming.

I began to realise that autism is more than a diagnosis. It is a culture and language. It is diverse within itself, with subcultures and generally unlabelled dialects. Often, we use the colour wheel to explain how varied autistic functioning is in terms of medically defined capacities. And just as intellectual disabilities can impact autistic presentation, so too can other intersections of culture, language and life experiences. This is why asking for accommodations in work or educational environments is challenging. It can be tough to distinguish the relatively obvious 'medical' accommodations from those required for genuine linguistic and cultural inclusion.

Further, most autistics, especially adults, have learned to mask our autism to try to mimic other people. If we do not mask, it tends to result in bullying and other forms of mistreatment. It is exhausting to be 'in character' all day in addition to being yourself underneath. But I have had to mask to succeed in the field. Masking can double the drain on internal resources, making the same task twice as hard for me as it is for someone who is neurotypical. For me, learning motivational interviewing felt like picking up a new language. The fluency gains felt very similar, and it was a definite clue-in to the similarity between my exhaustion and the exhaustion of someone who is immersed in a foreign language and culture.

I found myself, as a counsellor, frequently acting as an unsuspecting translator for a not-very-well-known language. For instance, a client might be agreeable verbally despite clear (nonverbal) reservations. I could see a stim or affect change and gently confront it, helping a client self-advocate. But, in my own personal treatment, who was my translator? If we do not see autism as a language, then we cannot accommodate a translator. Unfortunately, this causes problems. Imagine a man coming into an emergency room, asking for help in broken English. He may not sound capable of autonomy and informed choice, when actually perhaps he is a physicist, far more brilliant than most but simply not fluent enough in the language to convey complex information without translation, especially in crisis. When that is the case, others often presume the worst. They may think you are below your level of intellect. They may think you are being stubborn or noncompliant, especially if they believe you to be a native speaker of 'Neurotypical'.

As a patient, I have been excluded or treated differently due to stims. In one situation, I had to say I needed to use the restroom so I could get out of the room and go running up and down a flight of stairs until I could calm down from a trauma trigger. The staff did not realise what was happening and assumed noncompliance, so discharged me. I was only readmitted when a long-term therapist helped me translate this into language the treatment team understood and advocated for me to regain access. These days, even as a trained counsellor, I still need translators and advocates sometimes. Imagine going to a restaurant in a foreign country where you know only a modest amount of conversational language. If you are feeling great, your language is better. If you are distracted (such as from illness, pain or stress) you will find it harder to produce the right words, particularly if it is not your primary preferred language. We all need interpreters sometimes, even people who are not autistic and who live where their primary language is the accepted language. We all get kicked down sometimes and need help self-advocating. It is just harder when there is a language barrier, even if it is a well-masked barrier.

Culture is seldom addressed directly, especially in workplaces. We have months where we celebrate various cultures. Autism is frequently discussed in an 'awareness month', just like cancer. Because we get viewed as a disease. When the foundations of who you are are viewed so negatively, it contributes to complex trauma and poor self-image, making resilience much harder. Even if we are made of the toughest stuff, cracks will start to rupture our foundations and constant exposure to stress will break us down. This is about who we are and what we cannot change about ourselves. Even if you have a stable sense of self-worth, you will hear the echoes of exclusion in your mind based on comments such as people being shocked that we can marry, parents who 'wouldn't know what to do' if their child was autistic or being told what others think we cannot or should not be able to do.

It can take a lot of support and work to come back from the effects of trauma, especially with complexities such as being neurodivergent in a world that tends to find neurodivergency intimidating. Although there are many excellent practitioners out there who try very hard to be understanding, there are also therapists who, for various reasons, can resort to things like indifference or even cruelty. Or, more commonly, practitioners will simply say, with a concerned frown, that they do not have any experience with autism and therefore cannot help you. Try not to be that person. Sometimes the very people who say they understand us are those who coercively do damage, despite seeing themselves as the experts and heroes of their own stories. We already work on fluency and understanding. Forcing conformity reinforces trauma, as trauma derives from loss of control that results in being harmed. Just as you can try to learn to speak a new language or learn about a culture, you can get to know us. You might like what you find! And know that you can adapt therapies to diverse clients. It may take a little bit of extra exploration and spending some time outside your comfort zone, but that is how you brave new growth. Most mental health training, at least historically, did not do much to help counsellors/therapists learn how to treat neurodivergent clients. Much is still unknown. It can and should be an active conversation with our patients.

You are likely to find more gentle understanding from practitioners with marginalised identities, as they have walked the walk. That includes autistic counsellors and therapists, as well as many other people in marginalised groups. However, I will carefully add, not being marginalised does not rule out kindness and understanding. Kindness is a choice we make every moment of every day. I have known clinicians, personally and professionally, who do not identify with any marginalised group and may not understand systemic adversity well. However, because they make an effort to understand, are open to learning and doing things differently and receptive to feedback, they can still be helpful. It is important for all of us to be open to learning about the things we may not yet understand.

If you are a therapist/counsellor/practitioner or are considering becoming one, you can help by getting to know autistic people. Become our friends and allies. Learn about our passions, patterns and roadblocks. Join online communities and observe. Do not ask us to explain everything and teach you. But be willing and ready to listen and learn. Look for information from autistic professionals, not just professionals who specialise in autism. Know that our entire field is always adapting: what we hold dear today may be regarded differently tomorrow. Most of us are doing our best, so be gentle. Above all, try to see the best in us. Look for the logic. Give us the benefit of the doubt. Life can be unfathomably complex, and we understand so little of what there is to learn. No matter how much of an expert you become, the client will almost always be the best expert on themselves, so include the client and be honest. Try not to push your prejudices onto us, such as what you might think we can or cannot do. Most of this is basic counselling etiquette but it bears repeating. And I know that sometimes those with power over us implicitly demand we mask, so masking can be required of us. You may feel like you have to sacrifice who you are to be able to keep masking. Don't sacrifice who you are. We need genuineness. You are not an automaton or a mere producer of metrics. Your role for your fellow humans is as sacred as the wind in the trees. We need one another on the most basic level of human primal instincts, being social creatures evolutionarily. Counselling is a series of algorithms. It is also deeper than that, as it brings a connection and a ripple effect that may help your clients grow as stewards of grace, growth, strength, resiliency and kindness.

If you are an autistic therapist, know that you are not alone. You are capable. You are valued. You do not have to overhaul the whole system; it is much bigger than you and you probably will not be able to win that fight alone.

If life is a pile of good, bad and neutral things, try to add to the good pile for everyone you can help. Life might not always feel worth living. Yet, even if you do not know it, you might be helping another person find hope that a life worth living can be built. The change you make is by being there and doing what you can. Do not be intimidated by any person – at the end of the day, we are all just people. Stay safe, set boundaries and protect yourself, but also stay open to new ideas, cultures and concepts. Take joy in learning. You will find that the field is demanding and often situations will arise that make you confront ethical questions. Follow your gut and do what you know is right. Do not buy into philosophies that see people as little or nothing more than metrics. Sometimes you will have to balance workplace and financial demands but always take time to see people as more than that. And I know it is hard not to compare yourself with others when you have to mask. Try to avoid becoming them. Try not to be bitter if others do well more easily in a world built for them to excel, while you struggle. They have a lot of growing to do too, and if that environment does not fit, take root where you can be safe and are welcomed. You have much to bring and so much good to do. To the profession, you might just be a counsellor. To the client, you might be the biggest reason they learn to have the power to change their world. So, boldly and bravely, allow your strengths to shine.

Last, I am taking a break from the field to focus on my own healing journey from my own recent and complex/compounded traumas and physical injury. Recently, someone still in the field who is trying to cope with complex trauma asked me, 'But what do I do? I can't just leave my patients behind and quit my job to focus on healing myself.' We talked about temporary medical leave and other paths forward. Being wounded can help you better see hidden pain. But it can also cause you to accidentally cause harm if you do not do the work to gain insights and help yourself rest and heal. Being able and willing to work on yourself can also help send your patients the message that therapy is normal and that even the wisest or strongest healers themselves can always grow. When I could, I helped my clients transition to other therapists, and was honest (though not in detail) as to why. Clients appreciate it. They trust me to not judge them for needing counselling because I too admit to needing help sometimes. We need balance and resiliency, not just reckless heroism. In the time I have already taken to slow down and heal, I have learned far more than I could have ever gained through any continuing education and, after healing, will be a better counsellor for it.

Chapter 16

To be the supervisor I wish I'd had

Amy Walters

If you'd told 15-year-old Amy that one day she would be a therapist and a clinical supervisor with a thriving practice and about to become a coach, she would never have believed you. I was a 'weirdo', struggling with school and relationships and life in general, tired of trying twice as hard to be half as good as my peers, skipping school and counting down the days until I could leave and get a job. I had found community and 'acceptance' in a high-demand religious group. It took the abandoning of my religious beliefs, a series of terrible relationships, becoming a single mother, falling back into religious beliefs because I was afraid of dying, training to become a counsellor, falling in love with existential theory, and then deconstructing my faith, before I finally found the most authentic version of me yet. Or so I thought. As it turned out, becoming authentically myself was a continuing journey, with many stops along the way.

Before my counselling training and self-discovery journey, relationships of all kinds had always been somewhat confusing. I was never really quite getting it right, always feeling like I was doing something wrong, or copying what I thought I was supposed to be doing in relationships based on what I had seen represented in films, TV shows and Mills & Boon books. I was really quite needy and insecure. A friend had given me the feedback that, in our relationship I made everything about me, and I can see that was true to a degree. So, with that new feedback, I made a conscious effort to let people talk and to take turns in conversations. I am still really conscious of not dominating conversations and being intentional in my listening. During my counselling training, a peer told me I was relentless.

Despite all my apparent learning, growing, self-development and many, many hours of counselling, I would still have regular meltdowns that often ended in self-harm. I would still regularly be overwhelmed and tired. I would still always feel like I was forgetting something, or missing something, or supposed to be doing something. I still experienced anger as my go-to emotion for any sensory experience or response to feelings. I still struggled to emotionally regulate with anything other than food. Why, when I had done all this work, was I still just not being a 'successful adult'? Other people managed to stay in one job, managed the demands of life that I seemed to still fail at, and managed not to cry when shopping at the supermarket.

Around two years ago, as I investigated my son's neurodivergence and sought help and diagnosis for him, I had a growing sense that this was absolutely me as well.

Learning that I was neurodivergent led to a whole new level of unpacking and unmasking. Reframing my past experiences and behaviours through the lens of being AuDHD (a dual diagnosis, or self-diagnosis, of autism and ADHD) led to an even greater freedom and acceptance that I didn't think was possible.

On embracing being a neurodivergent supervisor

So here I am (at time of writing). Ten years of being a counsellor, two years of being a supervisor and six months of being diagnosed ADHD and self-diagnosed autistic has been quite the ride. So how has all this fed into how I am as a supervisor to other counsellors? Obviously, I've always been AuDHD, but in analysing my approach to supervision post-diagnosis, I can see how my neurodivergence was always woven throughout my practice. The whole premise of my supervision style has been to 'be the supervisor I wish I'd had'.

What I think is very interesting and relevant is that my approach seems to draw to me supervisees who are also neurodivergent, like bees to a flower.

The kind of supervisor I wish I'd had is fun, down to earth, collaborative and collegiate. Someone who actively tries to minimise the power imbalance; someone to whom I genuinely feel I can bring all of me. I want my supervisees to look forward to coming to supervision. I want them to feel supported and confident in their practice, to leave my supervision feeling inspired. This wasn't my experience of supervision. I often felt as though I was going to give a report to the headteacher. I felt I had to prove I was doing a good job or I'd get into trouble. I felt judged and found wanting. Unsurprisingly, my rejection sensitivity (rejection sensitivity dysphoria (RSD) is the term used to explain the extreme sensitivity to rejection that many neurodivergent people experience) would often be activated in supervision. Challenge often felt like criticism, so I never really felt safe enough to be my honest self and bring all of me to sessions. And, as none of my supervisors ever really communicated how supervision with them was supposed to help, I also didn't realise that I could ask my supervisor the questions I really wanted to ask. But I also didn't know what I needed to ask.

It has been suggested to me that what I offer is surely good supervision, supervision as it should be offered, and therefore nothing special or anything to do with my neurodivergence. So perhaps the saddest thing of all is that my experience, and the experience of the vast majority of my supervisees and neurodivergent counsellors, tells me this isn't the case. Good supervision, with the deep, affirming understanding that lived experience brings, is rare. Supervision with the inbuilt accommodations that disabled and neurodivergent counsellors need is rare. This perhaps speaks to a lack of good supervision training, or how much good supervision depends on the supervisor's competency and training, and even personal beliefs. If what I do is just plain old good supervision, I think everyone would be doing it.

So, what is 'good supervision'? When I did my training, we were introduced to various models of supervision, most of which follow the same basic principles in terms of their functions and tasks (see, for example, van Ooijen, 2013). In the counselling context, supervision is:

- restorative/supportive
- formative/educative
- normative/managerial.

And its tasks are:

- to provide advice
- to teach within a learning relationship
- to monitor/evaluate ethical practice, according to the practitioner's ethical framework.

In terms of actual supervision process, what resonated for me was the Hawkins and Shohet seven-eyed model (Hawkins & Shohet, 2012), which I go into more detail later, as it aligned with the existential parts of my training. It covers all the areas that I believe are important in offering effective supervision.

A safe container

For me, the primary function of supervision is to provide a safe container for the supervisee to bring, share, critically examine and consolidate their confidence in their counselling practice.

The creation of my supervision container starts with my intake form before we even meet online. None of my supervisors ever sent me a form before our initial conversation, so I would find myself meeting them for the first time without really knowing what to expect. This meant I didn't know what I wanted to ask. I send a form to potential supervisees who approach me so that they have a chance to sit and reflect before we meet, which accommodates people's different processing styles. I try to make what I do as accessible as possible by explaining how I work, my expectations of my supervisees, and what they can expect from me. When I set this up, I didn't know I was AuDHD; I just thought it made sense to lay the groundwork for clear communication, but since I have gained a deeper understanding of my neurodivergence, I understand how common it is for we AuDHDers to put systems in place to accommodate our differences without even realising that's what we are doing.

One of the questions I ask my potential supervisees is, 'If you were interviewing me for the job of your supervisor, what would you want to ask me?' For me, it's an honour and privilege to have this job; I believe I should have to earn the right to be these counsellors' supervisor.

Some of the responses I get to that question are below, and I am sharing them here so that you get an idea of some of the things you could ask a potential supervisor.

- Can you help me explore the potential self-disclosure of my neurodivergence to my clients?
- How will you support a supervisee if a client presents as neurodivergent but doesn't realise it?
- How do your experiences as a human impact your role as a supervisor?
- Why did you become a counsellor and what approaches do you use?
- How will you challenge me and support me on my journey?
- Are you able to help me set up my private practice?
- How do you deal with ruptures in our relationship?
- Are you okay if I swear or will you be offended?
- What are your political leanings? I'd like to know if we are on the same wavelength.
- What do you do for self-care?
- Are you affirming of or have lived experience of neurodivergence and gender, sexuality and relationship diversity?
- What are the expectations you have of me in supervision?

- My confidence can be low. Is it okay if we sometimes look at that, instead of client work?
- Do you have a sense of humour?

I wonder if you have ever asked your supervisors any of these kinds of questions? I didn't think I was particularly radical in my approach to supervision, but the more I hear about other neurodivergent counsellors' experiences with supervisors, the more I think I might be a bit radical! When people are invited to be themselves unconditionally, it brings such freedom.

On communication about the container

I always knew I valued clear communication, mostly because it meant I knew the rules, so that I would not do anything wrong or risk being told off, which always felt devastating (thanks, RSD). I now understand that it is part of my AuDHD. Years of being misunderstood mean that I now strive to communicate really effectively, and that can only be of benefit to my supervisees. I am clear, deliberate and intentional in my communication, and that is a great basis for a supervisory relationship. My supervisees will never have to guess what I am feeling or thinking or why I do or say a particular thing: they are invited to ask, if I haven't shared it already. My supervisees know that, if they want to clarify anything I have said, or they can't interpret an expression on my face, or something just feels off, they can raise it without fear of judgement. It's a beautiful thing to see my supervisees own their needs. That a supervisee can say to me, 'I am feeling a bit unsure of how you are feeling about me at the moment,' and I can tell them, simply and honestly, has been a revelation for many of them.

I seek always to make explicit the energy and culture I am trying to create within supervision. On my directory profile, I state that I am down to earth, open, collaborative and authentic, and that supervision can be curious, playful and fun. I acknowledge that there has to be an element of oversight within the supervision relationship, but I make clear how I approach the power imbalance by naming it and reducing it through being collaborative and open and in my approach to challenge (gentle, and with curiosity).

On my intake form, I ask: 'Do you have any specific needs that you would like me to be aware of? (Any neurodiversity needs you would like met).' This allows supervisees to share their access needs. This should be normal for all therapists and supervisors, but the more I hear, the more I discover that it is far from normal.

Supervisees have told me that, if we are working online, they might need the camera switched off at times – they might need to be resting in bed, and they might need to use the chat function sometimes, instead of speaking. One supervisee told me they had been laughed at by a previous supervisor for extensively writing out their supervision notes. Some have asked me not to have a blurred background as they find it uncomfortable. Some have shared their hearing loss and told me what they need in order to be able to communicate most comfortably with me. Some have told me that they are worried about not being succinct as they have been shamed for talking too much in the past. Some have asked me to be patient if I have asked them for clarification, so they are able to process what they think I want to know, and that I may need to rephrase what I ask or say to them if they don't understand initially.

If asked, and if given a chance to share their needs, most people will take the risk to be honest. That my supervisees feel able to claim their needs makes me so happy. It tells me they are self-reflective, that they understand themselves, and that they can advocate for themselves. I believe there's an energy around standing firm in claiming our needs that flows into our counselling work. If counsellors are claiming their needs, they are more likely to be better counsellors and less likely to burn out. Which leads me to my next point.

On your supervisor caring about your entire existence

Although there are many models of supervision, as I've already said, it's generally agreed that its main elements include not just helping your supervisees in their professional development and providing ethical oversight but also supporting their wellbeing, or 'self-care'. Many supervisors seem to forget that last part, in my experience.

Hawkins & Shohet's seven-eyed model (Hawkins & Shohet, 2012) of supervision is quite clear about this. It states that the seven 'eyes' or 'modes' a supervisor should be paying attention to are as follows:

- Mode 1: Exploration of the story of the supervisee's client's life.
- Mode 2: Exploration of the work the supervisee is doing with the client, interventions, how it's going, what's working, and what's not.
- Mode 3: Exploration of what's going on between the supervisee and their client – any tensions, and ruptures, what's working well, what's not, what's going on, what's playing out.
- Mode 4: Exploration of the supervisee's world. How are they feeling, how is the work impacting them, how is their wellbeing, what is going on in their life? This mode also includes 'attending to the general wellbeing (resourcing aspect) and development (developmental aspect) of the supervisee's needs' (Hawkins & Shohet, 2012, p.98).
- Mode 5: Exploration of what's going on between me and the supervisee. How is our relationship? Are they getting their needs met? Any ruptures?

What aren't they saying? Is any of the client work entering the supervisory relationship?

- Mode 6: Exploration about what is going on for me. What am I feeling about my supervisee, their work, their world? Is anything being activated in me? What am I noticing in my body as we work together?
- Mode 7: Exploration of the wider context for my supervisee, their client and me. What is happening socially, politically, culturally? What is going on in our worlds that may be coming into the work?

I once read a comment from a supervisor that supervision is about the client, not the supervisee. Nothing could be further from the truth, in my view. The supervisee is key. How they are doing personally and in their professional practice and relationships is essential to their work with their clients. Counsellors bring all of themselves to their work. Although there is little current research, we are beginning to understand that autistic and neurodivergent people are in general more likely to burn out, and certainly experience burnout differently from their neurotypical peers.

In the words of the National Autistic Society (Raymaker, 2022):

> Autistic burnout is a syndrome conceptualised as resulting from chronic life stress and a mismatch of expectations and abilities without adequate support. It is characterised by pervasive, long-term (typically 3+ months) exhaustion, loss of function, and reduced tolerance to stimulus.

In their 2020 research paper, '"Having all of your internal resources exhausted beyond measure and being left with no clean-up crew": Defining autistic burnout', Raymaker and colleagues conclude (2020):

> Autistic burnout appears to be a phenomenon distinct from occupational burnout or clinical depression. Better understanding autistic burnout could lead to ways to recognize, relieve, or prevent it, including highlighting the potential dangers of teaching autistic people to mask or camouflage their autistic traits.

As a neurodivergent supervisor, I recognise that part of my role is to provide that 'adequate support'. A supervisor should be alert to the signs of burnout, and be able to raise them and support their supervisee through it. Ideally, they should be able to flag it up early and find ways with their supervisee to manage their working relationships and life balance to avoid the risk. Client and supervisee alike then benefit, and not at the expense of the supervisee or clients.

So, part of my supervision practice is burnout prevention. It's checking in to see how my supervisees are doing, and whether they are practising self-care and how that's going. Can they afford therapy? Can they access what they need to support them so they can support their clients? How are they coping in their lives as neurodivergent counsellors and managing all that life demands? Working in a deeply relational way is key in a supervision relationship, just as it is in a client-therapist relationship (Mearns & Cooper, 2017). Although I may only meet with my supervisees once a month, I want to foster an environment where we can move quickly into working deeply.

I believe that being AuDHD helps me be a better supervisor because I already naturally value depth and connection. If something feels superficial, I sense that and want more depth. This in turn benefits my supervisees, because working at depth in a trusting supervisory relationship means that counsellors have confidence in the support that is supporting them to be with their clients. Of course, neurotypical supervisors should be aware of burnout and how to support their neurotypical supervisees, but they need also to understand how it's different for their neurodivergent supervisees.

The needs of autistic and neurodivergent supervisees are different to those of neurotypicals, but neurotypical counsellors will also benefit from having a supervisor who approaches the supervision relationship this way. Which brings me to my next point.

On the space to unpack

Realising my own neurodivergence led to what I call 'the great unpacking'. A really important part of this unpacking was deconstructing my internalised ableism, which I realised meant I had not previously been challenging my supervisees' internalised ableism. Ableism when applied to neurodivergent folk can be thought of as the assumptions, discrimination and external barriers placed on us that stop us accessing the things we need to survive and thrive. It can be overt and intentional, or subtle and systemic. Some examples of ableism with regard to neurodivergence that I've seen among some supervisors is the belief that neurodivergence is just a result of trauma and an implication that it can be healed and cured. Another is the persistent belief that autistic people can't feel empathy, and a refusal to acknowledge that expressions of empathy come in many different forms, and are not always recognised by the receiver in the same positive ways, especially if they are themselves neurodivergent.

Internalised ableism is when we place those restrictions on ourselves through the internalising of society's ableist messages about our abilities. An example of internalised ableism might be: 'I don't deserve extra support because I should be able to do these things the same way neurotypical people can.' Or,

'Other counsellors manage busy practices, relationships, parenting and life, and I should be able to too.' And even, 'This model makes no sense to me, I must be too stupid to get it.'

Supervision should be about exploring these issues – the unconscious internal messages, but also the external manifestations, and the failure of neurotypical models adequately to reflect how neurodivergent folk feel and behave. No matter what the neurotype of the supervisee is, ableism that isn't acknowledged, explored and challenged can be really damaging. And it can perhaps be still more damaging when it has become a constant inner voice commenting in our heads.

It is important that we neurodivergent counsellors do not deny the harm done to us from a lifetime of masking or of being diagnosed or undiagnosed or late-diagnosed or self-diagnosed or misdiagnosed. Many of us will be processing this for years to come – maybe all of our lives. Many of us trained in programmes where neurodivergence was never even mentioned, or only under the heading of 'abnormal', as 'other people', not us. We were forced to adopt a neurotypical model of counselling that was designed to reinforce neurotypical ways of being. We were taught always to make eye contact with our clients. Don't fidget. Don't ask too many questions.

After my great unpacking, and after going through a period of burnout, one of the things that I began to understand about myself (the unpacking and processing is still a work in progress) is that I am far better suited to short-term, solution-focused work. The lack of structure in open-ended work was one of the things that contributed to burnout and ended up with me having to take 18 months off from counselling. My success in being able to explore this came from having great supervision, and also from finding my tribe of neurodivergent therapists and having a great neurodivergent counsellor.

I believe being AuDHD has made me a better supervisor because I am able to ask deeper questions about how being autistic or neurodivergent affects my supervisees, from a place of deep understanding, not academic observation or third-party learning. When supervisees talk about difficulties with admin, or missing sessions, or the energy it takes to keep on top of a busy practice, or unmasking, or dealing with clients' masks, they need support from a supervisor with a deep, inner understanding of all of that. It means there is no shame, no judgement, no attempts at 'fixing'; just curious, gentle interest, concern and exploration. Supervision here is about the supervisor collaboratively figuring out what their supervisee needs in order to continue to do the work they love and supporting them to be the best therapist they can be.

To summarise all this

To sum up, embracing my AuDHD has not only helped me feel more accepting of myself and my difference; I believe it has also helped me be a better supervisor. Does that mean that neurotypical counsellors can't ever work well with and be great supervisors to neurodivergent therapists? The answer is I hope a resounding 'No'. Despite some evidence to the contrary from my own experience and the experience of my supervisees, there are some great neurotypical supervisors who are open, learning, affirmative and supportive, and do try to understand – even empathise with – our neurodivergence and the impact it has on our lives and work. While I like to believe that my difference is a superpower, the traits that make me a good supervisor are not magic – they are human traits. No supervisor, neurodivergent or neurotypical, can have lived experience of every identity and difference experienced by their supervisees. Counsellors who have multiple marginalised identities, who are neurodivergent, chronically ill or disabled, queer, gay or trans, fat, racially minoritised or of colour, and combinations of more than one of these, arguably have to do extra work when seeking the right therapist or supervisor. We have to make sure that the professionals we are working with understand our differences and have beliefs that align with our experience. We have to know that they are learning and doing the work to own their privilege, even when they have their own intersecting identities. For example, I may be fat, queer and neurodivergent, but I also have privilege by being a white cis woman, so it's on me to do the ongoing and never-ending work of deconstructing my internalised racism and gender bias.

I hear some supervisees tell me they feel their entire identity is dismissed by supervisors with phrases such as 'Don't identify with your label too much,' or 'Diagnosis is just pathologising'. It can feel very limiting to hear that from a supervisor. I've had supervisees tell me that they had to become an educator, advocate and defender of their clients to their supervisors. How can you explore client work if your supervisor does not have a starting point of understanding and accepting who those clients and supervisees are?

Choosing a supervisor, much like choosing a counsellor, can feel like online dating: browsing profiles, seeing if there is a connection when you look at their photographs and whether you like what they are saying with their words. You reach out to them and wait to hear back. If they message you back, you take the first tentative steps to see if they might be a good fit for you. Armed with the knowledge from this chapter, I hope you will feel able to ask for what you need, to check out the supervisor's beliefs on difference and diversity, and to ask them what they are doing to work on their unconscious bias.

In the light of this chapter, how do you feel about your supervision? Is your supervisor good enough for you and can you take all your parts to supervision? A good supervisor is worth their weight in gold. They should be an essential part of your practice and support system and your burnout prevention kit. Embracing my AuDHD identity has been so empowering for me as an individual, but I didn't realise just how much it would impact my work as a supervisor. I can confidently say, 100%, that I am a better supervisor because of my neurodivergence.

References

Hawkins, P. & Shohet, R. (2012). *Supervision in the helping professions* (4th ed.). Open University Press.

Mearns, D. & Cooper, M. (2017). *Working at relational depth in counselling and psychotherapy* (2nd ed.). Sage.

Raymaker, D. (2022, March 1). Understanding autistic burnout. *National Autistic Society.* https://www.autism.org.uk/advice-and-guidance/professional-practice/autistic-burnout

Raymaker, D.M., Teo, A.R., Steckler, N.A., Lentz, B., Scharer, M., Delos Santos, A., Kapp, S.K., Hunter, M., Joyce, A. & Nicolaidis, C. (2020). 'Having all of your internal resources exhausted beyond measure and being left with no clean-up crew': Defining autistic burnout. *Autism in Adulthood, 2*(2), 132–143. http://doi.org/10.1089/aut.2019.0079

van Ooijen, E. (2013). *Clinical supervision made easy* (2nd ed.). PCCS Books.

Chapter 17

Making environments accessible: Permission to exist

Elinor Rowlands

Therapy can be life-affirming when autistic clients are given permission to exist in environments they deem relaxed and safe enough to explore in. These therapy environments reduce access barriers so that autistic clients are given space and time to explore their life experiences as they choose. Digital technology is also used to provide access needs and so removes barriers and risks found in neurotypical situations and empowers autistic clients. Accessible environments may include everybody, including non-autistic people. However, so many non-autistic practitioners fail autistic clients because their so-called inclusive environments may be facilitative but the practitioner lacks the ability to empathise with the client. This is often down to an unwillingness to listen to or learn about the lived experiences of autistic people. This chapter will reveal why the 'environment' is so essential to autistic people.

The therapeutic environment emphasises autonomy and ease over intimidation, dependency and urgency (Rowlands, 2019/2020). For my arts project *Magical Women*, I created an alternative model to existing systems and structures within the arts that are conventionally created with the neurotypical in mind (Rowlands, 2019/2020).[1] *Magical Women* is an autistic/ADHD-led project and is aimed mainly at women/non-binary artists who are also autistic/ADHD. It is primarily a virtual meeting space that enables creative collaboration within the digital environment, which is highly adaptable. This online environment allows individuals to determine their own levels of

---

1. You can find out more about Magical Women at www.magicalwomen.co.uk

engagement and to manage sensory processing needs within an environment they control, thereby limiting or removing anxiety from communication and social interaction barriers, with support from peers as and when appropriate (Rowlands, 2019).

Creating safe environments

When working with neurodivergent and disabled clients, it is fundamental that psychotherapy and counselling professionals work from within an environment that is situated in the social and human rights models of disability (Degener, 2017). These models distinguish between 'impairment' as personal challenges, and 'disability' as stemming from socially imposed barriers and limitations (Barnes, 2012). However, sadly, so many of my clients are coming to me after seeing other therapists (or coaches) because they have not accepted, acknowledged or validated my clients' neurodivergence. In turn, my clients have expressed how the therapeutic environment feels one-sided, with the therapist holding most of the power in the space, and this, in turn, distorts effective communication and collaboration. So many of my clients are rendered mute or feel unable to be themselves in the session. One of my clients described this experience as a very noticeable and visible wall between her and other therapists she had seen in the past. During our sessions, she explained, there is no wall, and she feels that, however she might present that day, she will always be held, seen and heard by me because she can sense and feel this environment more clearly in our sessions. It is an environment that she deems safe to explore in.

In environments that do not feel safe, autistic clients do not feel empowered to end therapy sessions with their therapist, despite this unequal power dynamic, and thus the environment is never considered by these professionals who fail autistic and/or ADHD clients. When an environment is situated in the social and human-rights disability models (Degener, 2017), the client is empowered, feels relaxed to explore themes and topics, and is given the space to think with ease, because there is no risk of being rushed or feeling a sense of urgency. Furthermore, this environment also references Jo Scott's concept of 'live intermedial spaces' (2016) as sites of activation and empathy through 'affective encounters' (Bennett, 2005).

This chapter will therefore emphasise the importance of collaboration within the therapeutic environment to meet the access needs of clients in ways that promote equality and social progression, including advocating for diversity of thought and greater recognition of the 'double empathy problem' (Milton, 2012, 2018). I will also explore key and central insights and recommendations as to how to use digital techniques (journeying and soundscapes) to increase accessibility in the therapeutic and autistic/ADHD-led space.

Mentoring and coaching

I have always worked, but due to my access barriers, which centred around my fatigue, chronic pain and exhaustion, I have had to seek out jobs where I can flexibly choose my hours. As much as I tried to stick to full-time employment, I soon had to drop out, due to the burnout and access and communication barriers around managements' expectations on me to do daily small talk. As a result of these obstacles, I worked as an employment coach with autistic adults and a specialist mentor for autistic/ADHD and mental health university students. I have also worked as a learning-support and study skills tutor to children and young people who are neurodivergent (e.g. dyslexic, dyspraxic, ADHD, autistic, epileptic, Tourette's, bipolar and so on). I have supported people across all ethnicities and socio-economic groups, and ages: the oldest person I have mentored was 73, who at that time wanted to be a priest. She died from cancer before she completed her training journey, but I mentored her while she was progressing with a goal that she felt she had to explore – it was a 'now or never' moment. She explained to me that she had always sacrificed her needs to everyone else's, and that in our sessions she felt completely heard and seen for the very first time in her entire life, because I made the space so visceral and exciting. She looked forward to our sessions because the environment and space I held for her made her feel closer to her goal, so she couldn't wait to 'work' in them.

I enjoy problem-solving and collaborating with clients to identify their barriers, empowering them to find the tools needed to reduce those obstacles and achieve their goals. In my sessions, clients can explore what works for them. For instance, as an employment coach, I helped one autistic client secure a £30,000 annual salary just two months after starting coaching, after 11 years of exclusion due to inadequate workplace support. They thrived in a supportive environment where they felt safe to express themselves. Sharing this environment with me during coaching and then finding it afterwards in their employment gave them autonomy – they could use their voice without fear of being corrected or patronised. I also work with clients who are hesitant to return to work due to past trauma. We focus instead on exploring their sense of self in a supportive space. This work has become my passion – mentoring autistic graduates and school leavers, helping them find employment or opportunities to use their skills in conducive environments. While I've enjoyed this process, I've noticed many autistic and AuADHD (autistic and ADHD) clients face continuing barriers because they don't understand the type of environment they need to thrive and feel empowered.

Creating environments that work for us

I have chronic fatigue syndrome and postural tachycardia syndrome, both of which I have managed since I was an adolescent. My specialist has recommended that I do as many tasks as possible sitting down, due to my vertigo. My mother would say it was as if attending school was too much for me; she would find me in bed after every school day. Even now, as a parent with a baby, I am still able to work because I take power naps and organise my days around them. I have created an environment that works for me and is sustainable. Whenever I try to meet the aims other people have set for me, I go back to crumbling, because I am not in an environment that works for me.

So many of my clients explained that, when they were experiencing burnout, severe anxiety or breakdown in mental health, they were taking on jobs or seeking out roles that other people wanted for them. Some autistic people don't want jobs, and yet society won't allow them this sense of peace for themselves. It is difficult to be able not to work unless you come from a privileged background, or you are able to stay at home and be cared for by family, which many autistic people struggle with, due to their need for space and their own identity. So they are forced to find paid work. Some autistic people would simply prefer to volunteer or work in a role that is not very demanding so they can take a break some days, or to work in a way that is manageable for them; others may wish to contribute their voices on the boards of charities or organisations as a trustee, to bring about social justice and change. My clients have shared that, once they identified the kinds of environment and support they needed, they were able to find suitable roles or activities that gave them joy – a feeling that could be quite novel for them.

Some of my clients had never been able to take on employment due to their crippling anxiety around how people would talk to or treat them, so instead we would focus solely on what brought them joy. Each and every client who focused on building an environment for themselves where they felt encouraged, supported and held was able to give themselves the opportunity to consider at least applying for a role, or developing one for themselves where they felt able to flourish and achieve their worth. I have helped so many autistic nurses, for example, who identified that they were able to reduce patients' barriers to treatment and make things happen for them that would otherwise be shrugged off or ignored by their colleagues. The autistic nurses I have supported have gone on to change the environments they found challenging to work in, in the same way that they were able to advocate for their patients. They were able to do this after using the therapy environment with me to discover how to advocate for themselves. It gave them a place to think with ease and without urgency.

In our sessions there is a lack of the risk found in situations and environments led by neurotypicals. Autistic clients feel able to lead the sessions and explore their own themes and topics. It is important to emphasise that there is a worldwide lack of social security and provisions to enable autistic people to thrive with autonomy and agency. They very often know themselves best but need practical support day to day and throughout the day, and that includes support from autistic psychotherapists. I receive about three emails a week from autistic people seeking free therapy but, sadly, I can't afford to offer that, as I have to pay my own living costs. I spend a lot of time seeking and applying for funding so I can provide free mentoring to low-income or no-income autistic clients.

Supportive spaces

I trained and qualified as an art psychotherapist. On placements, my clients told me I was an incredibly insightful and progressive psychotherapist. But, sadly, my training experiences were ableist, and I was bullied and ostracised by some of my fellow trainees on account of being autistic. I remember during one university-led supervision, the tutor allowed three of my peers to bully me. Only one international student, who spoke English as an additional language, approached me at the end of the session, as I held back my tears, to ask how I was. She was horrified that the supervisor had allowed that to happen, and it put her off practising art psychotherapy in the UK. There was a belief that autistic people should not train as psychotherapists. The content in our child development modules was so backward I held my tongue most of the time because I was horrified at how many trainees believed what they were learning was fact. Instead, I took it for what it was: a theory, deeply flawed (and wrong). As den Houting (2019) explains in her TED Talk:

> Most people understand autism through medical assumptions. They understand autism as a medical condition, a disorder, even as a tragedy. In the medical paradigm, we're taught to believe that there is a correct way to develop neurologically – the normal way – and that any other way of developing is wrong and needs to be treated and fixed.

The child development theory we were taught lacked the lived experience of an autistic person. I am connected on social media with an autistic art psychotherapist who did the same training 10 years after me and was awarded a first – it had taken the same institution more than 10 years to become accepting of autistic people becoming psychotherapists.

During the time I was working as a professional artist, I realised that there were no sacred or supportive spaces for autistic artists, especially women, to make art. Studios were often far too expensive or inaccessible and autistic women artists were looked upon as being unprofessional because they did not tick the boxes required by the arts organisations who worked with 'autistic artists'. We were deemed too 'high functioning', and yet we were excluded from mainstream spaces for reasons they could not explain. I knew so many autistic women artists who were at home, isolated, but were also prolific artists. Nobody knew about them because they did not have an audience or a place to make and share art, and I wanted to change this. In 2019, I went about developing a model of a therapeutic space where neurodivergent women and non-binary artists could spend two hours together making art or writing and then share their work. I noticed that, when autistic/neurodivergent artists came together to stim, make art or write, the collective unconscious (Jung, 1959) became very powerful. Furthermore, a silent collaboration happened to a point where we all became one strong voice. Working with other autistic artists was also re-energising for our own practice, and in turn I began to become even more prolific with mine.

Magical journeying

I also later developed online workshops called 'Magical Journeys', where I guide women and non-binary artists through storytelling and visualisations accompanied by soundscapes. These immersive experiences allow neurodivergent artists to explore new creative territories by creating a supportive and accessible environment, with a support worker present for participants, and also one for me or the facilitator. In these workshops, participants feel held and can choose to have their cameras on or off while receiving feedback through chat. Rather than asking for good or bad responses, we encourage participants to share their experiences with prompts like, 'What images or symbols did you see? What feelings arose? What did you create in response to the soundscape?' This cultivates an ongoing dialogue filled with compassion, validation and support. Many clients began using these soundscapes in their personal lives, finding them helpful for relaxation, emotional regulation, or sharing with their neurodivergent children, often noting the deep sense of calm this engendered.

Soundscapes

As an artist, I paint, write and play through sound, texts and site-specific work. I make phantasmagorical layered films, performances and soundscapes to engage, inspire and mesmerise audiences of all ages and from all walks of life. I believe my neurodivergent experience holds power and magic. My work explores this power and sense of being through an autistic and ADHD filter. Autism exists in my work intentionally, without being overtly placed at its centre. Autism, in this sense, is experienced as an alternative form of consciousness, distinguished as 'an oscillation of psychic energy between the unconscious and conscious mind, informing one's whole field of perception: cognitive, emotional, social, physical and spiritual' (Harris, 2021). This is pretty much how I create my soundscapes from an alternative form of consciousness (Harris, 2021). As a sound artist, I create soundscapes of real and imagined places.

So, what is a soundscape? Well, if we think about a landscape, it's usually a view of somewhere, whether it's beautiful or ugly. But it is usually a scene that interests people, that gets people excited or intrigued, or makes them feel relaxed – scenes of wild heather and green hills or the bubbling sea, transparent, turquoise and free, or marshy beaches that make for a tranquil and beautiful view and landscape. Each time we view a landscape, a story is being told. A soundscape is similar, but instead we hear sounds. It can be a mixture of dialogue or monologue, and gathered or found sounds like birdsong, the sound of the sea or the sound of a passing train. A soundscape arises from an immersive environment. The study of soundscape is known as acoustic ecology, and I feel this term fits nicely with this sense of creating environments with and for my clients to prolong this continued sense of peace or ease that they experience in environments that allow them to thrive.

Soundscapes also overlap with the traditional ideas around folktales. How are they closely related? Folktales come in the form of stories in the oral tradition, or tales that people tell each other out loud. They're closely related to many storytelling traditions, including fables, myths and fairytales. However, folktales are largely used in soundscapes with the retelling of people's memories or childhood experiences, often of places where they find respite, peace and encouragement. They can be places of magic and beauty, wildness and freedom. As an artist, I am interested in these stories. I will work with clients who often require a soundscape to listen back to or work with. This offers them the potential to have their voice heard, held and seen. If, for example, a soundscape is made in the likeness of an island, because the client remembers visiting one during their childhood and this brings back the smell of the sea and the sounds of the birds, then the client becomes part of the island, and the island part of them. This unity is an important element for the creation of a soundscape and also brings the client back to an environment that fills them with a sense of belonging. In this way, soundscapes are like a collage of sounds. They can help people visualise themselves within the story even if they have never visited the island before or have lost a sense of what it felt like there.

The soundscape gives purpose to change or action. This may be for climate change, or for the client to feel more attuned to an energy they want to tap into when working, creating or trying to sleep. Engaging with a soundscape helps them to preserve a sense of self that they rarely experience in a world that sets out to bruise, exclude or remind them why they are different. A soundscape is a call to notice, to pay attention and to remember the astonishing beauty there.

Occasionally, long-term clients request a specific soundscape, prompting me to blend various unused audio snippets I have collected from previous art projects. This approach allows me to recycle and repurpose these sound fragments to craft tailored soundscapes for particular clients or groups. While gathering sounds on an island for a client who shared their emotional connection to the place, I recorded an array of rich auditory experiences. This included the serene, almost sacred silence inside the Mound at West Mersea Barrow, the rhythmic bobbing of boats in the harbour, the diverse sounds of each wild beach I had explored, and the stories the client had recited to the sea. With their permission, I used texts they had shared in sessions and added snippets to the soundscape. I also made sure to capture the various sounds of the beaches under changing light, as the quality of light can profoundly alter the acoustic landscape.

In creating the soundscape, I focused on the nuances of silence as well, recognising that many autistic people are attuned to the subtle shifts in silence across different environments. For instance, the silence at Cudmore Grove felt distinct to me, especially when I stood on the spots where collaborative artists from the project I had recently completed had crafted spirals that endured various weather conditions. At that moment, I sensed a watchful energy around me. Gazing out at the sea, I was struck by the anxiety that arises from the land being gradually reclaimed by the water, and I pondered how these environmental energies resonate within our own bodies and senses. All these elements are woven into the soundscape I created, as we incorporated effects to enhance the auditory space. After all, sound itself is a unique environment – a room filled with the essence of place and emotion.

I don't work this way for all my clients or groups. However, for some who rely on sound as a vital environment, it serves as a therapeutic tool. For many autistic clients, sound helps to regulate emotions and engages the senses in calm and accessible ways, allowing them to express themselves, share their experiences and create in an independent and empowered way.

Clients bring a rich tapestry of stories and shared experiences to therapy or mentoring sessions. I often incorporate these narratives into soundscapes to support and enhance their therapeutic journeys. Soundscapes allow clients to reconnect with the feelings associated with various environments, helping them to envision and create their own. They honour the past, present and future, celebrating the boldness, courage and beauty that reside within them. Soundscapes also offer autistic individuals the chance to engage with the energy found in stimming, resulting in a powerful and joyful experience.

In my therapeutic and mentoring practice, as well as in the workshops I conduct for varied audiences, including neurodivergent artists and creatives, I integrate a range of materials such as digital technologies, paint, sand and clay. I use soundscapes to document and enrich these experiences, employing sounds and voices to transport clients, participants and audiences to realms that are forgotten, remembered or imagined. This provides additional, immersive magic to help them remember moments of awakening. It offers them mantras to use in their daily lives that validate their lived experiences. Some of my clients like to use these soundscapes for their own practice or development outside of our sessions, to encourage their rituals and to not feel ashamed of them. This also increases access for them.

The vast range of methods and forms within therapy and mentoring are essential in helping autistic and other neurodivergent people engage with art and everyday life. The environments within therapy help to develop clients' own practice and acknowledge their identity, language and culture. In turn this offers them empowerment in a way that it is rare for them to feel in a world set out to exclude, punish and dehumanise them.

References

Barnes, C. (2012). Understanding the social model of disability: Past, present and future. In: N. Watson, A. Roulstone & C. Thomas (Eds.). *Routledge handbook of disability studies* (pp.12–29). Routledge.

Bennett, J. (2005). *Empathic vision: Affect, trauma and contemporary art*. Stanford University Press.

Degener, T. (2017). A new human rights model of disability. In: V. Della Fina, R. Cera & G. Palmisano (Eds.). *The United Nations convention on the rights of persons with disabilities*. Springer. https://doi.org/10.1007/978-3-319-43790-3_2

den Houting, J. (2019, September). *Why everything you know about autism is wrong*. Ted Talk. www.ted.com/talks/jac_den_houting_why_everything_you_know_about_autism_is_wrong?language=en

Harris, R. (2021). *Pythiism: Reframing autism as an alternative form of consciousness*. Rachael Lee Harris

Jung, C.G. (1959). The archetypes and the collective unconscious. In *The Collected Works of C.G. Jung*, Vol. 9(1) (R.F.C. Hull, Trans.). Routledge & Kegan Paul.

Milton, D.E.M. (2012). On the ontological status of autism: The 'double empathy problem'. *Disability and Society, 27*(6), 883–887.

Milton, D. (2018, March 2). The double empathy problem. *National Autistic Society*. www.autism.org.uk/advice-and-guidance/professional-practice/double-empathy

Rowlands, E. (2019/2020). *Magical women*. www.magicalwomen.co.uk

Scott, J. (2016). 'Affective encounters': Live intermedial spaces in sites of trauma. *Research in Drama Education: The Journal of Applied Theatre and Performance, 21*(3), 332–336.

Chapter 18

Neurodiversity-affirming supervision

Romy Graichen

The supervisory relationship is an integral part of the clinical setting, and its quality can have profound impacts on supervisees. Unfortunately, experiences of being discounted or unwanted as an autistic or otherwise neurodivergent (ND) practitioner during counselling/psychotherapy training often continue after having qualified. The neurotypical (NT) standards that have been set for what 'good therapy' looks like, including the boundaries of therapy, emotional literacy, containment and even empathy, are at odds with neurodivergent experience. What is needed is a decentring of neuronormative ideas in therapy, therapy training and supervision (Leong & Graichen, 2024). Masking is a direct result, as autistic therapists-in-training change in order to belong, feel accepted and, most of all, pass their training. Masking then continues in supervision, where the supervisor is not aware of neurodivergence in the supervisee (or themselves). This often results in supervisees not engaging in the process of supervision.

The aim of good supervision is to help the practitioner to be more available for their clients, to hold and contain their material and facilitate change. I argue that neurotypically-informed supervision does not support the ND supervisee to do this. In addition, I believe ND clients are not brought to supervision or not adequately discussed and explored because supervisors lack confidence and competence to do so. Instead, they propose NT ideas and interpretations, or discount neurodivergent traits as deficits rather than strengths. Neurodivergence may also be mistaken for traumatic responses, meaning the client does not receive the care and support they need, or the prevalence and significance of neurodivergent issues are ignored. Thus, the supervisor's attitudes and beliefs can disrupt (and even harm) the therapeutic work, and also, importantly, the relationship supervisees have with their clients.

I have been working as a supervisor in a counselling context for more than 18 years. Increasingly I am seeing the value of my lived experience as a multiply neurodivergent practitioner, trainer and supervisor. Most of my work these days consists of offering clinical supervision, so I decided to share here my approach to supervision.

My hope is that this account may help supervisors to offer a more affirming space for supervisees of all neurotypes. I believe this would contribute to challenging oppressive frameworks and ableist ideas within the profession and its practice – ideas and approaches that serve neither supervisees nor their clients – and to a general shift towards acknowledging and normalising diversity in neurological make-up, experience and expression.

I asked some of my supervisees to offer me feedback on how they experience supervision with me, and I have woven their responses into this chapter. I use their words, and their responses may contain my name, but feel free to substitute 'neurodiversity-affirming supervisor', as I believe this is what my approach represents.

What is neurodiversity-affirming supervision?

Neurodiversity-affirming supervision (NDASV) moves away from neurotypical dominant standards and instead uses a framework of acceptance, attunement and empowerment. It is designed to help individuals who do not conform to traditional neurotypical concepts of capacity, ability and skill, and allows for greater opportunity for individuals to flourish and be their most authentic selves. NDASV provides a space in which all practitioners can begin to feel safe and supported to explore their full talents, attributes and abilities. Offering NDASV means offering a space in which the supervisory relationship is underpinned by appreciating and celebrating differences in the ways our brains function, as well as exploring and challenging implicit assumptions about intelligence, capabilities and healthy behaviours, and internalised ableism. This can support supervisees to feel more empowered and more confident in their work and in who they are. NDASV allows all of us to learn from mistakes in a supportive environment and grow into our fullest potential.

Autistic masking is a phenomenon in which an individual attempts to fit in by suppressing behaviours associated with autism. This can be both conscious and unconscious; the individual may not even be aware that they are masking. It is self-denying, incongruent (Rogers, 1957) and exhausting. It is also known to have devastating impacts on mental health (Bradley et al., 2021) and is correlated with higher rates of suicidal thoughts and behaviours (Cassidy et al.,

2020). I argue that any practice, including supervision, that encourages (or fails to recognise) masking is harmful and unethical.

NDASV is designed to support and empower individuals who do not conform to traditional neurotypical norms. In NDASV, there is no externally imposed need to mask. It allows individuals to feel accepted for who they are and encourages them to develop their own abilities and strengths. It also allows for more creativity and flexibility.

Key features of NDASV
Creating safety

Creating a space that is open and inviting, where both supervisor and supervisee can be curious about what is happening in the space between us and the space between supervisee and their client, is paramount so that trust can develop and grow. Within NDASV, the supervisor and supervisee can learn to trust each other so that we can be vulnerable, be ourselves and know our limits, be respectful, and seek to understand self and the other without judgement.

One of my supervisees summed this up to me as 'being unfailingly validating and supportive while ensuring a healthy level of gentle challenge and intellectual stimulation'. We know that we learn best when we feel safe, when we can allow for nuances that we do not have the capacity for when we are stressed, in fight or flight or shutdown. These nuanced ways of working are essential with our neurodiverse clients and supervisees. When we are masking (think of masking as a fawning[1] nervous-system response to threat or danger), we expend a lot of energy on hiding the things we cannot do well, to camouflage our differences and difficulties. This contradicts a major purpose of supervision, which is to provide a safe space for exploration of concerns, not-knowing, possible mistakes and how to address any lack of knowledge, skills or confidence. If we are nourished to develop the things we are good at, we can flourish, and so can our professional practice. In a safe environment, we can explore the issues we find difficult. We can explore further whether those issues are crucial to providing a therapeutic relationship and psychological interventions. We can also delve into our challenges and find creative ways for scaffolding and supporting us through them.

My supervisees have shared with me how they experienced non-affirming supervision as unsafe and oppressive, and how it therefore caused them to mask. This then led to them experiencing a drop in confidence in themselves and their abilities, and in supervision.

---

1. Fawning is the fourth mammalian autonomic nervous-system response after fight, flight and freeze, and describes our attempts to placate the forces threatening us.

One wrote:

> I had been becoming increasingly despondent and drained by supervision and noticing how little benefit I (and by extension my clients) really derived from it. I felt I could never be truly myself otherwise I had no workable way of communicating with my then supervisor. It felt like I had to filter everything through a kind of 'neurotypical translation tool' with a lot of stuff inevitably getting lost in the process.

In stark contrast to NDASV, we hear how, in non-affirming supervision, this supervisee felt they could not risk being fully themselves:

> [NDASV] somehow felt like it was the first 'real' supervision I ever had in my life because previously I tried to hide my struggles and often wondered why I didn't find supervision particularly helpful. I now realise that if I deny a big part of myself then I am actually not bringing myself into the room at all. It's like a dark secret that gets locked away, out of fear that one day someone will tell me that I am in the wrong job indeed because of the way I relate to people.

Being curious and avoiding assumptions

In a neurotypically dominant setting, it is assumed that both supervisees and their clients should be matched against a standard of neurotypical ideas of good mental health, relationships and progress, as well as therapeutic interventions. In NDASV, I try to mitigate this by striving to avoid assumptions in my approach. I take the time to get to know my supervisees and stay curious about their experience in the therapy room. Above all, I enquire and explore beyond a neurotypical perspective. I use an open framework that draws on multiple, diverse ways of explaining/interpreting client behaviours and experiences, as opposed to limiting us to a single neurotypical and pathologising model. This non-judgemental, inclusive approach is culturally sensitive and neuro-humble. The positive impact that I have witnessed in my supervisees and what they report is a more inclusive sense of belonging and a marked absence of judgement.

NDASV is also characterised by the practitioner's commitment to ongoing learning and curiosity about what it is like to be the other, to be in their sessions with clients, to experience their life, as well as bring our own stories and work collaboratively, as equal partners. It is about recognising and speaking to the imbalances of power inherent in the supervisor/supervisee and therapist/client relationships and aiming to address them in supervision. I share with my supervisees when I get things wrong, as well as when I don't know something, and use this as a guide to inform areas for more curiosity and learning. It is an open invitation to reflect on how one's biases impact on how one makes sense of others – which is particularly important when training has only been on making sense of people through neurotypical lenses.

NDASV is also about being open to exploring different ideas and therapeutic approaches in their broadest sense that may be more inclusive and may be outside of the neurotypical box. This is only possible if the relationship offers safety – safety to get it wrong and safety to share differences. As one supervisee said:

> What has been one of the best aspects of getting supervision from you is feeling safe – safe enough for us to disagree, to have debates, and for me to be open about areas which might feel shameful to me under other circumstances.

The culture of the counselling profession and its often ableist standards conflict with the growing acceptance of one's neurodivergence. In a space where difference is welcomed and celebrated, a supervisee is invited to reflect on dynamics at play inside and outside of them and the interplay between them. NDASV can help to navigate this by examining with curiosity our sense of self, how it fits with our work, and how we may be able to bridge any gaps that exist. In another supervisee's words:

> I need an opportunity to reflect with an autistic supervisor on the service and my role within it. It is important for me to consider how this impacts on my mental health and wellbeing, and Romy provides an independent perspective to explore issues around my own autism and the institutional dynamics I experience. There are ideological issues to consider when being in the minority, and it helps to know I have someone with whom to talk through points where my identity and judgements conflict with others and think about how I manage these situations. I think this is going to be more critical for me in the future, and I will value a steer through some of those issues with Romy when they come. For example, facing ableism or misconceptions when I advocate for myself and my autistic clients.

Attunement (*Einfühlung*)

Non-affirming supervision misses the mark when it comes to attunement to neurodiverse supervision needs. I believe that careful attunement with supervisees and their clients is vital to successful supervisory work.

I experience attunement in the way that Vischer (1873) called '*Einfühlung*', which literally means 'feeling into'. By this he meant the act of projecting oneself (and thereby entering) into another body or environment or object of art or piece of literature, in order to feel the emotions the artist has tried to evoke in others. It has been translated as 'empathy', but attunement seems to be a better fit for describing connection with the other at a level where words are not needed to communicate being in the other's experience. This also allows me to attune to the client through the supervisee's experience of themselves and the client. Sometimes this can bring up interesting ways of making sense of different experiences.

I find the double empathy problem (Milton, 2012) helpful in understanding how empathy is communicated differently across neurotypes. However, I choose to use the concept of attunement instead of empathy, as this allows me to feel into the supervisee's needs and communicate them more effectively. I tend to do this through facial expressions more than through words. Sometimes I may share what the supervisee's experience reminds me of, or what it evokes in me, which supervisees tell me they find helpful in their relationships with clients.

This seems to leave supervisees feeling more empowered and more confident in their work, and above all in who they are. This is done by balancing attunement to the supervisee (and also the client via the supervisee), accommodating their neurotype-specific needs and offering the space for growth, acceptance and celebrating who we are.

It is not uncommon for me to experience a sensation or pain or to notice a shift in my posture and, when I then share that with the supervisee, to hear that they themselves, or their clients, have had that same experience. Sometimes what is resonating in me does not make sense immediately, but by staying with the felt experience, we are able to work out what may be happening.

Here, one of my supervisees is reflecting on this, and what happens when we are differently attuned to the client and how we collaborate and work through this in the aid of the client:

> Sometimes what comes up for you when speaking of a client feels off course for me: i.e. it's not what I was thinking/bringing and at times I find this harder to go with than others. This is a challenge for me at times, but I don't see it as a negative aspect of your supervision style. It broadens my focus at times, brings subconscious into awareness at others. My challenge is sitting with it until we have it, as we're working somatically often at these times; perhaps my 'hurry up' part becomes activated.

I trust that the supervisee has a good relationship with and understanding of their client, and I often pick up underlying neurodivergence in a client and may offer this as a different way of making sense of what is happening with the client. This can help the supervisee themselves to see things in a non-pathologising and more accepting way than before. I enjoy using transferential processes and attunement to the supervisee's body to help gain a better understanding of the client and their unconscious processes.

Accommodations and clear agreements

Neuronormative dominance in supervision and therapy training dismisses diversity in learning and supervisory needs. NDASV, however, honours diversity in learning and supervisory needs, and thus offers accommodations. I do this by enquiring and giving space to supervisees to tell me about any individual needs and developing clear agreements and a co-created understanding of what I can do to accommodate them. When I sense an unmet need in supervision, I actively encourage my supervisees to be curious about it, and explore, identify and express it. This offer is often met with moving experiences of tears and deeper connection. I regularly ask if there are needs that I can meet differently and what I can do to accommodate them. It is vital for me to establish clear agreements around these accommodations and to continually review them to ensure they still meet the dynamic and ever-changing needs of supervisees.

When teaching this approach to my supervisees, I am equally explicit and transparent about any accommodations I may need, and I encourage them to think about their own needs as well as those of their clients. This means that I enquire about their lived experience of gender, of structures of oppression and marginalisation, of learning needs, and of privilege and power.

Conclusion

Neurotypically informed theories of therapy and supervision have long been commonplace. Nevertheless, this conventional approach has the potential to be damaging both for supervisors and for those they supervise by forcing them to hide their real identities in order to conform with neuronormative standards. It leads supervisees and supervisors to present an inauthentic version of themselves, which then adds an additional level of constraint within therapeutic sessions that can hinder personal and professional growth. This in turn may carry over into the therapeutic relationships of the supervisee with their own clients. Practitioners are compelled to adhere exclusively to standards based on neurotypical principles that ignore important aspects of being neurodivergent. Ultimately this can be damaging both professionally and ethically when providing therapy sessions or supervision.

The affirmative NDASV framework for supervision centres on creating an environment that is both responsive and accommodating to the individual needs of supervisees and supervisor, regardless of neurological makeup. By being curious about how each can make sense of their experiences in a supportive space, we are able to create safety not just for the supervisee receiving supervision but also for their clients. In essence, this framework works towards bringing understanding through teaching while providing safety nets so mistakes may be owned and explored without reservation or fear of consequence.

My hope is that reading this chapter will spark a positive shift for supervisors, encouraging them to embrace and affirm neurodiversity, thereby creating a safer environment and experience for supervisees and clients.

References

Bradley, L., Shaw, R., Baron-Cohen, S., & Cassidy, S. (2021). Autistic adults' experiences of camouflaging and its perceived impact on mental health. *Autism in Adulthood, 3*(4), 320–329. doi:10.1089/aut.2020.0071

Cassidy, S.A., Gould, K., Townsend, E., Pelton, M., Robertson, A.E. & Rodgers J. (2020). Is camouflaging autistic traits associated with suicidal thoughts and behaviours? Expanding the interpersonal psychological theory of suicide in an undergraduate student sample. *Journal of Autism Developmental Disorders, 50*(10), 3638–3648. doi: 10.1007/s10803-019-04323-3. PMID: 31820344; PMCID: PMC7502035.

Leong, C. & Graichen, R. (2024). Decentering neuronormativity: A transactional analysis impasse theory perspective for understanding ADHD masking and authentically honoring the Da Vinci archetype within. *Transactional Analysis Journal, 54*(1), 91–106. DOI:10.1080/03621537.2024.2286581

Milton, D.E.M. (2012). On the ontological status of autism: The double empathy problem. *Disability and Society, 27*(6), 883–887.

Rogers, C.R. (1957). The necessary and sufficient conditions of therapeutic personality change. *Journal of Consulting Psychology, 21*, 95–103.

Vischer, R. (1873). *Über das optische Formgefühl: Ein Beitrag zur Ästhetik* (The optical sense of form: Its contribution to aesthetics). Herman Credner.

Chapter 19

Kathryn's call: The lost generation

Wilma Wake

I had one more phone call to return that evening: Kathryn's. 'Kathryn' is a composite of a number of clients I have worked with. Her message had the same theme as many others I get every day: 'I found your name online. I'm looking for a therapist who understands autism. My nephew was recently diagnosed, and I've started doing some reading. I'm almost 67… and for the first time think I might be autistic! That's a terrifying thought! I want to work with an autistic therapist. Can you help me figure this out, please? I don't know where else to go for help…'

I called back and got her answering machine. I left a message that I could schedule her for a 30-minute free consult so she could decide if she wanted to go on my waiting list for therapy. If she wants to see me, I will find a way to fit her in. Older autistic adults are 'my people'.

Kathryn is almost 67, so was born around 1957. I'm 77; born in 1947. My father was a US soldier stationed in Japan during World War II. When the war ended, soldiers returned to their lives. My father came back to Illinois to marry his childhood sweetheart, and I was born soon afterwards. I was born in the midst of the post-war exhilaration, as the post-war world was taking shape and moving ahead. The 'baby boomer' generation includes those born between 1946 and 1964. I was in the 'first wave' of baby boomers, and Kathryn came along 10 years into the era.

That's the generation I interviewed for my research with older autistic adults, together with my co-authors Robert S. Lagos and Eric Endlich, both autistics diagnosed late in life (Wake et al., 2021). So many of us have had a similar journey of having struggled all of our lives to make sense of the world and communicate with others.

These are my people. So much of who we are comes from the political and social concepts during our lifetimes.

As a fellow autistic, I share many of the life views and experiences of my clients. My therapy is not a bland listening to my client. It is an impassioned interactive journey together. We are fellow travellers on the same road, and we talk about the scenery along the way. Traditional therapeutic norms say not to self-disclose to the client. For me, the essence of my therapy is that my autistic clients know I am autistic, too. And, like most of them, I was diagnosed late in life.

I think this is important. Until recently, the experience of growing up autistic but not knowing it has been excruciating. The bewilderment at how the world works and the inability to communicate with its people are overwhelming.

If Kathryn and I work together, I'll want to help her put her autism into historical context. To be diagnosed now, at age 67, is a completely different experience to that of a 10-year-old child getting diagnosed today. As an older autistic adult, I want to help Kathryn on the journey that is unique to each generation. That's a specialty that I can offer to her, as we are in the same generation and diagnosed later in life.

I was diagnosed at age 66. I'm a licensed clinical social worker in the state of Maine and also received a masters of divinity and doctorate of ministry in feminist liberation theology. I view mental health through the lens of the social and political factors involved. I 'came of age' in these programmes, as I awakened to social and political oppression. When one is in an oppressed minority group, one must seek solidarity within the group. Because of the shame we baby boomers have about autism, we keep it hidden and live in secrecy. Sometimes we share a bit with a neurotypical. But we older autistics tend not to seek out each other's company.

Our tribe

The day I was diagnosed as autistic, I went online to find a support group for autistic adults, and started attending a group that weekend. I was terrified when I walked in the door of the community centre where we met, but was welcomed by friendly adults, with snacks and coffee. When I left the meeting a couple of hours later, I knew I had been transformed forever. I had found my people. My tribe. Never before had I knowingly spent time with other autistic adults. I've always felt that I don't know who I am, but I left that meeting knowing for the first time where I belong and who my people are. I was one of 'them'. That's my tribe and my heritage.

Finding 'my people' has been the most significant healing experience on my autistic journey. Yet I am rarely able to convince a client who is discovering their autism to attend a support group. It's not in our nature to go to groups. But the healing is so profound, I at least want Kathryn to know that. I'll give her material on support groups in our area and online. She may never attend, but I'll be sharing from time to time about my own experiences in groups with autistic adults. I might let her know that I'll be attending the group that day, so she will see a familiar face.

When I initially started as a social worker, I worked in addictions. I helped addicts understand that recovery involved being with other addicts and healing together. The 12-step and similar communities have developed tools for addicts to be in community with each other. So, too, must autistics support each other in community. I'm not sure we can claim full wholeness in isolation from the tribe.

Other articles in this book discuss the issue of disclosure. Many of us believe that disclosing our autism to clients can be beneficial to the client.

I'll probably encourage Kathryn to read *Neurotribes* (Silberman, 2016), which gives a great understanding of autism as 'tribal'. You can't understand who you are without spending time with your people. Autism is not just another diagnosis; it's a mindset; an approach to life. It's a minority neurotype that is misunderstood and ignored.

Often, when a client is diagnosed/recognises their diagnosis, I'll ask, 'What other autistic adults do you know?' Often they will say, 'Only you.'

Can you imagine the people of any other minority group not knowing each other? You have to meet 'your people'. You are part of a tribe.

Our political support

After I found a support group, I began looking for our political and social activists who helped us define our journey in the world. I discovered ASAN, the Autistic Self-Advocacy Network. I love their slogan: 'Nothing about us without us.' Where had I heard that before? I had first encountered it as the title of a book about disabled people by James Charlton (2000). In the book, he explains that people with disabilities are not the problem; rather, society is the problem when it does not accommodate us. ASAN believes that, instead of trying to change disabled people, we should work to make sure people with disabilities can access what we need.

Our masks

Most of us grew up learning to live behind masks. We never knew who we were – only who we were expected to be. I might encourage Kathryn to read a book like Devon Price's *Unmasking Autism* (2022). Then we can talk about it together and look at how masking impacts her life. Once she realises why she does it, she can make conscious decisions about when and how to mask.

Diagnosis

One of Kathryn's therapy goals might be to get a diagnosis. Adult autism diagnosis has become a politically charged issue, with long waiting lists for therapists who can legally diagnose conditions listed in *DSM-5*, the American Psychiatric Association's professional reference book on mental health and brain-related conditions (APA, 2013). I'll help her look at the political dimensions of this issue. As a licensed social worker in the US, I can give a diagnosis. However, I prefer that we take this journey together. Neuropsychologist Laura Slap-Shelton and I are starting a 'collaborative diagnosis' group for adults exploring an autism diagnosis. Together we will go through the diagnostic criteria and see if it explains the context of the client's life.

Increasingly, autistic adults are self-diagnosing. It is empowering, in that it is hard to find a practitioner who understands adult autism – and who is able to take on new clients. Within the support communities of autistic adults that I'm familiar with, it is totally accepted to self-diagnose; indeed, it is seen as a bold move to take one's own power for diagnosis.

Questions and answers

Kathryn called me back the next day, and we arranged for tele-therapy consult at the end of the week to go over her questions. She had a lot of them.

She started with: 'How do I know if I'm really autistic? Should I get a diagnosis? Where would I go?'

'This is such a complicated question,' I told her. 'Different countries have different standards about how to diagnose for autism, and who is authorised to do it. Diagnosing children is different from adults. I specialise in seeing older adults. Most of us have grown into older adults without knowing about our autism or how to explain it to others. For older adults, some of us use a "collaborative" model where you and a professional go through the criteria and look at what applies to you and together we reach a conclusion. That's primarily what I do.'

'Should I tell others about being autistic? How will people react to me?'

'Well,' I said, 'there are different perspectives. Sometimes newly diagnosed people like to tell others in their lives about the autism. Yet few understand the situation of late-diagnosed adults. Mostly we need to explain to others what it means for an older adult to get this diagnosis late in life, and help others understand our journey.'

'So what is therapy like for autistic adults? Can it make us normal?'

'That's a great question,' I noted. 'Many of us have come to see our autism as an important aspect of who we are. Many of us see ourselves as having our own autistic culture and communication. We don't want to give it up to try and look "normal". We want to understand who we are, and help others understand us. So the point in therapy is not to try to be "neurotypical", but rather to discover who you really are and learn how to express your real self.'

'Wow!' Kathryn exclaimed, 'that makes therapy sound like a great adventure.'

'Yes, it is,' I responded. 'It's a journey to discover a real self that most of us have hidden all of our lives. And it's a search to find "our people". I share information about support groups and books and programmes that help us discover who we really are. It's like taking off a mask and allowing the real inner self to emerge!'

Defining who we are and where we are going

We are living in an exciting period of history where autistic people are taking the power to define who we are and how we want to live our lives. It's a gratifying time to be an autistic therapist working with autistic adults. Together, we are defining who we have been, who we are now, and where we are going.

As autistic therapists, we have no guidebook. But we are all writing one every day in our work and sharing our experiences with each other.

I'll help Kathryn put together a treatment plan to reach her goals. Here is a sample treatment plan that I recommend for autistic baby-boomers:

Treatment goals

1. Gain confidence in your own perceptions about the neurology of your brain. Whether or not you get a formal diagnosis, you have an inner wisdom that is elderly and wise. If it's important to you to get a diagnosis, then go for it. If it's not a strong inner push, let it go.
2. Find your tribe and spend time with them. Notice how different you feel from when you are with neurotypicals. This is who you are. You're home. Who else do you know in your life who is autistic? Spend time with them. Find more.
3. Consider political action with a group such as ASAN (https://autisticadvocacy.org).
4. Speak the secrets. 'Should we tell Grandpa?' How dare you NOT tell him, when you can potentially greatly enhance the quality of the rest of his life?
5. Consider 'coming out' – for our comrades.

6. Notice the mask. Choose when to take it off and for how long. You own it; it doesn't own you.
7. Feel the regrets from all the years of not knowing. Now feel the joy of knowing.

References

American Psychiatric Association. (2013). *Diagnostic and statistical manual of mental disorders* (5th ed.) (DSM-5). APA.

Charlton, J. (2000). *Nothing about us without us: Disability, oppression, and empowerment.* University of California Press.

Price, D. (2022). *Unmasking autism: Discovering the new faces of neurodiversity.* Harmony.

Silberman, S. (2016). *Neurotribes: The legacy of autism and the future of diversity.* Penguin Random House.

Wake, W., Endlich, E. & Lagos, R.S. (2021). *Older autistic adults in their own words: The lost generation.* Future Horizons.

Chapter 20

Working with my neurokin

Kathy Carter

I am 50 at the time of writing. A milestone indeed. It was 44 years before I was diagnosed as autistic, and 45 years before I started training as a therapist. Hence, I have been an autistic-identifying therapist from the start. It is a role that I embrace, and it is a real fit for me. My journey to this point, both personal and professional, now makes great sense in light of my relatively recent autism diagnosis, but it hasn't all been plain sailing.

My childhood was punctuated with difficulty fitting into the world: a general sense of difference, without the language or understanding to describe it. Realising that I am autistic, followed by diagnosis, has given me that language and understanding, both of myself and of my clients. Despite an overarching and sometimes confusing sense of difference that has been ever-present, being autistic has had a positive effect on my professional life.

There are, of course, negatives as well as positives to my autisticness. By the time I was diagnosed, I was well into my professional, social and relational life. Forty-four years is a long period to have an unsettled sense of self. In my diagnosis year, on paper, my career looked good, and I had been happily married for more than 20 years. I was also a mother and experiencing all of the highs and lows that come with that remarkable journey.

But throughout my life there had always been a strong and unsettling sense of being an imposter. I rarely felt a true sense of inclusion, except in my own home. Where did that anxiety come from? Why did I just burst into tears? Why am I so tired to my core? Why are certain things, such as remembering a set of procedures, so hard for me, when other people somehow just get it? I often felt – and this is a common metaphor, which recurs throughout this book – like an alien, slightly bemused by the unpredictable land that it inhabits, repeatedly trying to 'get it right', yet feeling out of place.

I left the employed workforce 15 years ago; it was probably one of the best things I ever did. Being employed in a non-autistic environment is difficult for many autistic people; we tend to excel in fields where we can be creative, autonomous and flexible.

Talking therapy, as a counsellor and hypnotherapist, fits me well, professionally and personally; like most autistic people, however, I have to be mindful of my available energy units in a given time period – my 'spoons', as Christine Miserandino puts it (Miserandino, 2010). I currently see around 13 clients a week, which includes some young people at their school, and have no plans to increase this number significantly. The state of my own nervous system and my general wellness potentially affect my therapy work, and it is important to me to be able to hold my clients from a place of good health and energy. Today, I am much clearer about my needs for personal autonomy and self-care, and therefore also what my neurodivergent clients may be experiencing or may be needing.

And this is the clue to the way I work, as a talking therapist, with my autistic clients, and why talking therapy is a good professional fit for me. My very autisticness is my strength, especially in working with other autistic people. It has, for example, been posited that autistic people engage well in talking therapy roles because we know the rules, and I concur. There are time boundaries, a pattern of 'one at a time' conversation that both parties understand, a sense of congruence with each other, and a non-judgemental space. These are aspects of life that make our interactions as autistic people much easier. Unfortunately, life outside the therapy room is less structured and the rules less clear; and of course, they are less congruent and less non-judgemental.

It is important, when discussing being an autistic therapist, to counter the old cliché that autistic people lack empathy. Damian Milton has done this elegantly by expressing the frequent misunderstandings between autistic and non-autistic people as a double, two-way problem: the 'double empathy problem' (Milton, 2012). Both sides experience the problem: it is not a problem located in the autistic person, as the stereotype suggests; it is simply a difference in experiencing and processing. It is true that it can be difficult for autistic people to express how they are feeling, if they are required to do so in the moment and, above all, in terms that come naturally to non-autistic people, but not to autistic people. I will discuss this in the context of therapy below. Emotions – including empathy – are by no means absent in autistic people, but they are likely to be both experienced and expressed in a different way.

So how do I, as an autistic therapist, work with my autistic clients? As a neurodiversity-affirming talking therapist, I have many different influences in my work, including humanistic models, some behavioural theories, hypnotherapy and mindfulness. I have found that some cognitive behavioural techniques can be beneficial with clients who experience compulsions, phobias and issues around addictions, but it is essential that the interventions are neurodivergence-affirming in the context of the autistic community.

For example, some behavioural therapies encourage the removal of anxiety-driven 'safety-seeking behaviours', which a client might be using to avoid or escape from a perceived threat, especially if they are consistently intolerant of uncertainty (Clark & Beck, 2011). However, for autistic people, avoidance or escape from a situation that runs counter to our needs is often a healthy boundary, and a preference for certainty, and a matching intolerance of uncertainty, is intrinsic to many autistic people (Jenkinson et al., 2020). It is not therapeutic to use behavioural techniques to challenge an autistic client's intrinsic needs. It is essential to consider the effect of external factors on our thoughts, emotions and behaviour. As Luke Beardon puts it (2021), 'Autism + environment = outcome' (p.4).

Probably the commonest thread among all of the different client groups that I work with, which includes individuals affected by addiction, young people of school age and neurodivergent people, is a tendency towards dysregulation of the nervous system. It is therefore a priority for both therapist and client to understand the patterns of the client's autonomic nervous system states.

A propensity to dysregulation of the nervous system is one of the characteristics of the autistic experience. In the same way that people who have experienced trauma are easily triggered into (and get stuck in) different states, such as fight, flight, shutdown or freeze (Porges, 2009), I find that neurodivergent, and especially autistic, people tend to have a propensity to heightened arousal of the nervous system. I see so many overlaps and links with trauma among the neurodivergent population.

I would say that most, if not all, the autistic people I meet have experienced trauma in some way. Even those who had attuned and caring parents have grown up and lived in a non-autistic environment ('autism + environment = outcome') and will have experienced unmet basic needs – for example, around sensory regulation and the double empathy problem. There are also multiple intersections with other challenges, many of which are discussed elsewhere in this book – physical health issues, additional neurodivergent conditions, gender identity and the effects of marginalisation – that can cause responses akin to trauma reactions.

Therefore, a lot of the work I do with clients can be around regulating the nervous system and recognising triggers for overwhelm or dysregulation: for example, heightened anxiety responses and a disconnection from the body.

Many autistic people experience alexithymia: we may struggle to identify and describe our emotions, and sometimes the emotions of others, too. It may be true that autistic individuals are at higher risk of developing insecure attachment patterns (McKenzie & Dallos, 2017), but being autistic can also affect other people's perception of our attachment style: we experience and express things differently. Perhaps an example of the double empathy problem in action!

Alexithymic clients do seem to find it harder to interpret the early signs of overwhelm in their own bodies, and may also have imaginal differences, such as aphantasia (the inability to picture things in your mind), which is a factor if a therapist is using imagination-based interventions like hypnotherapy.

In addition, the alexithymic difficulty in recognising emotional responses results in difficulty in modulating them. A system in overwhelm is like a weapon that needs discharging, or a water tank that needs draining. If the client has difficulty recognising the triggers for what they are feeling, or finds the feelings too unmanageable, the energy can overflow. This is when people may experience meltdowns, compulsions or unhelpful coping mechanisms, and some alexithymic clients find themselves perpetually stuck in heightened or elevated states. If, as van der Kolk puts it, 'the body keeps the score' (2014), it is hardly surprising that a perpetual stuckness in heightened states may lead to physical health problems.

In clients who struggle to describe their emotions, I find it can be useful to work on the release of physical tension. Progressive muscle relaxation, a simple exercise performed with the eyes shut, is one example. Also, a client can develop a connection to current somatic sensations, such as heaviness in the chest.

Connecting to our holistic systems – body, mind, neurotype and nervous system – is key. It does not matter to me as a therapist if our notion of 'the correct language' for what we are feeling does not meet neurotypical expectations. With young people especially, my client and I may use made-up names that reflect the movement or effect of the sensation they have. Even if we have previously struggled to describe an emotion, if we can relate to a feeling or sensation as an imagined word, an animal or a metaphor, this can help the client differentiate between their emotions and learn regulatory skills.

If our family of origin and challenges surrounding our neurotype did not give us a secure base for attunement, connecting to our holistic systems – body, mind, neurotype and nervous system – in adulthood can help give a feeling of autonomy, and even empowerment.

Rather than seeing a list of disorders (for example, personality disorder, attachment disorder, autism spectrum disorder, eating disorder, substance use disorder and so on), I prefer to look at neurodivergence – as well as addictions, compulsions, phobias and other mental health conditions – through a less judgemental lens. I try to see the person fully as who they are.

It is my autisticness that helps drive my style of being relational with clients, as it means I am not judging a client based on what medical diagnosis or type of physical or mental dysregulation they have been assigned. Instead, I am focusing on how they are showing up today, in the room or on my screen, with the knowledge that their way of interacting with the world is changeable and affected by neurotype, environment, stress, self-care, medication, nervous system state, trauma and many other factors. I know very well that some days my own neurotype gives me more challenges than others! This autistic congruence and lack of judgement feels intrinsic to many of us.

I do, however, notice certain patterns, and spotting these patterns – or even personality types – can be very useful in therapy.

Some people – I'm talking about the general population here – have the skills to self-regulate their emotions and their autonomic nervous system; they can feel safe and connected, rather than be triggered into a fear state, without the need for extensive co-regulation from others. They are seemingly more likely to enjoy secure relational attachments and are less affected by trauma or marginalisation.

In other people, I can often see a spectrum of responses and personality traits. Some seem more independently and internally focused. A challenge for those who function in this way could be unhelpful coping mechanisms that are more rigid, restrictive or punitive, and anxiety that is not always outwardly expressed. Perhaps because of their internal focus, I find that they can be innovative when it comes to visualising and using their imagination therapeutically – for example, with hypnosis.

I have found that many autistic people, especially those who do not have an additional diagnosis such as ADHD, tend to interact with the world in this way. Many people in the general population share similar traits, and this is because they are human traits! But for those who are born autistic, it is not a question of personality traits; it's a matter of a different neurotype. The autistic experience of 'traits' can be more intense and experienced and expressed differently from that of neurotypical people.

Some people may seem more emotionally unregulated, may struggle to set and maintain boundaries, and may have unhealthy coping mechanisms that are less rigid and more about gratification. They may seek more awareness of their triggers for overwhelm or flight responses, and tools that connect them to the present moment and their body's responses. This may be more characteristic of people with a diagnosis of ADHD.

There are people who have more than one neurodivergence: for example, autism and ADHD (sometimes referred to as AuDHD). They may have a mix of the above patterns. For example, the AuDHD people I meet may excel at hyperfocus, which can be very productive. However, they often describe needing support with mindfulness, as if focusing on the now and their current need is unproductive.

As I have said, spotting and considering these patterns can be very helpful in developing ways to support clients with similar processing and experiencing patterns.

I am always interested in how we, as autistics, see ourselves. Many neurodivergent people grow up with strong introjects (the unconscious adoption of the attitudes of others) as their own inner voice. They may grow up believing that they are too much, or not enough, or experience negative self-judgement. Psychotherapist Anna Robinson describes how, for autistic clients, a fragile sense of self may develop as a consequence of what they perceive to be 'failed interpersonal encounters' (Robinson, 2018). Neurodivergent people may mask or camouflage their way through life (National Autistic Society, 2022), especially if they are assigned female at birth (Wood-Downie et al., 2020), and somewhere along the way, can lose touch with their authentic selves.

With all clients, I encourage connection with both nervous system state and feelings. I also prize the link between thoughts, emotions, sensations and behaviours. I take a very embodied, holistic view of therapy, and (bearing in mind any trigger risks) encourage clients to 'Say hello to the restriction, converse with the heaviness, and ask questions of the butterflies'.

Certainly, connecting to my authentic self, and my own feelings – for example, the unsettling sense of being an outsider, the shameful heaviness of 'not enoughness' it brought, the confused withdrawal from interactions and the critical imposter thoughts – have led me to a place of acceptance in my mid-life and beyond. It is precisely my own experience of connecting that has given me a more secure base.

Some people, including therapists, consider labels to be negative, believing that a label is a stereotype or 'others' the individual – that is, it treats them as intrinsically different from oneself in a negative sense. However, I see an autism diagnosis or self-identification as liberating. We become part of a kinship with other people; we learn to understand and prize ourselves, and by understanding and prizing ourselves, we can help others to do likewise.

References

Beardon, L. (2021). *Avoiding anxiety in autistic children: A guide for autistic wellbeing*. John Murray Press.

Clark, D.A., & Beck, A. T. (2011). *Cognitive therapy of anxiety disorders: Science and practice*. Guilford Press.

Jenkinson, R., Milne, E. & Thompson, A. (2020). The relationship between intolerance of uncertainty and anxiety in autism: A systematic literature review and meta-analysis. *Autism, 24*(8), 1933–1944.

McKenzie, R. & Dallos, R. (2017). Autism and attachment difficulties: Overlap of symptoms, implications and innovative solutions. *Clinical Child Psychology and Psychiatry, 22*(4), 632–648. doi:10.1177/1359104517707323.

Milton, D.E.M. (2012). On the ontological status of autism: The 'double empathy problem'. *Disability & Society, 27*(6), 883–887. doi:10.1080

Miserandino, C. (2010). *The spoon theory*. Butyoudon'tlooksick.com. https://butyoudontlooksick.com/articles/written-by-christine/the-spoon-theory/

National Autistic Society. (2022). *Autistic people and masking*. www.autism.org.uk/advice-and-guidance/professional-practice/autistic-masking

Porges, S.W. (2009). The polyvagal theory: New insights into adaptive reactions of the autonomic nervous system. *Cleveland Clinic Journal of Medicine, 76*(Suppl.2), S86–S90. doi:10.3949/ccjm.76.s2.17

Robinson, A. (2018). Emotion-focused therapy for autism spectrum disorder: A case conceptualization model for trauma-related experiences. *Journal of Contemporary Psychotherapy, 48*(3), 133–143. doi:10.1007/s10879-018-9383-1

Van der Kolk, B. (2014). *The body keeps the score: Brain, mind, and body in the healing of trauma*. Penguin Books.

Wood-Downie, H., Wong, B., Kovshoff, H., Mandy, W., Hull, L. & Hawin, L.A. (2020). Sex/gender differences in camouflaging in children and adolescents with autism. *Journal of Autism and Developmental Disorders, 51*(4), 1353-1364. doi:10.1007/s10803-020-04615-z

Chapter 21

The autistic therapist and chronic illness

Rebecca Antrim

Autistic people, particularly women, are more likely to experience chronic physical health conditions than the general population, although it is not yet clear why. A study by researchers at the University of Cambridge shows that autistic people are, on average, 1.5 to 4.3 times as likely as the general population to have a wide variety of health conditions (Weir et al., 2021).

Some of the physical/neurological conditions that frequently affect autistic people are dyspraxia, disordered sleeping, epilepsy and problems with joints and other parts of the body: for example, flexible or painful joints, 'stretchy' skin that bruises easily, and persistent diarrhoea or constipation (NHS Choices, 2020). There is also a heightened risk of low blood pressure and heart, lung and diabetic conditions in autistic adults (Weir et al., 2021).

There are other disorders that are closely related to autism, such as Fragile X syndrome and Prader-Willi syndrome (Baker et al., 2018), but this chapter will focus on my own experience with myalgic encephalomyelitis (ME)/chronic fatigue syndrome (CFS). ME is perhaps better known as CFS; however, I feel that since CFS focuses on just one symptom of many, it does not truly reflect the illness, which is why I choose to use ME/CFS.

Central sensitivity syndromes (CSS) are a group of disorders such as ME/CFS, fibromyalgia, irritable bowel syndrome, pelvic pain syndromes (including vulvodynia), chronic headache, restless leg syndrome, idiopathic low back pain, and temporomandibular disorders. These disorders share some common symptoms, the most notable being pain.

Heightened sensory sensitivity is a common feature of central sensitivity syndromes, perhaps because there is a common underlying sensitisation of the nervous system within the syndromes. A 2022 study concluded that:

> central sensitivity syndromes diagnoses and symptoms appear to be very common in the autistic population. Increased awareness of an association between autism and central sensitisation should inform clinicians and guide diagnostic practice, particularly for women where CSS are common and autism underrecognised. (Grant et al., 2022)

My school and work history pre-diagnoses

I knew nothing about any of this until my 30s: it took a coincidence, a trauma, and the onset of chronic illness for me to understand myself.

Both my school life and my early work life disguised my autism effectively, as they suited my way of being so well. It is therefore not surprising that nobody – including me – picked up on my neurodivergence until a combination of circumstances brought it to the fore.

It was only later in life, following trauma, workplace bullying and the breakdown of my physical health, that I recognised that I was autistic. Looking at the first part of my working life now, I can hardly believe how much energy I had.

I attended a rather progressive school and then worked for 10 years for Heritage Services in various local authority-owned museum and gallery spaces across the county, spending my days in dark, quiet buildings, often the only person on site, surrounded by things that I loved and was deeply fascinated by. Pure bliss.

It was while working for Heritage Services that I connected with vulnerable people in the community. At weekends, people with various challenges and little support would gravitate toward the museum, killing time until their support workers and the services that they were engaged with would re-open on Monday. It was somewhere that they could exist without being expected to pay or hurry. I loved getting to know and understand these regulars, and it was that experience that led me to begin training as a counsellor.

I completed my foundation degree in person-centred counselling in 2012. When the time came to choose a placement, I did not feel ready to specialise and so, rather than choosing one of the very specific placements on offer, I founded my own.

Having noticed how poor local transport was a barrier to people accessing therapy (my home city is divided by the river into 'North Side' and 'South Side', with the South Side being very much the poor relation), I wanted to do something about this. Due to poor transport and through no fault of their own, people would be late to sessions and inevitably were told that they could no longer continue to have counselling if they couldn't be on time. This put many people off seeking help and support, since they felt that there was little that they could do.

I saw a very clear gap that needed to be addressed and set about finding out how I could bring a service to the South Side. I was the first student at my university to set up their own counselling service as their placement, and in its first year the service was nominated for a British Association of Counselling and Psychotherapy (BACP) award for improving access to therapy. We were told that we had scored highly against other well-established organisations, which was incredibly exciting. The service went on to run for 10 years, in partnership with the University of Worcester and later the University of South Wales.

I later became the manager of the community centre where the service was launched, so was able to continue to work closely with it as placement manager. Being trusted and having the freedom to do things in my own way was hugely beneficial to my work and has helped me to consistently deliver, especially in terms of working in a way that can be tailored to each client, rather than having to fit everything into boxes.

My discovery of autism

Later, I was working in a position where part of my role was to visit various local charities, services and organisations and deliver a presentation on the work we did and how we could benefit their clients. It was while I was doing my research for the local branch of the National Autistic Society that it all suddenly clicked into place, and I realised I was reading about myself.

I had not known much at all about autism before then, so it was hugely eye-opening to see all these pieces of me laid out on the page. It was scary. It was also exciting: it made sense at last. There was so much that I had just accepted without question. I had felt it was explained by my interest in and embodiment of the alternative subculture. The bottom line is that, since it was all I had ever known, I had no alternative frame of reference. I thought that everyone experienced what I did, and they were all just better at coping with it than I was.

I felt euphoric at my discovery as I had just been through a significant trauma that had blown to smithereens any protective casing I might have built around myself, and I was now struggling significantly with things that had not been as challenging before. My sensory sensitivities were amplified; I was struggling to focus and prioritise; I felt continually on the verge of what I now know were meltdowns, as I was so wired from the stress and therefore constantly overstimulated. It was exhausting. I now know that I was experiencing not just autistic burnout but the first symptoms of ME/CFS.

In August 2019, at the age of 37, my autism diagnosis was confirmed. Just weeks later, I received a diagnosis of ME/CFS. For around three years, I had had symptoms that I had put down to 'stress'. Between the previously mentioned traumatic incident and the workplace bullying that took place in the aftermath, my body had been stuck in 'fight or flight' mode for three years or so, and this had led to everything imploding. Which came first – the burnout, the trauma, the bullying, the ME/CFS? I find it hard to say whether the stress of that job brought on autistic burnout that triggered the ME/CFS and was cemented by the trauma, or whether what I thought was burnout was in fact ME/CFS, and that and the trauma heightened my autistic traits/symptoms.

My experience of managing the diagnoses

Before having ME/CFS, I had the energy to effectively manage and mask or camouflage my autism (and ADHD, diagnosed in 2022 at age 40). I had no idea, of course, that that is what I was doing, since I did not know that I was autistic or had ADHD.

I had often been told how calming my presence was, which always made me chuckle, as that's not how I felt inside. Inside, it was more like the cartoon 'On Fire' by K.C. Green, in which a dog sits at his table, staring ahead with a rictus grin and drinking his coffee while the room around him is on fire. The caption reads: 'This is fine.' And I had thought I didn't mask!

As soon as ME/CFS entered the equation, that energy simply was not there, and I believe that this was the reason that my neurodivergence seemed to 'burst forth' around the same time. I simply no longer had the energy to put into acting my way through each day on top of everything else I had to do.

Receiving both diagnoses was a confusing and often alarming time, although not as alarming as before I had the diagnoses: the unknown was much more troubling, so I ultimately found comfort in the explanation that my diagnoses provided. I experienced the common feelings of imposter syndrome: grief, denial, anger, bargaining, depression, and eventually a partial, reluctant acceptance.

Clinically speaking, there is an overlap of symptoms between ME/CFS and autism, including (but not limited to) fatigue, brain fog/cognitive impairments, sensory sensitivity (particularly to light and sound), and increased levels of pain. Additionally, the symptoms of ME/CFS (extreme tiredness/exhaustion, disordered sleeping, muscle and/or joint pain, headaches, sore throat, nausea, dizziness, palpitations and 'flu-like symptoms) can deplete us to the point where we struggle even more with challenging aspects of autism, such as sensory overload. I am also fighting a constant battle between the need to rest and pace to manage the ME/CFS and the impulsivity and restlessness that my ADHD brings.

In 2022, I also received a diagnosis of postural tachycardia syndrome (PoTS: an abnormal increase in heart rate that can occur after sitting or standing, which is most common in girls and women aged 15 to 50). The significant symptomatic overlap between the various conditions led me to conclude that my time and energy might be better spent responding to and managing the symptom first, instead of trying to figure out which condition might have triggered it. It made sense to me to focus on managing how I feel instead of using up precious energy trying to solve the unsolvable.

A key feature of ME/CFS is post-exertional malaise (PEM), which is a worsening of symptoms following mental or physical activity. This can be something as minor as taking a shower or watching television. Typically, PEM occurs 12 to 48 hours after the activity or event responsible and can last for days or even weeks. The difficulty is that, before having worked out what one's baseline is, it can be exceedingly difficult to know when to stop, particularly when in hyperfocus, since the effects do not rear their heads until afterwards, by which time it might already be too late.

Even when, after months of observation and reflection, which is exhausting in itself, one has a general idea of one's baseline, it is still possible to get it wrong, since ME/CFS is a fluctuating condition.

Autism and chronic illness

When we consider that PEM is not just caused by physical activity, but also by mental exertion, the effects that autism can have on ME/CFS are clear to see. For example, masking and sensory overload take up a significant amount of mental energy that causes autistic fatigue and can lead to burnout. This depletion can lead to increased sensory sensitivity and brain fog, which can lead to meltdowns and shutdowns, which again use up significant reserves of energy, and all the above can result in yet another increase of PEM. It is truly a balancing act, which can be extremely unpredictable and uncertain. That uncertainty can be a significant cause of worry and stress, which also impacts energy levels, continuing the cycle of push-pull and crash.

Since I live in a rural area with limited access to health care, I had no choice but to do my own research, my own experiments and self-advocacy, and I feel deeply for those not in a position to do so for themselves.

The effect on my practice

My experience gives me a unique perspective as a physically disabled AuDHD therapist in that I know what it's like to feel like an 'offshoot of an offshoot' and to experience the mixed emotions of dealing with both a mental *and* physical diagnosis and the impacts that this can have.

I have come away with some strategies to help me to create more balance in my life and health: resting and pacing being key elements. I feel privileged to be able to pass these strategies on to the people I work with. This balance has been difficult to achieve with ADHD as part of the equation, since both mental and physical hyperactivity impact on the ability to rest and pace when needed. However, it has been one of my most invaluable discoveries and has truly taught me the value of slowing down, even when it is an enforced slowing down that I have often resented.

For example, I had always worked with a broad range of people of all ages and gender identities and from a wide variety of backgrounds, and I thoroughly enjoyed it. The diversity of the work was exciting and challenging in a way that I found very stimulating and motivating. I particularly enjoyed the high-intensity crisis work, which is not uncommon in people with ADHD. Since becoming physically ill, it has naturally no longer been sustainable for me to continue to work in this way.

However, it slowly became clear to me that, despite my deep reluctance to exclude anyone, it made sense for me to narrow down my client base and availability. Focusing more on drawing from my own lived experience and areas that came more intuitively to me is a way for me to conserve energy so that I can continue to work with people, which is extremely important to me. In fact, I believe that one of the best things you can do as a helper of any sort is to recognise your own limits.

In slowing down, I began to notice changes to the way that I was working. It became more about acceptance and choosing a different, more meaningful perspective. I became increasingly drawn to thinking more about changing the way we relate to our thoughts and feelings, rather than using up precious energy resisting or fighting them, trying to control the uncontrollable.

I had also been thinking more about how to live a more meaningful life since my priorities had so drastically changed, by necessity rather than choice. This led me to reflect on my values as a means to take back some control and feel more empowered. Alongside the work I was doing on myself, I noticed that many of my clients' difficulties also stemmed from a remoteness from their own values, so I began introducing more work on values into my client sessions, where appropriate. I was interested to see how quickly many of my clients responded to this approach, which reinforced my belief that, for many people, particularly those with limited reserves, this might be a more efficient way of working.

Since I was seeing such remarkable results, both in myself and my clients, I decided to investigate further to see how I might enhance my new way of working. That is when I discovered acceptance and commitment therapy (ACT). ACT (pronounced as the word 'act', rather than A-C-T, since in ACT, we act!) is a type of mindful psychotherapy (a 'third wave' cognitive behavioural intervention (Cullen, 2008)) aimed at enhancing our psychological flexibility. It helps us to stay focused on the present moment and accept thoughts and feelings without judgement. As we acknowledge and accept those thoughts and feelings, the hold they have over us lessens. We are free to continue to move forward in life alongside those thoughts and feelings, rather than being in a constant battle with them. Continually resisting or avoiding unpleasant thoughts and feelings usually creates additional pain and suffering and keeps us stuck firmly where we are, preventing us from moving forward and living and engaging with our lives fully in a meaningful way.

As well as being drawn to the aspect of using mindfulness to savour and make the most of the positive moments, the sense of fun in ACT appeals to me, as there is a certain playfulness to many of the techniques and exercises, and fun is something that has been in short supply for many of us after the Covid-19 pandemic. Additionally, the acceptance element is something that I find particularly neurodivergent-affirming, since it is about being and embracing who we are and doing what is right for ourselves, based on our own needs and desires, not those placed on us by the expectations of others.

Whether my clients are experiencing autistic burnout, chronic illness or both, those in themselves are a huge challenge on top of whatever else they are already dealing with, and can create a barrier to effective therapy. We cannot expect to be healthy by eating just one apple a day or working out once a week, so how can therapy work for us and help us to be mentally healthy, if we do not have the energy or reserves to put in the work consistently?

Autism and chronic illness have many overlapping symptoms that make day-to-day life increasingly difficult. Since chronic illnesses are often fluctuating conditions, even the best laid plans can sometimes come to nothing, which can be frustrating and demoralising.

Managing the health condition(s) alone can use up significant swathes of energy in terms of attending medical appointments and check-ups. There may also be the added fear that a symptom flare could alter our baseline permanently, and that puts even more pressure on us, both physically and psychologically.

Introducing complex and intensive therapy when we already feel we are at our lowest ebb is not helpful. Many ACT techniques are very straightforward and simple to apply, which is ideal for people with limited energy or mental 'bandwidth'. It is also highly adaptable, in that it is flexible enough to be used in a way that meets clients where they are on any given day, whatever their energy levels, making it particularly accessible.

In terms of my personal experience, ACT has been a highly effective form of therapy, and alongside the simplicity of it, the playfulness and joy incorporated by the values work makes it irresistible to me. Having got such phenomenal results from it myself, I am eager to share it with others in my position who may also benefit from this modality.

I experienced debilitating anger and grief over the loss of life as I knew it, and the future that I had been working toward. Through using ACT, I have been able to acknowledge and accept those feelings, which has helped me to find new meaning and move forward, creating a new life. It might look and feel very different to my original plan, but it is significantly more meaningful and more fulfilling than I could have dreamt of.

I will never forget how debilitating, dark and depressing those early days were, yet I can now look back on them with gratitude, because they sent me in a new direction of self-discovery and personal growth. This has enhanced my practice in that it has made me a more compassionate therapist with invaluable lived experience that I can use to help others with very specific needs. This is one of the silver linings I had been looking for.

It has driven me to focus on working with my autistic clients, so many of whom share my experience of chronic illness, to help and support them in self-actualising, being who they want to be and living the life that they want to live with their needs in mind and on their own terms.

References

Baker, E.K., Godler, D.E., Bui, M., Hickerton, C., Rogers, C., Field, M., Amor, D.J. & Bretherton, L. (2018). Exploring autism symptoms in an Australian cohort of patients with Prader-Willi and Angelman syndromes. *Journal of Neurodevelopmental Disorders, 10*, 24. https://doi.org/10.1186/s11689-018-9242-0

Cullen, C. (2008). Acceptance and commitment therapy (ACT): A third wave behaviour therapy. *Behavioural and Cognitive Psychotherapy, 36*(6), 667–673. doi:10.1017/S1352465808004797

Grant, S., Norton, S., Weiland, R.F., Scheeren, A.M., Begeer, S. & Hoekstra, R.A. (2022). Autism and chronic ill health: An observational study of symptoms and diagnoses of central sensitivity syndromes in autistic adults. *Molecular Autism, 13*(1), 7. doi:10.1186/s13229-022-00486-6

NHS Choices. (2020). *Other conditions that affect autistic people*. NHS Choices. www.nhs.uk/conditions/autism/other-conditions

Weir, E. Allison, C., Warrier, V. & Baron-Cohen, S. (2021). Increased prevalence of non-communicable physical health conditions among autistic adults. *Autism, 5*(3), 681–694.

SECTION D

Training, trainers and trainees

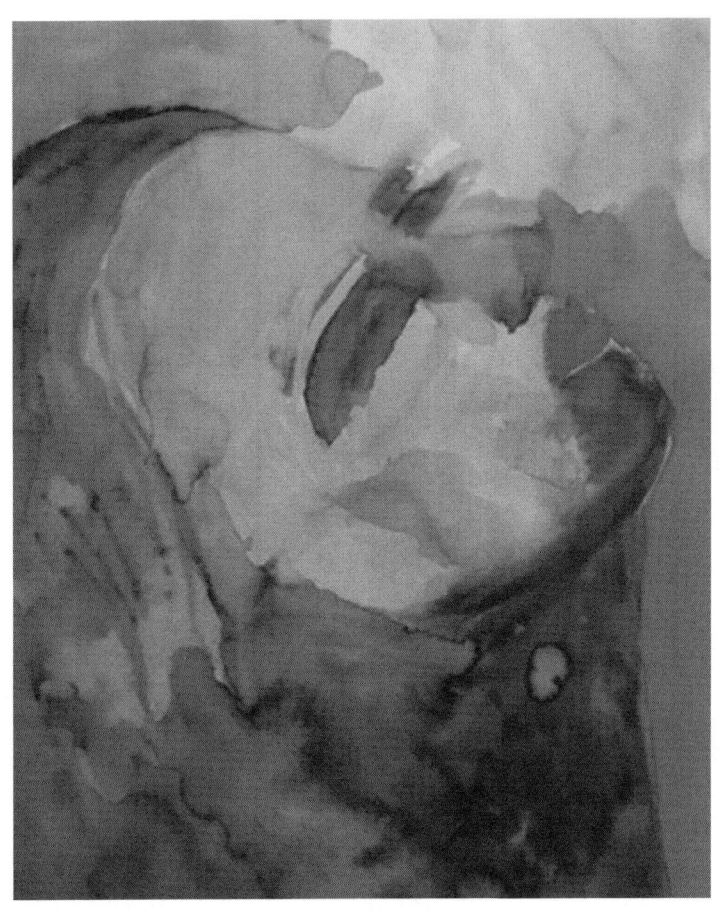

'Awakened' (watercolour on paper – greyscale repro from colour)
© Elinor Rowlands

Introduction

We hope that the preceding chapters will have given readers an insight into our autistic experience and how we work as therapists and supervisors. We hope also that they will have provided ideas and insights into the most effective ways of working with autistic clients and supervisees. We finish with two chapters specifically on the subject of training.

First, an interview with Vauna Beauvais and Eoin Stephens, founders of Vanguard Neurodiversity Training. The organisation exists to teach therapists about autism from an autistic point of view, so they can rightfully state that they are autism-informed, and their clients can be confident they will not be approached and judged from a neurotypical point of view, and that they will not have to educate their therapists. In this chapter, Vauna and Eoin talk about their own experiences of being diagnosed as autistic when they were already experienced therapists; the current absence of anything about autism in current training; its failure to challenge stereotypes, and why and how they decided to set up their training organisation to redress that balance. Yet, despite this dismal picture, Eoin finishes on an optimistic note:

> Understanding of autism and autistic people's ways of thinking, being and doing, is moving at a very fast pace now. This can improve the quality of therapeutic services for autistic people. We're living in such an exciting time.

So much for the trainers; what was our experience of being trainees, whether or not we were aware of being autistic? What was good about our training, what could have been better, and what suggestions would we make? We finish the book with a collective chapter; again, each contributor was given a free hand to say whatever they felt was important about their own experience as trainees.

Max Marnau

Chapter 22

The autistic trainer's perspective: Educating therapists

An interview with Vauna Beauvais and Eoin Stephens

Interviewer: Vauna and Eoin, you are both very experienced psychotherapists, supervisors and trainers, and you are both autistic. What I find intriguing is that not only did you both discover after the age of 40 that you were autistic, but also that you were already qualified, accredited and experienced therapists when you made the self-discovery.

Vauna: That's right – it's quite amazing, isn't it? I was already qualified as a therapist, already had a master's degree in understanding people and relationships, and here I was not knowing that I'm autistic. Eight years post-qualification, with many years of private practice under my belt, along with four years working in a GP surgery, running groups in the NHS, and all kinds of things.

I was seeing a client who was talking a lot about it. A mature client was telling me about their autistic partner, who was a professional person in their 40s. And, because I had not had any formal training on autism and wanted to understand my client's life better, I thought, 'Oh, I should know about this, really.' I thought, 'I'm going to read intensely about this, so that I can really be fair to my client.' So, I started to do that. And, as I read about autism and learned more about the reality of being a real autistic person through the client work, the penny gradually dropped. And I said, 'This is you, Vauna. This is you.'

Interviewer: Wow! Through your work you saw yourself?

Vauna: Yes. Yes, I did.

Interviewer: And you, Eoin...?

Eoin: Well, I'm interested in anxiety disorders in general, and I discovered a subset of my socially anxious clients who were different. Who, it turns out, were autistic. Like Vauna, it wasn't just meeting clients but meeting clients and then going and doing lots of reading. But yes, that was the route for both of us.

It was, 'That's interesting – professionally'; then, 'Ahh, it's kind of interesting *for* me,' and finally, 'Oh, it's relevant *to* me.'

And then that's what started to click. By the way, it's an interesting time to be talking about all of this, because it's 10 years since I discovered I'm autistic. On that day 10 years ago, I woke up in the morning thinking I'm probably autistic and I finished the day thinking, 'Now that's it. Look, yeah, this is it, you're autistic. Now we know.'

Interviewer: You are a mature adult. And so, 10 years ago, you would have already lived a long time as an adult, yet you did not know?

Eoin: I definitely felt there was something missing, you know? When I was leading up to it, I was thinking, 'I'm a bit autistic-ey', even before I had that day where I realised, 'Actually, I'm just autistic.'

But I did have a sense before that – as somebody who was in lots of therapy throughout their life – that there was some bit of my self-understanding that I still hadn't got. And I got that 10 years ago and it's been solid since. As in, it was the missing bit, you know?

Number one, it has clarified a million things that hadn't been clarified before in therapy. And number two: I don't really feel I'm missing anything in particular now. It's not like there's something else that has to come along. I mean, that's why it's such an exciting issue to be working with it as well. Because that's the other thing we are talking about here: you have a very exciting issue, a very exciting discovery, personally. Very rewarding. Very vital.

Vauna: I really can relate to that thing about the 'finding'. You know when you've reached the end of your searching. As a child, I knew from very early on that almost everyone else was very different to me. And later, as a trainee therapist. My core training to become a psychotherapist was seven and a half years. And during that time, I read every word in the *DSM-IV* (APA, 1994). Every single thing. And I would look at things and think, 'Oh, this, this is explaining me!' and I would read it and read it, and think: 'It's not quite that, but it is sort of saying something about me. I must be that.' And then, a few months later, we'd have a different workshop on a different topic. 'Aah, this is it, this is it. This is it. This is it?' And I did about six or seven of those. But nobody at all, ever, in the whole time, spoke about autism on our training programme. The covert message was, 'You don't need to know about autism because as a psychotherapist you will not work with autistic clients.'

Interviewer: I see. So, psychotherapists and counsellors have not been professionally trained to understand autistic people?

Eoin: As things stand, no. I mean, not if their training has occurred more than a few years ago, anyway. Things may be changing now in terms of training, but there are thousands and thousands of therapists who have not had useful information about autism, and nor have they been trained and supported in working with autistic people.

Interviewer: And would you say that there are a lot of myths about autistic people?

Eoin: Yes there are. I think three of the big ones are: 'Autistic people are unsociable; they're not interested in people'. Then 'Autistic people are unemotional – they don't really feel – they don't have much feeling or are a bit robotic.' And then, 'Autistic people are un-empathic. They don't have any empathy for other people.'

We do love people, but our way of having friendships can be quite different. We express emotion differently. As you can see, I'm expressing plenty right now. But other times I can sit with very much of a poker face. Not consciously; it's just that I'm listening intensely, so my face doesn't change. But to some people, that can seem strange.

The big one of course was: 'If autistic people are un-empathic then what am I doing as a therapist?' There was a little bit of a fear there. Then I thought, 'Hold on a second. Let's just do a quick self-scan. No, I am empathic. So, I must have just learned to do it. Yeah. I must have just learned this, you know – autistic people must learn it. And, I spent years learning it, so… Anyway, I'm empathic, so let's get on with this.' But I suppose I was still buying a bit into the myths that autistic people aren't empathic by nature. That's not true, though, and it is becoming clear from what actual autistic people are saying, that many autistic people are in fact hyper-empathic. A lot of these myths need to be just thrown in the bin.

Vauna: Yes. It can be that empathy might be shown differently or expressed or communicated or shared differently. It's not that it's not there. The whole understanding of autistic people and empathy has to be thought through again.

Interviewer: So, you think that people might think that a therapist who is autistic may not be empathic?

Vauna: I think that is possible, yes. Because you never know what somebody thinks autism is. So, when you're saying, 'I'm autistic,' you know yourself what it's a shorthand word for, but you don't know what they think autism is. When I am saying 'I am autistic', I am letting people know my cognitive style in advance and helping them to expect differences in my processing and emoting. And yet, if I say I am a therapist and I am autistic, people may tap into ideas of mythical stereotypes to imagine (wrongly) what that means about me, and ask themselves – as Eoin said – 'How can you be a therapist if you're un-empathic?' So these myths do need to be busted, in society in general, and, of course, in the therapy room.

Interviewer: What concerns you about therapists being uninformed about autism?

Vauna: Once you become aware of the huge number of people – and therapists are among those people, too – who misunderstand autistic people, you have to be concerned. You have to think, 'Well, who's out there who needs accurate information or help?'

When Eoin and I first started talking about offering training courses to work with this population, we did so because, although we are concerned about therapists, our primary concern is autistic clients – autistic adults in therapy. Autistic adults who are seeking therapy or who need therapy. We are wanting them to be well served by the therapist population. So offering training is our main focus. Training and supporting therapists to work therapeutically with autistic adult clients.

Eoin: Another concern – just following on from what you were talking about there, Vauna – is supporting autistic and otherwise neurodivergent counselling/psychotherapy trainees. I used to work in the field of counselling and psychotherapy training, running a college. I no longer do that, but I have recently acquired a couple of supervisees who are trainees. They are currently in counselling and psychotherapy training and are autistic. And for me, that's a very necessary and very gratifying piece of work to be doing.

But I worry about the ones out there who aren't getting supervision from an autistic (or at least very neurodiversity-affirming) supervisor. And I worry about what I hear from these supervisees of their experience in college. It's not that it's deliberately negative, necessarily. But, at much subtler but very important levels, they are not really being properly accepted, or enough accommodation being made, or enough up-to-date adjustments being made – not even in the minds of the people around them, whether it's their fellow students, their teachers or their lecturers.

And then there are presumably lots of therapists out there who may be working with autistic adults, or want to. There are also therapists out there who are autistic and haven't realised it yet. So we're not trying to force that knowledge on them, but we do want to offer it.

And certainly any time I've done a bit of training myself with a group of therapists, there has been that mix. Usually, once the group gets talking, and once they feel a bit safe, one of them will say, 'By the way, I am interested in this for myself, as well. I'm wondering about myself and autism.'

Vauna: Yes, that's right. And, of course, some therapists are already autistic, because it's not something that comes on later in life. Even if the recognition might only be validated later in life, you are born autistic. If therapists who are working with clients have been trained that everybody's the same and are not aware of diversity of neurotype, there are huge consequences for autistic clients, because the therapy has to be different to be actually therapeutic.

Interviewer: Does that lead us into why you set up Vanguard Neurodiversity Training?

Vauna: There are going to be many autistic clients going to see therapists. The client may not know that they are autistic, or they may partially know, or they may fully know. And what is going to be understood by the therapist? How is the therapist going to comprehend that client's concepts of quality of life, or the way that they think and feel? Can they appreciate their desires, their needs, their communications, the things that they want, or the ways in which they're trying to get their needs met? Are those things being understood in a neurodivergent kind of way, or in the dominant neurotype kind of way?

Damian Milton wrote a great paper called 'The normalisation agenda and the psycho-emotional disablement of autistic people' (Milton & Moon, 2012) about how society equates 'normal' (typical) with healthy and that there is an unconscious agenda to normalise autistic people (that is, 'make them healthy'), instead of understanding their frame of reference and working to autistic clients' own outcomes.

So, yes, that is why Vanguard Neurodiversity Training was set up. We are aware of adult autistic clients having a need for therapists who understand them and know how to work with them. In 2020, the National Autistic Society in the UK did a survey of autistic adults and there were some shocking findings, and some interesting ones. One very interesting finding was the order in which autistic people listed the things that were most important to them when they were accessing mental health services. It was as follows, in reverse order (NAS Good Practice Guide, 2021). Third, autistic adults wanted the process for accessing therapy to be made easy and clear. Second, they wanted to have information about what therapy would be like before it starts. And then first on the list, the most important thing for autistic adults was that they wanted therapists to understand autism.

Eoin: Yes. I hear that all of the time from clients.

Vauna: [Sigh] Yes. Clients said that they don't want to educate the therapist – it's exhausting, even if it works, and it's devastating if it doesn't because the therapist doesn't understand. The client feels that they're failing. They blame themselves.

Eoin: Yes. [Sigh]

Vauna: The 2018 NICE guidance on suicide prevention recognised autistic people as among those at the highest risk. Yet they are getting the least help. They said that, when they've gone to therapy, they've found that, even though the therapy has been marketed as being inclusive of autistic people, they have found that it isn't.

Interviewer: So you see yourselves training therapists so that this doesn't happen?

Eoin: There are lots of therapists who may well be working with autistic clients and who may not think they need to learn anything new. And therefore won't do any training in it. That's the way the world is. I'm not saying we're going to change all of that, but obviously the message from us is to get training to ensure you ethically serve your autistic clients. Again, getting back to what you were asking about, there's a political dimension here. There's a movement, there's an advocacy that needs to happen. There is some persuasion needed, you know. It's not just about, 'Here, this is what we offer.' There is an element of, 'People need to know this' addressed to as many therapists, as many trainee therapists, and as many training colleges as possible. That's the reality.

Vauna: I feel that it does need to happen because it seems to me that the clients know, now. Because neurodiversity and autism are all over social media, and in those groups people are talking with each other. And so now clients are going to be seeking someone who does understand them properly. And they feel that they have a right to have that; they feel, 'If I'm having therapy, I want the therapist to understand properly what I'm about and what I need and how I view the world and what matters to me.' And that starts with understanding real autistic people.

Eoin: There are difficult questions for therapists, I think. People in general can find it hard to be sufficiently motivated to do the work of adjusting their notion of what being autistic means, and that goes for therapists as well, personally and professionally. I think there are a good few shifts that have to be made, and some big ones. For instance, understanding that a very important aspect of some clients is something they were born with.

Because therapists are used to thinking, 'There are things you learn through experience,' and if a person is very different from other people in certain significant ways, therapists commonly attribute that to something like traumatic experiences. Which is sometimes the correct explanation, but not always. Sometimes it's, 'Yes, I was born autistic.' There could be trauma involved as well. And that's quite a mental shift.

And there is more on the nature–nurture mixture. For example, we learn very specific things – such as eye-contact is important, and empathy happens in particular ways. And part of the reality is that, with eye contact and empathy, quite different rules apply for autistic people. And if you don't know those rules, you will completely misinterpret an autistic client and the effect may be oppression, even though you were just trying to do what you were taught. So this is pretty big. It is a paradigm shift. People do have to be prepared to make quite a shift in their thinking. It's never an easy thing to do.

Vauna: As therapists, we are seeking to have a relationship with a client. That's the bedrock on which we are building the ability to have a working alliance. And so, to be able to build trust and to be able to interact and express empathetic responses to each other, and for those to be understood, is really important in the therapeutic relationship. So, even just using the two examples of eye contact and empathy, as you were saying, Eoin, the quality of relating could be different with an autistic person, and that could impact greatly on the success or otherwise of rapport and establishing safety and trust.

Interviewer: You are both talking about how working with autistic clients can be a little different, and I just wondered a few things. You talked about eye contact, and I realised how little I know and how much the training would benefit therapists. And that the two founders of the training company are autistic gives it a different slant, doesn't it? Rather than people who aren't autistic writing and delivering training courses?

Eoin: There's something. There's an energy. And a connection. And an excitement to an autistic therapist working with an autistic client. Assuming that your personalities match well. We don't always just get on well with someone else just because they're autistic. But there is a sort of freedom.

Vauna: It's based on the freedom of a natural mutual comprehension of each other's minds.

Eoin: Yes, there's more of a sense of inhabiting the same worlds. And validation, and an acceptance that we're different, and we know that so well. Both of us. There's a straightness and a congruence in the genuineness. Which there should be in therapy anyway, but between autistic therapist and autistic client, often that really takes off. Just that strong sense of straightness.

I'm not saying that only autistic therapists can work successfully with autistic clients. Of course, non-autistic therapists can. But they would have to do the learning. Those therapists would have to become much more clued in to the world of the autistic person. The world of the autistic person isn't an entirely different world to the world of the non-autistic person. Obviously – we're humans, and there's lots of overlap. But there's also a huge domain that is just different. And so, at the very least, the therapist needs to meet and learn to understand that world. A good analogy is that this is cross-cultural counselling. Culturally aware counselling and therapy. You need to become aware of the fact that this client has a very different culture and a lot of very different ways of seeing things. And you can learn to empathise with those and see them that way.

Vauna: Yes, it definitely is like cross-cultural counselling.

Eoin: Yes, and it's also like dating somebody from a very different culture. You need to adjust to the different ways.

Vauna: Sure, such as with the communication differences and in terms of social understanding. Autism is about having differences in perception and attention – the brain perceiving things differently and attending differently. So, when you're talking, your client might be perceiving something different to what you thought, or may attend to a slightly different area of focus of the conversation from what you were expecting them to. All of that needs to be understood by therapists. And it does mean that therapy has to be done differently with autistic adults. And these things won't usually occur to a therapist naturally. Therapists need to be explicitly informed of these things.

It doesn't mean totally relearning the art and science of therapy from scratch, though. The way I see it is that the more you learn about real autism in real people, and how that really looks, feels and sounds, as well as how it really is in relationships, behaviours, interactions, and just in everyday life, the more you can apply the principles of what you already know as a qualified therapist.

Taking the time to properly understand autistic people will bring myriad rewards. As a clinician, when you already know and understand people, you already know how to do compassionate, supportive, life-enhancing therapy. If you also know how to understand your autistic client, you can then apply those principles effectively to an autistic person with great success.

Let's be honest, you don't get many clients – you do get some, actually, but you don't get many adult clients – coming in and saying, 'So I found out I'm autistic. I've done some self-discovery work, and now I want to have help. I'm finding myself and, by the way, here's a little manual of how I work – just to help you to be able to do therapy with me.' That would be wonderful, but the client is probably not going to steer you so clearly around their operating system, so to speak. Instead, the client is going to come in and they're going to start talking about their relationships, their life-choice disappointments, or their work stress. And that's what they want to talk about. That's what they want to focus on, just like any client. And we need to understand those things because this is a human being's life and their situation and feelings and desires and pain that is being presented to us. And we need to make meaning of it all.

Interviewer: I can see that you are both extremely passionate about improving the experience of therapy for autistic clients and going about it by training the therapists. I'm just curious about the two of you, and how you came together and decided to do this work?

Eoin: An autistic therapist has felt like a strange and rare thing to be. As I said, when I first discovered I'm autistic 10 years ago, I did think, 'To be autistic and be a therapist is probably a bit of an odd thing. And I had better not say too much about it for the moment.' But I did feel, 'Yes, I would love to meet other autistic therapists.' And then a few years ago that started to grow a bit on the internet.

By the way, before I come back to the specifics of that, in the last few years, my mind has shifted in the direction of 'I think there are loads of autistic therapists, not even just the occasional one.' I wonder if it's even maybe higher than the average general population. A bit like in some other professions. But that's another story. Vauna and I met in an online Facebook group for autistic therapists.

Vauna: Yes, we were in the same Facebook group for autistic counsellors and psychotherapists. I decided to start a monthly video conference session for any of the interested members of the group. Eoin came along and we hit it off. We realised that we had a similar level of experience and qualifications, and that we were a similar age and had discovered that we were autistic at a similar age, too – both later in life. We were just interested in talking about a few things in more depth, and so we did that outside of the group.

I also thought when I met Eoin, 'Oh, this is somebody like me. How rare is that?' It was exciting! Being an autistic person has meant I have not had that happen very often. So, I had to contact this person. Initially we started talking about our own selves. Then we started to talk about the work and the theory, and then the political scene and the whole wider view of autism, being autistic and doing therapy with autistic clients.

Eoin: Those discussions were very exciting for both of us. We are both interested in training and have been for a long time. So it is part of our professional history.

Vauna: And I suppose, ultimately, what we're wanting to do is to help. Well, we are not wanting the autistic clients to suffer, for a start. We are, instead, wanting a therapeutic outcome for those clients.

Eoin: Yes. We firmly agree on that.

Vauna: We both are very passionate about what we've just been talking about today – the fact that there is a long way to go before the access to truly therapeutic therapy is as easy for autistic clients as it is for non-autistic clients. Exchanging ideas was satisfying and seemingly never-ending. We ultimately went from talking about it to the decision to do something about it, to work together on it. And here we are.

Eoin: The training events and the learning points are the details. The paradigm shifts make up the bigger picture. I think we're all just on a huge learning curve.

Vauna: And how do you make sure that autistic adult clients are safe and being served properly by all therapists? It will be good to be able to be more sure of that. Seeing best practice for working with autistic clients included in core therapy training would be a dream come true.

Eoin: Training has to be up-to-date and good quality and accurate. It also needs to be neurodiversity-affirming. So there's a lot to do and we're not going to do all of it, but we'll do our bit.

Interviewer: It seems you also want to build some kind of community so that people have somewhere to turn to for support. And it seems important that it's not just about education, but that you want to build a community of therapists who can support one another as well.

Vauna: Yes, that is true. Because, although reading and reading and reading about it is fine, when you start to interact with other therapists, just as we have done, that's when you learn what you need to learn and validate what you are already thinking and doing with clients. So the coming together is crucial. You need a framework to hang it all on. Talking about the real, lived experiences of autistic people, of ourselves as autistic therapists, and sharing information about how we actually operate as human beings can help a person make sense of their own selves, or of their work, or of each other.

It's just fantastic to congregate, for the purposes of meeting the need for human connection, and also helps builds the picture more – the landscape of the autistic therapist and the adult autistic client.

Because there isn't a manual on how to work with an autistic client. Or how to be an autistic therapist. There is no manual to follow. Together, we are writing it right now.

Eoin: Ten, 15, 20 years ago, we weren't dealing with this at all. Maybe in 30 years' time, it may largely be about working with autistic adults who discovered they were autistic when they were younger and who didn't have to mask very much because society was more accepting of it. Right now, we're mostly dealing with late-discovery, highly masked autistic adults.

Vauna: People who did not show themselves, do not know themselves very well, or are conflicted.

Eoin: That's our population as therapists at the moment. And all therapists are seeing masked autistic clients; they may just not know it. That's the reality. As we go forward now, we will understand autism much more – and society will gain more acceptance.

Vauna: Until then we will work with clients to help them emerge as their true selves, while honouring their self-protective impulses. We are learning more and more each day about being a real autistic person living in the socially constructed world, and the impacts on us. And that helps us in our work with autistic clients.

Eoin: Understanding of autism and autistic people's ways of thinking, being and doing, is moving at a very fast pace now. This can improve the quality of therapeutic service for autistic people. We're living in such an exciting time.

References

American Psychiatric Association. (1994). *Diagnostic and statistical manual of mental disorders* (4th ed.). (DSM-IV). American Psychiatric Association.

Milton, D. & Moon, L. (2012). The normalisation agenda and the psycho-emotional disablement of autistic people. *Autonomy: The Critical Journal of Interdisciplinary Autism Studies, 1*(1).

National Autistic Society. (2021). *Good practice guide.* www.autism.org.uk/what-we-do/news/adapt-mental-health-talking-therapies

NICE. (2018). *Preventing suicide in community and custodial settings.* NG105. National Institute for Health and Care Excellence. https://www.nice.org.uk/guidance/ng105

Chapter 23

Our experiences as trainees

Katherine Balthazor

In an introductory class at university, Professor Kimber Wilkerson discussed increased correlation between college dropout rates and disabilities. On a reflective assignment that day, I shared that my own withdrawal felt imminent due to barriers I was facing. She requested to talk individually. She noted I could get accommodations like testing in a quieter room. We discussed scholarships to overcome resource barriers, such as a grant from another programme professor. She was exceptional in doing everything she reasonably could to help me succeed. Her social investment in my success was a turning point for me. Her ongoing promotion of my inclusion helped with overcoming many obstacles. Acceptance (or rejection) can be contagious! Other department staff were unusually welcoming too.

Inclusion and understanding of language, culture and medical differences by staff like Dr Wilkerson made my career possible. Scholarships and accommodations helped me overcome resource and medical barriers common to autistic students. Caring and advocacy were social investments she and other staff made to promote equity for me within the programme. Staff sometimes afforded me access to quiet, safe areas to rest or study on campus when life was chaotic. These factors made all the difference for me in terms of completion versus terminal overwhelm. For my fellow students: share your experiences, ask for help, and build relationships with academic and field staff.

College staff: make an effort to know and care about your students as people. Look for signs that they may be struggling. Staff mentors can advocate for students with their social capital, systemic expertise, and support for students in need. The support of a single staff member can make all the difference.

Danielle Goddard

During my training, I was fortunate to have a personal tutor who had lived experience of neurodivergence. I was given a space to speak freely about areas that I might have found difficult on the course and was encouraged to consider potential solutions.

My tutor also helped me reflect on areas that I was doing particularly well in, which neurotypical colleagues may not have found so straightforward. I found this reflective space invaluable, and it encouraged me to continue with my education, even when things were feeling tricky. As my tutor was also a supervisory lead on the course, I was able to take ideas to them that could improve the accessibility of the course. We were able to start organising a peer support space for neurodivergent students and had sensory needs considered in the lecture rooms. Being able to advocate for my own learning needs was empowering and it opened up broader conversations with other trainees about their particular needs.

The communication between the staff and students was strong and our ideas were listened to. I am hopeful that the course will continue to make positive changes to allow future neurodivergent students to thrive.

Silvia Liu

For me, during my doctoral programme in clinical psychology, my problem was with supervision. I noticed during my training that supervisors wanted me to deduce clinical issues based on what felt like very little information. I felt that it was presumptuous and unfair to assume. It reminded me of how one of my therapists had misunderstood my problems without demonstrating curiosity or asking first. I understood that supervisors wanted to see my skills in clinical judgement and ability to home in on important clinical issues, but it was important for me not to assume a narrative without sufficient evidence. I might, for example, be slow to realise if clients chose to lie to me or withhold information, but I preferred that to doing harm through hurtful assumptions.

I prefer to gather details through observation and discussions before coming up with a conceptualisation or hypothesis to test. My favourite supervisors throughout graduate school were ones who would honour this type of bottom-up processing and meet me where I was at.

Similarly, I needed concrete details and examples to understand what was expected of me in training and practice. Supervisors who were truly accommodating understood that I required feedback that was sufficiently detailed, with concrete examples, rather than perceiving me as 'anxious' or 'too caught up in details'.

Neurodiversity-affirming supervision for autistic therapists is culturally competent supervision. Neurodivergent people have a different culture from neurotypical people. Looking back on my training, I think that it would have been helpful to have a space for me, as an autistic therapist, to discuss any difficulties and challenges around navigating therapeutic relationships with neurotypical people. It is also important for this to be done in a way that is not shaming or pathologising. These difficulties were about navigating cultural differences and should not be conceptualised as incompetence.

River Marino

The most impactful trainings I've attended have been unapologetically and authentically autistic, led by autistics, with the understanding that autism is a neurotype, not a condition to be fixed or a disorder to be resolved. These trainings consistently emphasise the underlying premise that autism is a naturally occurring neurotype, heritable, and neutral – meaning it is simply a neurotype and not categorised as good/bad or right/wrong. My favourite autistic-affirming trainings have also recognised autism as a unique culture. It would be amazing to see therapist training programmes include a curriculum that celebrates autistic identity and culture. This would encourage a more inclusive lens on what it means to be autistic, centring autistic people as the experts of our neurotype and culture.

To make counsellor and therapist training programmes more autistic affirming, a crucial addition would be comprehensive coursework on ableism. Ideally, this would include specific content and assignments addressing internalised ableism. Learning about internalised ableism is essential because it helps individuals recognise and challenge harmful beliefs or stereotypes they may hold about themselves or others. Understanding the subtle ways that ableism and internalised ableism can show up in a therapy session is important in not perpetuating this form of oppression.

Additionally, ongoing continuing education for professors and teachers is essential to ensure a sustained commitment to not engaging in ableism. Ideally, this education would delve into nuanced aspects of all forms of ableism, equipping educators with the knowledge and skills to create an inclusive learning environment for students with diverse needs.

By integrating these elements into training programmes and embracing autistic-led perspectives, we can transform the learning environment into a space that both acknowledges the neurodiversity-affirming paradigm and actively affirms and celebrates it.

Max Marnau

I didn't know I was autistic when I trained but I knew I was different. Certain elements of the training were almost unbearable: forced overnight stays, although I lived only a few miles away; forced socialising; and the 'whole group meeting' where all 30 of us were expected to 'contribute' (contribute what?), with no guidelines, no shape and no facilitation. Sometimes that meant awkward silence, sometimes the most shocking attacks on each other. I effectively opted out; the only contribution I remember was when a group of women turned on the only man in the group and attacked him… just for being a man. I protested, which did not go down well.

My salvation was the small 'personal development group'. The facilitator started by inviting each of us to present a piece telling the group who we were, what was important to us, what we loved, what we hated. The only rule was, 'What you really want us to hear about you.' We all took that literally and our five contributions were academic, quirky, creative, serious, funny. For the following two years, that was my sanctuary, the one place where people really knew who I was and appreciated me for that. I doubt that I could have survived the course without that safe place.

So, course organisers: consider whether certain non-negotiables really are non-negotiable. Consider who your trainees are, and what might make it easier for them to learn and flourish. And if the numbers on the course are too high for that – well, maybe the numbers on the course are too high. And provide a safe place where nobody will be attacked, mocked, or required to conform.

Shirley Moore

Counselling and psychotherapy training programmes attract a diverse array of individuals, each bringing unique life experiences, career and carer backgrounds. Trainers may have no training in training yet have teachers as students. They may be a critic of the medical model yet have doctors as trainees or be expected to teach legal and ethical aspects of counselling to lawyers. All students can offer invaluable insights derived from their distinctive perspectives and this is certainly true for autistic trainees, who offer a wealth of relevant knowledge that educators can tap into. By embracing this diversity, while maintaining appropriate academic and professional boundaries, trainers can facilitate an environment where everyone is encouraged to learn from one another, promoting an atmosphere of equality and respect, minimising power differentials and transcending traditional roles of instruction.

There are two quotes I would like to share.

> The really bright student, the eager questioner, the probing searcher, especially if he is brighter than his teacher, is too often seen as a 'wise guy', a threat to discipline, a challenger of his teacher's authority. (Maslow, 1998, p.74)

Understanding perhaps a bit more about autistic counsellors by now, it is hopefully easy to see how this quote might apply to autistic trainees and why I and other autistic students have found themselves in difficulty during training.

The second quote is from my very first teacher of counselling skills and it had more impact than she will ever know!

> I do wonder if I have learnt as much from you as you have hopefully learnt from me!

Wendy Reiersen

I get the impression that counsellor training is very different in the US and in the UK. Here in the US, when I trained, there was a set curriculum of courses to be taken in order. There were no options for electives; I would like to think that most graduate programmes are at least a bit more flexible. We were not trained in a particular modality. It was more like a checklist designed to cover the credits required for licensing, with nothing more, nothing less.

We were assigned to 'learning teams', which were groups of about four students to meet together outside of class and do collaborative projects and assignments and experiential activities. I would have liked more of the experiential activities, but it always seemed as if my classmates were trying to do the minimum and cut it short. Sometimes I thought that they just weren't taking it seriously – just going through the motions. To me, this was real life. I wanted to connect, but didn't know how, especially when my classmates didn't seem to be into it.

I really wanted the experiences, so that I could be a good therapist, but that was not what the others were wanting.

It was after I burned out from being overworked and in toxic work settings, when I had been a crisis worker for several years and wasn't sure that I remembered how to be a therapist, that I trained in NARM (neuroaffective relational therapy – see my Chapter 9). That was what counsellor education should have been! It was a large main group led by a senior faculty member, with breakout groups facilitated by practitioners with experience in the modality. I lost touch with everybody from my first training at graduate school, but NARM is ongoing and is a real community. If you didn't get the experiences that you needed or wanted in training, consider training in a specific modality that resonates with you. It's not too late!

Elinor Rowlands

On my course, staff and trainees were aware I was disabled. I had been explicit from the start about my access needs as a person with both an invisible disability and some difficulty in walking. But on the last day of training, it was announced, without any advance warning, that we were to climb a hill and do an eco-installation to honour the past two years' work. A lovely idea, but with no attempt to understand what that might mean for a disabled person. With prior warning, I would have come in supportive shoes, not light sandals, for the planned long walk and steep climb. Just one trainee took notice of this inaccessibility: the only one who was non-white and not of UK origin. She asked if I needed help as she could see me struggling to get down the hill independently in those sandals.

The tutors and the other trainees seemed unwilling to acknowledge the access needs of disabled or neurodivergent people. A surprise can be exciting for people who do not need to consider access. However, for people who need preparation for a change of plan, such a 'surprise' may make the event inaccessible. Other trainees suggested that I was the problem, and there was no understanding or input from the tutors. I am unable to stand for long periods, but whenever I tried to sit the tutors insisted that we all stand, out of respect for the work. They did not appear to see that this was both disabling and insensitive.

We need to identify the ableism within our profession to know how best to serve our communities. Training is always important, especially if you are not sure how to work with disabled practitioners, or disabled clients. The first essential is to read your disabled trainees' access statements, note their access needs, and plan events with that in mind.

Chan Shu Yin

I was unaware of my different access needs during my training. If I had known about them and disclosed them, I am confident that the faculty would have been both willing and able to accommodate them. It would be ideal if there were more knowledge about neurodivergence and the possibility of therapy trainees being neurodivergent, especially challenging the assumption that autistic people are unable to empathise.

This could be achieved with formal training of staff and students on the subject: for example, by incorporating it into the syllabus as a stand-alone topic. With increasing awareness, seemingly unusual behaviours would be more accepted and no longer seen as inappropriate. That therapists are to socialise and communicate in a certain way only would be challenged, together with the other assumptions. For example, questioning social hierarchies would be more accepted as part of critical discourse and viewed less as intentionally challenging authority. Incorporating an attitude of ongoing inquiry into assumptions during practical sessions such as group therapy, role-play and group supervision, would help elevate everyone's views on neurodivergence beyond being merely a deficit to the natural diversity of humanness.

I am encouraged to note that there is now more dialogue on neurodivergence in the art therapy training programme here in Singapore, and in the therapy world and the community more generally. However, being biased against those who are different is often said to be part of human nature; we still need to be constantly reminded of this ongoing and subconscious issue, and so of the importance of being affirming in practice.

Kristina Takashina

What helped me most during my training was that so much of it was non-verbal and not interpreted. We were just given space to access our bodies and to sensorily interact with props or the environment (the walls, the floor, space, each other) in whatever way we wanted, and for the vast majority of the time, this meant moving on our own in the space without needing to be with others in any other way than simply sharing the space. Dance movement psychotherapy makes use of props that can be used in whatever way you like, and much of that can be a real sensory joy for an AuDHDer like me. For example, there were stretchy Lycra bags to get into, hoops to move in and out of, and full access to walls and empty wooden floors to slide along or use for balance or pressure. There were big chiffon pieces of material to fold yourself inside or swish or just make pictures and shapes with on the ground. And all of this was made much easier without the need for interpretation. No eyes to judge and say it was either right or wrong, or that it needed to have meaning, to be bigger, smaller, more or less. The meaning was in the moment, the pleasure and the sensations, and there was no need for any other structure or framework; nothing would have been gained by it.

Amy Walters

If I could have a wish that would change anything about counselling training, it would be a requirement that all courses have to prove they are accessible. Accessibility comes in all shapes and forms, but something needs to change to address why counselling is predominately full of white, middle-aged women. It is changing, but for counsellors to start reflecting the multitudes of difference we see in society, we have to look at the barriers to accessing training.

Are the buildings accessible? Are funding and scholarships available? Is the course content and structure accessible? Does the course content cover specific training on disability, race, LGBTQIA+, equality and discrimination?

A client looking for a counsellor deserves to see themselves represented in the counsellors they are looking at – someone of their race and culture, their gender, their disability. Right now, it's slim pickings. We deserve to see ourselves represented by the counsellors we might want to work with. Representation is so important to show other people who are different, like us, that they too could become a therapist.

Although my counselling training was good, when I trained, I didn't know I was neurodivergent. I was highly masked and struggling with procrastination, but essay extensions did help, and the practical nature of the course kept me very hooked. The joy of self-discovery, the journey of self-awareness and the special interest in understanding humans was naturally part of the course that really appealed.

References

Maslow, A. (1998). *Toward a psychology of being* (3rd ed.). John Wiley & Sons.

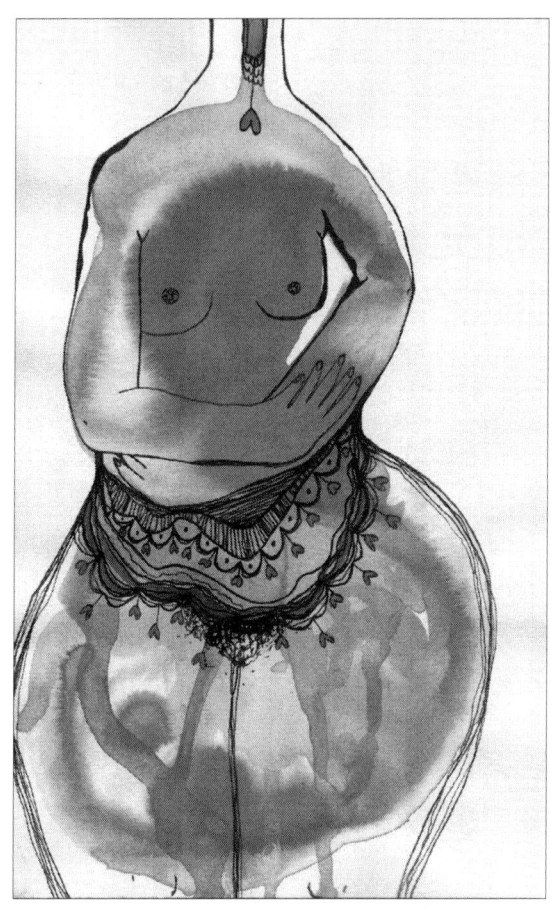

'Love Story to Self' (India ink on paper)
© River Marino

About the contributors

Rebecca Antrim
Rebecca has worked as a therapist since 2010 and was diagnosed with autism and ME/CFS in 2019, followed by a diagnosis of ADHD in 2022. Rebecca has worked with people from a variety of backgrounds and contexts, from children and young people experiencing a family health crisis to survivors of trafficking and people in the prison service. While she enjoyed and thrived on the challenge of high-intensity crisis work, following the ME/CFS diagnosis there was a need for a much slower pace, so Rebecca chose to largely focus on working part-time with neurodivergent women. In March 2023, Rebecca devised and developed her neurodiversity consultancy service, which launched in April 2023. Her lived experience of neurodivergence and years of therapeutic work give her consultancy work a unique edge.

Rebecca lives in Herefordshire with her miniature dachshund, Hoggle, and enjoys creating abstract art, plant-based cooking, drumming and taking care of her house plants.

Katherine Balthazor
Katherine is an American AuDHD licensed professional counsellor and certified rehabilitation counsellor with a master's degree in rehabilitation psychology. She has more than a decade of experience counselling people with all types of disabilities in diverse settings. Her career has included work experience in both the private and public sectors, most recently for a Fortune 500 company providing specialised vocational counselling.

Vauna Beauvais

Vauna is a UKCP registered psychotherapist specialising in working with neurodivergent adults. She has been seeing clients for more than 20 years in private practice. She is also a clinical supervisor for counsellors and psychotherapists who are seeing neurodivergent clients and for therapists who are autistic themselves. Discovering, aged over 40 years old, that she is autistic with ADHD, she turned her interest towards understanding the autistic experience and what that means for therapists, trainers, supervisors and for autistic clients. Areas of interest include understanding the nuances of masking and facilitating the emergence of the self, as well as clarifying ways that psychotherapy, counselling and therapy training needs to be different for autistic adults. Vauna has postgraduate qualifications in autism, is a qualified coach and trainer, a certified transactional analyst, and a certified cybertherapist. She is currently serving on the board of directors for The Association for Counselling and Psychotherapy Online (ACTO), where she also chairs an autism interest group for the professional members.

Kathy Carter

Kathy works in private practice, including as a talk therapist with the social enterprise Thriving Autistic. She also has experience of working with young people with social, emotional and mental health support needs, as well as adults in recovery from addiction. Kathy's passion in life, outside of work and family, is music. She especially enjoys going to see live music from different genres and has always had a special fascination with the 1960s pop group The Monkees. As a teenager in the 1980s, this was widely considered to be uncool. But now, finally in possession of an 'I am autistic' badge, Kathy understands this inclination towards rather obscure interests much better. Kathy is also a mum and an animal lover. She finds that therapy, music and family encapsulate her entire life. She's been married to her own 'daydream believer' for 24 years.

Chan Shu Yin

Shu Yin is an artist, art therapist and somatic experiencing practitioner based between Singapore and Sydney, Australia. She founded Creative Trauma Healing, a private practice serving adolescents and adults. She also works with other organisations to bring art therapy to various populations. Shu Yin has facilitated and co-created public art with the community at Singapore Art Week '20, and Light to Night Festival '21 at the National Gallery Singapore. As an artist and illustrator, she has illustrated books and worked for non-profits and performing arts groups. She formerly worked as a film visual effects artist and taught herself watercolour painting. She makes art about nature, human beings' relationship with it, and the human condition. She enjoys creating as a form of self-care and a way to tell personal stories.

Natalie Furdek

Natalie is a licensed professional counsellor in Texas (USA) who provides therapy to autistic and ADHD clients. She received a bachelor's and master's degree from Texas Tech University in Lubbock, Texas, and was licensed in 2002. She has exclusively worked online since just before the pandemic and enjoys finally thriving in a counselling career as a result. Working remotely has allowed Natalie to move away from the city to a quieter environment and to focus more on simply providing counselling services (and less on the stressful logistics and overstimulation of life in the city). She teaches her clients to find the same kinds of relief in their own lives wherever possible.

Danielle Goddard

Danielle is a qualified education mental health practitioner and cognitive behavioural therapist. She self-identifies as autistic and likely ADHD after several years of research and learning. She currently works for an NHS mental health support team and is passionate about increasing accessibility for neurodivergent people. When Danielle isn't working or studying, she spends time with her partner Davey and their six dogs. In true ADHD fashion, Danielle has far too many hobbies and interests to list, but her current interests include gaming, reading and book collecting.

Romy Graichen

Romi is multiply neurodivergent and late diagnosed, like most of her colleagues in this book. She trained in a variety of modalities, including transactional analysis psychotherapy, person-centred counselling, EMDR, brainspotting, imago, somatic trauma therapy and others. She specialises in neurodiversity and trauma and offers therapy, training and supervision around these topics.

Silvia Liu

Silvia is a humanistic clinical psychologist in California who enjoys helping individuals and families across their lifespan. Her deepest desire is to bring innovation to the global psychological field and inspire a new wave of psychological awareness in human beings. She believes that music and anime are essential parts of life. She also hugs trees.

Debbie Luck

Debbie is a UK-based therapist and founder of Nymah Healing, which was created to provide a safe, accepting, supportive and therapeutic space for those on an alternative path.

Healing is Debbie's sole passion in life. She is an integrative counsellor, coach, teacher, meditation facilitator, energy worker and shadow healing practitioner. She has also travelled extensively, gathering knowledge of healing techniques from around the globe. In her work, Debbie infuses spiritual tools and ancient healing practices with modern therapeutic modalities. Her mission is to help people move out of the shadows of shame and trauma and into the sovereignty of true Self.

River Marino

River (they/them) is an artist, writer, therapist and Kripalu-certified yoga teacher. River fell in love with meditation and mindfulness when they were 20 years old and has been practising ever since. Writing and creating art began as ways to cope when River was in high school and over the years have become nourishing practices of self-care and personal expression. As an autistic therapist, River is trauma-sensitive and social justice-informed, and views therapy through an intersectional lens (bodymind, environment, culture, etc.). River's approach to therapy is both collaborative and holistic, centring around values of embodied presence, empathy, connection and deep listening. River provides an autistic-affirming perspective in therapy and believes autism is a genetically based neurotype, not a medical disorder.

Max Marnau

Max Marnau is a person-centred therapist, artist and poet living in the Scottish Borders. As the autistic daughter of refugees from Hitler's Nazis, she feels a particular affinity with all the exiled, the othered and the displaced. Her special interest is Gaelic language, poetry, and music.

> *Chan eil adhar no speur*
> *sa bhaile choimheach chruaidh*
> *Chan eil gàire ann.*

> There's no air nor sky
> in the alien harsh town
> There's no smiling there.

> *Sàmhchair bhòidheach*
> *Aiteas òran na h-aibhne*
> *Gaoth às na beanntan.*

A lovely silence
The joy of the river's song
A wind from the hills.

Shirley Moore

Shirley is a person-centred counsellor with a portfolio career, living in Scotland. She arrived in the therapy world having explored a number of different professions, including engineering, IT and medicine. She is considering adding a law degree to the mix if she doesn't run away with the circus first, and spends much of her spare time hanging from a trapeze or spinning fire poi.

Sally Nilsson

Sally is a Human Givens practitioner and hypnotherapist. With a humanistic approach, she works in a solution-focused model, giving practical tools and techniques around trauma, nervous system regulation, co-occurring differences and physical challenges, working to tailor-make her holistic approach by meeting clients' needs. Sally lives in Frome, Somerset, with her Swedish husband, and has two sons aged 21 and 24. As well as counselling and coaching, Sally is a published author (*The Man Who Sank Titanic*), with a new book in progress. She is also a public speaker. She hosts the Neurodivergence and Mental Health Podcast and presented nine shows on Frome FM, called *Love Your Mind*, speaking to guests about their neurodivergent and mental health journeys. A keen vegetable grower and nature lover, Sally has many hobbies and is curious to the core.

Wendy Reiersen

Wendy is a wounded healer. She has been many other things as well – a mother, a musician, a textile artist, a dairy goat farmer, a cheesemaker, a blogger… She is first-generation American, as a daughter of a Norwegian immigrant, and also a descendent of many travellers and explorers who were among the Mormon pioneers and aboard the Mayflower. Wendy dreams of some day having the time and the space and the balance to do and be all of these things, to travel, and perhaps to return home to a place where she has never lived, maybe somewhere in south-western Norway.

Leo Ricketts

Leo trained in relational transactional analysis and has been practising since 2014. At 55, he was diagnosed autistic, having suspected as much for years. This came with a bonus ADHD diagnosis, which surprised precisely no one in his personal life. Leo has what his psychologist described as a very AuDHD

CV, having had careers as a drummer, DJ, journalist, radio presenter, graphic designer, digital producer and project manager. In his work as a therapist with a practice of 90% neurodivergent people, he feels he has finally come home. Outside of his client work, Leo teaches, writes about and advocates for neurodivergence inclusion. Leo co-hosts the Autistic Licence podcast with fellow autistic therapist Siana McGarvey. He finds writing about himself in the third person jarring but oddly liberating.

Elinor Rowlands
Elinor is a person-centred Jungian art psychotherapist (HCPC). Elinor has worked in various roles as autistic mentor, study skills tutor, employment coach, academic advisor and manager of disability and wellbeing in higher education. As an artist, she works with text, sound, collage, installation and video, and is doing a PhD. She examines autistic stimming through journeying as an act of power, self-expression and creativity. She creates work in collaboration with neurodivergent artists and musicians. She is founder of Magical Women, a project that reduces barriers faced by neurodivergent women, trans women and non-binary artists (often also survivors of violence). As a psychotherapist, her services address access barriers that fail autistic people who encounter barriers to quality mental health support and mentoring. She advocates for radical changes in the way we approach neurodivergent access in higher education, mental health services, and access in the arts.

Eoin Stephens
Eoin is an Irish counsellor/psychotherapist and trainer who has worked in the areas of disability, addiction treatment, training and counselling/psychotherapy private practice for more than 30 years, using a humanistic, pragmatic approach to cognitive behavioural therapy. After specialising primarily in the areas of behavioural addictions and anxiety disorders for a number of years and working at a senior level in counselling/psychotherapy education, his focus is currently on understanding the problems faced by autistic adults and their specific therapeutic needs.

Kristina Takashina
Kristina (she/them) is an AuDHD dance movement psychotherapist based in the UK and has two dachshunds and two rescue cats. Kristina has had a varied career prior to training as a psychotherapist, including doing voice-overs for Nintendo games, appearing on Japanese TV and singing opera. As well as her MA in dance movement psychotherapy, Kristina has a BA (Hons) in modern

and mediaeval languages and literature from Keble College, Oxford, an MA in literary translation and a PG Dip. Mus. from The Royal Conservatoire of Scotland. Kristina is interested in trauma, adverse social conditions, the ways in which self and social development intersect, the influence of social class on psychology, all facets of social change, gender, voice, music, embodiment of all types including energy work and spirituality, and all aspects of neurodiversity, including the concept of neurotypicality.

Fiona Villarreal
Fiona is an art psychotherapist from the UK. Art for emotional expression changed the path of her life and now she offers space to others to explore their internal world through the creative process. Fiona is passionate about neurodiversity and encouraging people to express their authentic selves. Fiona believes everyone is an artist and that the creative self is there waiting to be unlocked. In her down-time, Fiona is most content painting and drawing for hours to many random sub-genres of music or wandering in the great outdoors.

Wilma Wake
Wilma was shocked but relieved to be diagnosed autistic in her late 60s. Now 77, she lives in Maine in the US, where she is a licensed clinical social worker and retired ordained (Swedenborgian) minister. She has a PhD in social foundations of education and a DMin. in feminist-liberation theology. Her social work practice is devoted primarily to working with other older autistic adults. She has co-authored a book with two other autistic adults, *Older Autistic Adults in Their Own Words: The lost generation*, for which they surveyed 150 older autistic adults around the world to learn about their experiences with autism. She co-leads two online discussion groups for older autistic adults through AANE (the Association for Autism and Neurodiversity – aane.org). She enjoys connecting with other autistic adults through CASY (Cultural Autism Studies at Yale – https://culturalautismstudiesatyale.space).

Amy Walters
Amy is a fat, queer, ADHD/autistic counsellor, coach and clinical supervisor. She is well known for starting lots of things and never finishing them, so it's a miracle this chapter got written at all. Amy is a mum and a mediocre musician. An eternal starter of new and exciting hobbies. A collector of all the cute things. A wild, free-spirited rule keeper. Amy is absolutely passionate about enabling people to be utterly true to themselves.

Sharon Xie

Sharon Xie loves nature, art and creative expression, and finding connection and beauty in the mundane. She is mother to a delightful young person and is a dubious yet hopeful gardener, as well as a loyal subject to her two hilarious cats. She was duly warned by her forefathers to be quiet on matters of politics and social justice but struggles mightily with compliance and joined this collaboration to find and use her voice. Sharon envisions the field of psychology transformed to lift those voices that were previously silenced and oppressed. You can find her in Seattle, working closely with others in building their empowering narratives, or eagerly tending to the reluctant seedlings in her patches of dirt, and captivated by the gentle buzzing and fluttering of pollinators.

Name index

A
Accardo, A.L. 26
Ackerman, C. 89
Adams, C.A. 89
Adams, D. 133
American Psychiatric Association (APA) 76, 92, 186, 210
Anderson, F. 17–18
Anna, M. 135, 137
Anna Freud Centre 20
Arnold, C. 139
Attwood, T. 94, 135
Autistic Advocate 12
Autistic Counsellors and Psychotherapists (ACP) 1–3, 4, 77, 130
Autistic Self-Advocacy Network (ASAN) 185, 187

B
Baker, E.K. 196
Barnes, C. 167
Baron-Cohen, S. 103
Beardon, L. 3, 127, 191
Beck, A.T. 191
Bennett, J. 167
Blackburn, I.M. 21, 22
Bradley, L. 176
Brede, J. 78
British Association of Counselling and Psychotherapy (BACP) 198
Brown, L.S. 103

C
Caldwell, C. 38
Case, C. 42, 45
Casement, P. 43
Cassidy, S.A. 127, 176
Chapman, L. 63
Charlton, J. 185
Chiang, H.M. 61
Chick, N. 108
Chong, C.Y.J. 43
Clark, D.A. 191
Clark, D.M. 25
Conan Doyle, A. 120
Cooper, M. 162
Crane, L. 78
Creative Trauma Healing 232
Crompton, C.J. 76
Csikszentmihalyi, M. 15
Cullen, C. 202

D
Dalley, T. 42, 45
Dallos, R. 192
Dana, D. 110–111
Degener, T. 167
De Mille, A. 36
den Houting, J. 170
Desaulnier, C.L. 92
Doherty, M. 22, 132
Donovan, M.P. 97

E
Elisabeth, J. 12, 86
Endlich, E. 183
European Council of Autistic People (EUCAP) 97
Evans, H. 135, 136

F

Feminist Therapy Institute 125
Freyd, J.J. 138
Furdek, N. 71

G

Garcia Dominguez, L. 103
Garrett, C. 22
Gibson, L.C. 91
Gillott, A. 26
Graham, M. 36
Graichen, R. 175
Grand, D. 103
Grant, S. 197
Green, K.C. 199

H

Hanna, J. 38
Harris, R. 172
Hassan, S. 128
Hawkins, P. 157, 160
Heller, L. 95
Heritage Services 197
Heyworth, M. 26
Hicks-Wilson, D. 16
Higgins, J.M. 22
Horvath, A.O. 63–64
Hu, Y. 136

J

Jaarsma, P. 102
Jenkinson, G. 128
Jenkinson, R. 191
Johnsson, G. 78
Joseph, B. 44
Jung, C.G. 171

K

Kaku, S.M. 78
Kammer, B. 95
Kierkegaard, S. 71
King, R. 92

L

Ladinsky, D. 11
Lagos. R.S. 183
Laugeson, E.A. 99
Lauria, A. 15, 17
Lawson, W. 14

Leong, C. 175
Lesser, M. 14
Levens, M. 44
Levin, A. 92
Levine, P.A. 63
Lewis, D.B. 135, 136
Lim, C.R. 135
Linden, M. 139
Linehan, M. 91–92
Litz, B.T. 134
Liu, S. 71, 94
Lobregt-van Buuren, E. 92
Lowry, M. 15, 17
Luck, D. 72

M

Mahalik, J.R. 125, 127, 130
Manning, M. 90–91
Marnau, M. 123
Maslow, A. 225
May, T. 89, 135
McCowan, S. 135
McDonald, T.A. 22
McKenzie, R. 192
McNiff, S. 42, 67
McQuaid, G. 92
Mearns, D. 162
Medavarapu, S. 99
Milton, D.E.M. 23, 66, 77, 120, 138, 167, 180, 190, 213
Miserandino, C. 120, 190
Montgomery, L.M. 107
Moody, C.T. 99
Moon, L. 213
Moore, S. 72, 132
Murray, D. 14
Murray, F. 14

N

Nannery, L. 108
Nannery, S. 108
NAS Good Practice Guide 214
National Autistic Society 161, 194, 198
Nerenberg, J. 52
NHS 20, 132, 209
    NHS Choices 196
NICE 214

O
O'Brien, F. 43
Owens, L.R. 13

P
Pardo, C.A. 103
Pearson, A. 22
Perls, F. 129
Poissant, S. 108
Porges, S.W. 112, 191
Price, D. 63, 88, 186
Protect 134
Psychotherapy and Counselling Union 133

R
Raymaker, D. 161
Reiersen, W. 72
Ricketts, L. 71, 80
Robinson, A. 194
Rogers, C.R. 43, 71, 74, 113, 124, 125, 176
Rose, K. 12, 22
Royal Conservatoire of Scotland 31
Rumi, J. al-D. 14

S
Sarris, M. 89
Schank, J.A. 123
Schwartz, R.C. 17, 18, 114
Scott, J. 167
Scottish Women's Autism Network (SWAN) 2
Selhub, E. 32
Shapiro, R. 103
Shay, J. 134
Shirazi, H. 11
Shohet, R. 158, 160
Siegel, D.J. 139
Sifneos, P.E. 23
Silberman, S. 77, 185
Singer, M.T. 127–128
Slap-Shelton, L. 186
South, M. 88
Spock, Mr 116, 120
Standen, P.J. 26
Stephen, C. 67
Stewart, J. 97
Stop ABA, Support Autistics 97
Sullivan, K. 107
Supekar, K. 103

T
The Awetist 103
Thurm, A. 22
Trauma Geek 12
Turnock, A. 22

U
University of California, Los Angeles (UCLA) 99
University of South Wales 198
University of Worcester 198

V
van Ooijen, E. 157
Vance, T. 103
Vancouver Crisis Center 99
van der Kolk, B. 43, 192
Vischer, R. 180

W
Waheed, N. 17
Wake, W. 183
Walker, N. 12, 77
Weir, E. 198
Welin, S. 102
Wells, A. 25
Wheelwright, S. 103
Wilding, T. 74
Wilkerson, K. 221
Wood-Downie, H. 194
World Health Organization 92

X
Xie, S. 72

Y
Yalom, I.D. 33, 111–112, 130–131

Z
Zener, D. 22
Zheng, S. 99
Zur, O. 122

Subject index

A

ABA (applied behaviour analysis) 94, 97, 98, 99, 101, 103, 119, 148
ableism 163, 179, 223, 226
   internalised, 120, 162, 176, 223
   vulnerable to, 139
abuse
   child, 100
   emotional, 95
   spiritual, 124, 125, 127, 128, 129
   substance, 74
acceptance 46, 54, 91, 112, 115, 119, 145, 155, 156, 176, 180, 194, 199, 201, 202, 216, 219, 221
   of neurodivergence 179
   radical, 71, 103
access
   in the arts 244
   barriers to, 244
   to healthcare 93, 200
   to help 150
   in higher education 244
   in mental health services 244
   needs 159, 167, 185, 226
   to other autistic people 77
   to quiet 221
   to resources 89
   to self 17, 128
   to self-energy 18
   to skills 92
   statement 226
   to support 139, 162
   to therapy 78, 198, 218
   to training 1

accessible/ility 100, 158, 173, 202
   buildings 228
   courses 227, 228
   environments 17, 166–174
   increase in, 167, 227, 233
   presentations 27
   in universities 26
accommodations 181, 212, 221
   asking for, 151
   inbuilt, 157
   'medical', 151
   need for, 133
accountability 135, 141
ACT (acceptance and commitment therapy) 2, 95, 101, 201, 202
addiction 9, 42, 53, 185, 191, 193, 232
   DBT for, 92
   treatment 41, 236
ADHD 3, 21, 22, 26, 30, 37, 39, 41, 42, 52, 53, 55, 59, 65, 66, 78, 81, 82, 84, 102, 119, 156, 166, 167, 168, 171, 193, 194, 199, 201, 231, 232, 233, 236, 237
advocacy 214, 221
   self, 200,
   systemic, 139
advocate 3, 115, 140, 152, 160, 164, 169, 179, 222, 236
   autistic community and neurodiversity, 97
   self-, 151
affirming 16, 157, 158, 227
   autistic-, 235
   life-, 166

neurodivergent-, 202
neurodiversity-, 4, 12, 102, 119, 120, 146, 175–182, 191, 212, 218, 223
non-, 177, 179
agency 10, 32, 33, 94, 95, 99,115, 170
alexithymia/alexithymic 10, 23, 35, 53, 77, 192
alien 3, 11, 115–121, 234
  blue 58, 59
  feel, 87, 128, 190
  feel less, 149
alienation/alienating 135, 136
anxiety 40, 75, 76, 100, 111, 118, 119, 128, 167, 169, 173, 189, 193
  DBT for, 92
  disorders 210, 236
  -driven 191
  generalised, 129
  label of, 26
  -provoking 130
  responses 192
  sense of, 35
  separation, 149
  social, 25,
  symptoms 9, 53
  treatment 25
aphantasia 192
arousal
  emotional, 139
  heightened, 191
  hyper-, 25
  sensory, 43,
Asperger's syndrome 94, 124, 135
assessment 74, 130, 135
  for autism 21, 22, 52, 54, 77, 81
  for dyspraxia 81
assumption(s) 42, 102, 162
  about autism 170
  avoiding, 178
  challenging, 226, 227
  concerning psychic unity of humans 38
  hurtful, 222
  implicit, 176
  less likely to make, 27, 86, 150
  negative, 135
attachment
  disorder 193
  insecure, 192
  relationships 42
  style 192

theory 42
attention tunnel 14, 15
attunement 176, 179–181, 192
AuDHD 3, 39, 40, 41, 42, 44, 46, 48, 50, 81, 82, 83, 84, 86, 156, 158, 159, 162, 163, 164, 165, 194, 200, 227, 231, 236
authentic 71, 74, 159
  nature 113, 126
  self/ves 43, 49, 59, 62, 126, 176, 194, 223, 237
  version of self 155
authentically
  autistic 223
  myself 155
autonomy 35, 41, 63, 74, 76, 151, 166, 168, 190, 192

B

baby-boomers 182–187
barrier(s) 26, 166, 168, 221, 236
  access, 166, 168, 236
    to therapy 197, 202
    to training 227
  communication, 168
  communication and social interaction, 167
  external, 162
  invisible, 112
  language, 152
  logistical, 78
  medical, 221
  organisational, 136
  political, 136
  resource, 221
  socially imposed, 167
  to treatment 169
  well-masked, 152
behaviour 37, 63, 71, 94, 100, 102, 103, 108, 109, 112, 113, 119, 130, 140, 156, 191, 194, 216
  adapting, 52
  animal, 149
  atypical moral, 136
  changing/change, 53, 119, 130
  client, 178
  complainant, 136, 137
  disruptive, 99
  focused, 119
  habits of, 32

healthy, 176
human, 99, 149
mimicking, 109
patterns in, 31
observable, 119
prosocial, 99
safety-seeking, 191
suicidal, 176
suppressing, 176
taken from movies and stereotypes 30
undesirable, 119
unethical, 75
unusual, 55, 226
behavioural
   addictions 236
   health policy work 74
   intervention(s) 101, 202,
   interventionist, 99
   lens, predominant 98
   techniques 191
   theories 191
   therapist (cognitive) 4, 20–29, 233, 236
   therapy 2, 94, 97, 99, 107, 191, 199, 203, 233, 236
behaviourism 99, 104
blame 65, 95, 140, 214
body 10, 16, 106, 108, 111, 112, 113, 161, 180, 194, 196, 199
   autism and the, 30–38
   disconnection from, 192
   keeps the score 192
   language 24, 26, 44
   posture 54
   reactions 63
   sensations 54
bodymind/mindbody 12, 235
borderline personality disorder (BPD) 92
boundaried
   safe and, 45
   self-disclosure 72
boundary (ies) 32, 34, 35, 43, 44, 65, 125, 126, 193
   better, 65
   crossings 122
   healthy, 191
   holding, 130
   maintaining, 194
   navigating, 61
   professional, 224

set, 154
of therapy 175
time, 190
violations 122
brainspotting 103, 233
broken
   English 151
   feeling, 71, 100, 103, 100, 119,
   not, 53, 54, 77
bullying 34, 83, 89, 151, 170
   workplace, 135, 197, 199
burnout 57, 70, 139, 162, 163, 165, 168, 169, 200
   autistic, 22, 132, 161, 198, 199, 202
   consequences of, 102
   overwhelm and, 55

C

camouflage/camouflaging 3, 116,
   autism 199
   autistic traits 161
   detriments of, 120
   differences and difficulties 177
   to fit in 127
   learning to, 117
   as marker for suicide risk 127
   not, 125
   risk of, for health 88
   struggle to, 124
   through life 194
CBT (cognitive behavioural therapy) 10, 20–28, 99, 100, 101, 103, 119
CFS/ME (see ME/CFS)
childhood 40, 74, 99, 124, 172, 183, 189
   conditioning 56
   experiences 172
   goal of, 102
   trauma 88,
   traumatic events 118, 124
click 81, 85, 198, 210
   neurodivergent, 82, 84
coach/coaching 52, 55, 155, 167, 168, 232, 234, 235, 236, 237
   autistic, 52
   employment, 168
   life, 49
collaboration 3, 59, 65, 94, 166, 167, 168, 171, 156, 159, 163, 173, 178, 180, 186, 225, 235, 236, 238

communication 93, 130, 159, 167, 222
    atypical, 137
    autistic style, 12, 76, 159, 187
    barriers 168
    between therapist and client 41, 148, 150, 213
    breakdown in, 137
    challenges 52
    clear, 158, 159, 167
    complaining as, 137
    deficits 135
    differences 65, 137, 141, 213, 216
    difficulties 55
    direct, 102, 137
    skills 91
    style 114, 141
    verbal, 147
community 1, 5, 54, 55, 56, 73, 89, 93, 115, 116, 156, 185, 197, 227, 232
    academic, 22
    autistic, 22, 97, 191
    build, 218
    centre 184, 198
    network 132
    neurodivergent, 9, 53, 94
    neurokin, 60
    one's own, 122–131
    online, 91
    real, 226
compassion 18, 78, 111, 115, 119, 171
    fatigue 41
compassionate(ly) 113, 114, 145, 203, 217
complaint 133–141
conform/ity 176, 177
    forced, 152
    hiding identity in order to, 181
    of industry standards 59
    to neurotypical standards 94
    primed for, 116,
    required to, 36, 55, 224
    struggle to, 128
confusion 3, 11, 55
congruence 3, 70, 71, 73–79, 125, 193, 216
    autistic, 193
    goal of therapy 85
    own, 85
    sense of, 190
containment 37, 44, 175
    emotional and psychological, 43
    provide, 49
    sense of, 47
co-occurring conditions 3, 145
co-regulation 63, 101, 110, 111, 193
    experience, 113
    extensive, 193
    safe space for, 114
creative(s) 3, 13, 18, 177, 190, 224
    collaboration 166
    expression 238
    fellow, 40
    neurodivergent, 173
    process 237
    self 237
    territories 171
cult(s) 127–131
culturally 161
    aware 216
    competent 223
    sensitive 178
culture iv, 36, 38, 100, 101, 102, 103, 116, 117, 118, 159, 174, 179, 221, 228, 235
    allistic, 11
    autistic, 4, 5, 12, 15, 16, 145, 147–154, 187, 216
    Chinese 118
    cross- 216
    differences 223
    inclusion 151
    and neurodivergence 38, 56, 223
    neuronormative, 119
    norms, neurotypical 150

D

DBT 91, 92, 95, 99, 101, 119
deficiency 128
    feelings of, 117,
    in terms of, 124, 126
deficient 120
depression 9, 26, 53, 76, 90, 91, 99, 100, 102, 118, 119, 125, 127, 129, 161, 199
destigmatise 45
developmental 160
    age 44
    condition 127
    disorders 88, 92
    language impairments 29
    trauma 72, 88, 90, 92, 95

diagnosis 124, 129
  ADHD, 21, 119, 193, 194, 231, 236
  autism, 4, 5, 21, 22, 26, 35, 52, 54, 61, 77, 81, 82, 84, 85, 88, 94, 95, 119, 124, 128, 132, 145, 150, 151, 156, 164, 185, 186, 187, 189, 193, 199
  central sensitivity syndrome, 197, 203
  comorbid, 150
  c-PTSD, 92
  dyslexia, 84
  ME/CFS, 145, 199, 231
  OCD, 119
  personality disorder, 92
  PoTS, 200
  PTSD, 119
diagnostic
  categories 139
  criteria 14, 76, 134, 186,
  manuals 137
  practice 197
  process 124
Diagnostic and Statistical Manual of Mental Disorders (DSM)
  -IV 210
  -5 76, 92, 186
difference(s) 2, 13, 23, 25, 43, 78, 83, 85, 115, 132, 134, 138, 148, 151, 222, 227
  accept, 152, 164
  accommodate, 158
  attention, 216
  aware of, 52
  between a meltdown and a tantrum 114
  brain, 102
  camouflage, 177
  celebrate, 176
  communication, 216
  in communication 65, 137
  co-occurring, 235
  cultural, 223, 227, 235
  embrace, 164
  in experiencing 190
  imaginal, 192
  inconvenient, 118
  mask, 116, 119
  medical, 221
  perception, 216
  processing, 212
  sense of, 189
  sensory, 120
  share, 179
  sleep, 54
  use our, 3
digital 166, 167, 174, 236
disability (ies) 61, 93, 147, 185, 221, 228, 231, 236
  intellectual, 22, 150, 151
  models of, 120, 167, 221, 226
  service 26
disabled 3, 157, 164, 167, 185, 200, 226
disablement 213
disabling 3
disclosure (*see also* self-disclosure)
  of neurodivergence 84, 85, 185
  protected, 135
  whistleblowing, 133
discomfort 25, 40, 43, 63, 83, 117, 129, 138
disorder 12, 124, 170, 223, 235
  anxiety, 129, 195, 210, 236
  attachment, 193
  attention deficit hyperactivity disorder (ADHD), 21
  autism spectrum, 135, 136, 193, 195
  borderline personality, 92, 99,
  common co-occurring, 196
  communicative, 90
  developmental, 88, 92
  eating, 193
  mood, 92
  obsessive compulsive, 5, 81
  oppositional-defiant, 118
  personality, 92, 119, 135, 193
  post-traumatic embitterment, 139, 141
  post-traumatic stress, 128, 134
  substance use, 193
double empathy problem 23, 24, 77, 120, 138, 167, 180, 190, 191, 192
dyslexia 3, 26, 53, 81, 84, 85
dyspraxia 3, 53, 81, 196
dysregulation 191, 192, 193

E

Einfühlung 179, 180
EMDR 93, 103, 233
emotion(s) 10, 23, 24, 27, 35, 53, 55, 84, 89, 91, 94, 112, 149, 150, 156, 180, 190, 191, 192, 193, 194, 211
  abstract, 33
  client's, 10, 63

communicating, 40, 95
heavy, 48, 113
mixed, 145, 200
regulate, 65, 173
sit with, 63
very grand, 103
emotional(ly) 27, 59, 85, 90, 149
   abuse 95
   appropriate, 23,
   arousal 139
   connection 173
   containment 43
   cues 24
   demands 67
   discomfort 138
   distress 110
   embarrassment 110
   expression 41, 237
   fear 110
   healthy, 80
   hurt 16
   labour 116
   learning 35
   literacy 175
   memories 43
   needs 54
   needs audit 55
   overwhelm 64
   pain 40
   regulation 156, 171
   responses 24, 192
   shame 110
   stress 58
   support needs 232
   unregulated, 193
   vocabulary 108
empathy 2, 10, 23, 34, 37, 57–68, 77, 86, 88, 111, 112, 119, 126, 162, 167, 175, 190, 211, 215, 236
   affective, 24
   capacity for, 22,
   cognitive, 24
   communicate, 24,
   experience, 23
   quotient test 103
   somatic, 41
employment 127, 139, 169
   appropriate, 93
   coach 168, 236

   departure from, 75
   full-time 61, 63, 168
   government, 150
   troubles 77
empower 4, 5, 22, 56, 95, 127, 165, 166, 167, 168, 173, 177, 180, 186, 201, 222, 238
empowerment 48, 77, 174, 176, 188, 192
environment iv, 25, 74, 106, 110, 113, 116, 134, 154, 162, 174, 180, 193, 224, 235
   accessible, 166–174
   autistic-friendly, 3
   conducive, 168
   contained in, 43
   create, 71, 169, 172, 181, 182
   digital, 166
   discomfort in, 40
   educational, 151
   home, 132
   immersive, 172
   learning, 223
   noisy, 41
   non-autistic, 127, 191
   online, 166
   quieter, 233
   relate to, 37
   safe, 12, 112, 167, 177
   of safety and trust, 72
   sensory, 36
   supportive, 168, 176
   therapeutic, 38, 166, 167
   therapy, 166, 169
   uncomfortable, 23
   unique, 173
   utopian, 73
   vital, 173
   work/working, 43 78, 132, 151
equality 167, 224, 228
exhaustion 78, 151, 168, 199
   long-term, 161
expert/ise 52, 74, 122, 152
   on autistic culture 12
   clients, on themselves 95, 115, 153, 223
   by experience 29, 124
   by study 124
   in theory 124
eye contact 26, 39, 215
   ability to make, 81, 86
   minimal, in art therapy, 45
   taught, 163, 215

F

face (concept of: 面子(miàn zi)) 116–119
fairness
    sense of, 75, 136, 139
fatigue 66, 168, 199
    autistic, 200
    compassion, 41
    feelings of, 31
female(s) 89, 123, 194
feminist 38
    liberation theology 184, 237
    theory 125
flow, autistic, 11–19, 33, 36, 37, 41,
framework 74, 91, 176, 178, 182, 219, 227
    affirmative, 181
    ethical, 122, 157
    neurodiversity-affirming, 120
    oppressive, 176
    pathologising, behaviour-focused, 119
freedom 65, 126, 128, 156, 159, 172, 198, 215, 216
friendship 61, 211
functioning 139
    autistic, 151
    executive, 133
    high, 3, 127, 171
funding 170, 228

G

gaslighting 55, 61, 150
gender 82, 83, 84, 123, 126, 228, 237
    bias 164
    cis, 82
    diversity 158
    dysphoria 83
    identity 83, 191, 201
    lived experience of, 181
    trans 77
Gestalt therapy 2
gifted 107, 108, 118
goal 61, 74, 100, 148, 168
    of childhood 102
    of meltdown 108, 186
    of therapy 85, 148, 186
    treatment, 187
golden equation 3
grief 17, 19, 49, 52, 98, 199, 203
grievance 72, 134–140

group(s) 42, 45, 98, 116, 126, 127, 168, 173, 184, 185, 213, 214, 224, 225
    adult addiction, 42
    approved behaviour 127
    autism interest, 232
    autistic doctors, 135
    of autistic therapists 1, 2, 3
    client, 66, 72, 191
    clinical skills, 26
    collaborative diagnosis, 186
    discussion, 237
    Facebook, 102, 103, 104, 217
    feeling out of place in, 58
    high-demand religious, 155
    less likely to receive autism diagnosis 22
    marginalised, 153
    minority, 4, 125, 184
    neurodivergent, 33
    of neurodivergent people 86
    NHS, 209
    personal development, 224
    settings 47
    supervision 227
    support, 184, 185, 187
    of therapists 213
    therapy 36, 65, 227
    training, 26, 34

H

healing 42, 67, 77, 94, 104, 110, 113, 114, 140, 154, 185, 234
    art for, 40
    flow 17, 19
    perspective 76
    qualities of self-energy 9, 11,
    together 185
    trauma, 18, 95, 114
health 201
    behavioural, 74
    care 93, 200
    condition(s) 197, 202
    crisis 231
    good, 190
    ill-, 203
    mental, 21, 26, 40, 41, 51, 52, 55, 64, 65, 66, 88, 89, 90, 91, 92, 93, 118, 119, 122, 129, 134, 135, 138, 139, 148, 153, 168, 169, 176, 178, 179, 184, 186, 193, 214, 232, 233, 235, 236

physical, 3, 88, 190, 192, 196, 197
practitioners, autistic medical care 22
healthy 46, 117, 136, 177, 213
    behaviours 176
    boundary 191
    emotionally, 80
    mentally, 202
Human Givens 2, 9, 51, 53, 54, 235
humour, sense of 89, 159
hyperactive/hyperactivity 40, 41, 81, 201
hyperfocus 15, 41, 44, 66, 194, 200
hypermobility 35, 102
hypnotherapist/hypnotherapy 51, 190, 191, 192, 235

I

identity 21, 45, 54, 83, 115, 116,
    autistic, 16, 67, 90, 102, 104
    autistic therapist, 82
    AuDHD, 83, 84
    gender, 83
    immigrant, 117
illness 55, 152
    chronic, iv, 145, 196–203
    mental, 102, 134
imagination 45, 106, 107, 193
    -based 192
immigrant 115, 117
    1.5 generation, 116
    Asian, 102
    experience 116
    Norwegian, 235
imposter syndrome 52, 199
inclusive 179
    approach 178
    of autistic people 214
    environments 166
    learning environment 223
    lens 223
    sense of belonging 178
independent 106, 108
    and empowered 173
    learning 62, 95
    perspective 179
    practice 73
    study 91
inflexible/bility 136, 137
infodump 17, 86
injustice 139, 140

internal family systems (IFS) 16–18
internet 91, 217
interoception 35, 53, 108
introject 128, 129, 194
invalidation 95
isolation 64, 113
    from peers 40,
    sense of, 47
    shame and, 110
    from the tribe 185

J

journey(ing) 5, 51, 54, 130, 147, 158, 184, 186, 187, 190, 236
    arduous, 56
    into art therapy practice 57, 67
    autistic, 185
    healing, 154
    interactive, 145, 184
    magical, 171
    mental health, 235
    from research knowledge to lived wisdom 97–104
    of self-awareness 228
    of self-discovery 115, 155
    therapeutic, 173
    into therapist career 49
    therapy, 54
    training, 132, 168

L

language iv, 32, 34, 54, 56, 76, 77, 114, 116, 117, 118, 170, 174, 190, 192, 222, 234, 237
    autism as, 5, 145, 146 147–154
    body, 24, 26, 44
    figurative, 9
    loaded, 128
    of music 126
    non-verbal, 112
    of therapy 33
LGBTQI(A)+ 34, 126, 228
lived experience 41, 65, 67, 157, 158, 164, 181, 201
    of autistic people 166, 170, 219
    of depression 125
    invalidation of, 95,
    invaluable, 145, 203
    of neurodivergence 222, 232

understanding from, 124
validate, 174
value of, 176
wisdom of, 102

M

marginalisation 88, 181, 191, 193
mask 71, 98, 124, 151, 153, 154, 161, 177, 188, 194, 199, 219
   able to, 22
   clients', 163
   creation of, 128
   de-, 45
   differences 116
   learning how to, 3
   living behind, 185
   need to, 25
   social, 10, 63
   take off, 187
   wearing the, 109
masked 71, 74, 119
   highly, 219, 228
masking 24, 29, 67, 75, 87, 98, 102, 120, 125, 139, 151, 153, 175, 232
   act of, 88
   autistic, 55, 176
   differences 119
   enforced, 128
   exhaustion associated with, 78
   as fawning 177
   high, 127, 129
   lifetime of, 163
   opposite of, 127
   risk factor 127
   and sensory overload 200
ME/CFS 145, 196, 198, 199, 200, 231
meditation 8–18, 28, 110, 234
meltdown 71, 75, 106–114, 119, 120, 156, 192, 198, 200
   adult, 110, 111, 113
   client, 148, 200
   private, 118,
   public, 109
memory (ies) 172
   earliest, 71
   early, 39
   emotional, 43
   of struggles 59
   traumatic, 63

mentor 55, 114, 119, 168, 170, 173, 174, 222, 236
metaphor 9, 25, 49, 190, 192
metaphorical 44, 139
mindfulness 28, 91, 140, 191, 194, 202, 234
   healing benefits of, 13
minority 125, 179,
   challenges of being, 67
   group 4, 185
   minority within a, 116
   multiple, 72,
   neurotype 66, 185
   oppressed, 184
   stress of being, 58
misdiagnosis 92, 135, 163
misunderstanding 22, 118, 130,
   constant, 129,
   frequent, 190
modality (ies) 2, 7, 28, 71, 87, 91, 94, 95, 112, 120, 125, 203, 225, 226 233, 234
   brainspotting, 103
   established, 65
   mystery, 42
   scientific and effective, 99
model 14, 43, 45, 72, 80, 85, 103, 119, 133, 163, 171
   alternate, 166
   collaborative, 186
   of disability 120
   fidelity to, 99
   Human Givens, 9, 53, 54
   human rights, 167
   humanistic, 120, 191
   medical, 74, 137, 224
   neurotypical, 163
   pathologising, 178
   pathology, 77
   relationship, 82
   role, 125
   seven-eyed, of supervision 157, 160
   SIBAM, 63
   social, 120, 167
   solution-focused, 235
   therapeutic, 17
   of therapy 54
monotropic 18
   attention 15
   experiences 9, 11
   flow 13, 15, 16, 17

focus 15, 17
meditative state 14
mind 14
monotropism 11–19
mute
computer 25
go, 109
rendered, 167
situationally, 118
myth(s) 77, 122, 172,
about autistic people 211, 212

N

NARM (neuroaffective relational therapy) 95, 225
neuro-developmental 68
art therapy 63, 68
disorders 203
neurodivergence 3, 22, 26, 33, 37, 58, 64, 118, 156, 157, 163, 165, 167, 175, 180, 193, 197, 199, 226, 236
ableism with regard to, 162
acceptance of, 179
-affirming 191
awareness of, 20
disclosure of, 84
experience of, 83
exploring, 82
lived experience of, 222, 231
mentions of, 23
more than one, 194
open about, 85
radar for, 86
reality of, 119
recognise, 9, 72, 134
specific, 148
as social and cultural issue 38
umbrella 54
understanding, 87, 102, 120, 158
views on, 227
neurodivergent 20, 55, 85, 88, 102, 150, 151, 158, 168, 181, 213, 228
access 236
adults 232
-affirming 202
artists 173, 236
click 82, 84
clients 21, 36, 45, 52, 54, 56, 64, 78, 82, 86, 115, 119, 120, 153, 167, 190, 232
community 9, 53, 94
conditions 191
counselling/psychotherapy trainees 212
counsellors 157, 159, 162, 163
diagnosis 84
experience 36, 37, 175
flow 33
folk 162, 163
-friendly 45
group 33
individuals 21
issues 175
journeys 235
late-diagnosed, 5
mind 41
path 82
person 35
people 54, 55, 56, 66, 81, 86, 103, 120, 153, 161, 174, 191, 194, 223, 226, 233, 236
population 191
practitioner 175, 176
psychotherapist 52
spaces 33
supervisee 146, 162
supervisor 156, 161
therapist 22, 25, 37, 54, 65, 124, 163, 164
traits 175
trauma 34
ways of being 81
whiskers 86
women 231, 236
neurodiverse 81, 177, 179
neurodiversity 4, 26, 53, 76, 82, 214, 237 (*see also* affirming, neurodiversity)
concepts 77
consultancy 231
movement 76, 102, 104
needs 159
and trauma 233
neurokin 3
community of, 60, 124, 145
working with, iv, 189–195
neuronormativity 83
neurotype 37, 71, 73, 74, 82, 86, 124, 163, 180, 192, 193
autism as, 12, 16, 223, 235
differences in, 65
diversity of, 213

minority, 66, 185
similar, 66
unique, 103
neurotypical 22, 23, 61, 81, 86, 127, 135, 138, 151, 169, 184, 187
  behaviours 98
  clients 25, 78
  colleagues 222
  concepts 176
  counsellors 164
  cultural norms 150
  expectations 24, 94
  ideas 178
  lenses 179
  life 33
  majority 54
  mimic, 127
  model of counselling 163
  norms 177
  peers 161
  perspective 178
  point of view 207
  practitioners 65
  situations 166
  social skills 37
  society 127
  space 133
  standards 71, 94, 175, 176
  supervisors 164
  therapists 137
  therapy 33
  'translation tool' 178
  ways of being 163
  world 150
non-directive 42, 95
non-speaking 35
  skills 147
non-verbal 35, 227
  aspect of art 66
  children 90
  clues in conversation 76
  commands 106
  skills 147

O

occupational
  burnout 161
  therapists 150
OCD (obsessive-compulsive disorder) 81, 119
online 16, 52, 132, 158, 160, 164, 183, 184, 185, 233
  autistic community 123
  community 91, 153
  counselling 75
  discussion groups 237
  environment 166
  Facebook group 217
  method 78
  moving, 2
  relationships 91
  services 75, 78
  test 81
  therapy 2, 123
  working 26, 76, 78
  workshops 171
oppression 181, 184, 215, 223
othered/othering 94, 130, 234
outcome 15, 213
  autism + environment =, 3, 191
  desired, 139
  improve, 148
  positive, 138
  therapeutic, 218
outsider 40, 43, 44, 115, 194
over-stimulation 25, 108, 233
overwhelm 16, 55, 64, 72, 118, 192, 193, 221
overwhelmed 63, 108, 156
overwhelming 12, 40, 100, 107, 111, 112, 127, 184

P

pain 53, 152, 180, 196, 199, 217
  chronic, 168
  emotional, 40
  hidden, 154
  physical, 21, 109, 111
painful 129, 148
  content 17
  experiences 11, 125
pandemic 47, 59, 76, 78, 123, 233
  Covid-19, 2, 29, 58, 75, 79, 150, 202
paradigm
  medical, 170
  neurodiversity-affirming, 223
  shift 215, 218
pathologise 9, 37, 53, 136, 137
pathologising 138, 164, 223
  behaviour 102

of complaints 137
framework 119
ideology 118
model 178
non-, 17, 181
PDA (pathological demand avoidance/ pervasive drive for autonomy) 74
person-centred 2, 9, 53, 125, 133, 197, 233, 234, 235
phobias 191, 193
power/ful 3, 16, 71, 83, 130, 153, 171, 187
　act of, 236
　differentials 224
　higher, 106
　imbalance 159, 178
　naps 169
　privilege and, 181
　relations 34
　violations of, 141
private practice iv, 2, 57, 58, 61, 64, 80, 133, 158, 209, 232, 236
privilege 22, 61, 158, 164, 169, 181, 201
processing 41, 120, 139, 163, 190
　bottom-up, 63, 222
　challenges 52
　differences 127, 212
　feelings 44
　language 34
　multiple information streams 51
　needs, sensory 167
　resources 14
　similar, 194
　speeds 12, 33
　styles 158
　symptoms, sensory 92
proprioception 35
pseudo-identity 127
pseudo-personality 127, 128
psychodynamic 2, 42, 103
PTSD 51, 92, 119, 129, 134

Q
queer 38, 82, 164, 27

R
race 126, 228
rapport 51, 55, 61, 77, 78, 140, 215
regulation 37, 111, 149, 171, 235
　co-, 63, 101, 110, 111, 113, 114, 193

rejection 113, 117, 118, 221
　sensitivity 64, 156
relational 162, 193
　approach 80
　attachments 193
　dynamics 65
　life 189
　therapist 81
　therapy 95
　togetherness 101
　trauma 92
relational transactional analysis 80, 235
relationship 10, 17, 33, 34, 35, 36, 41, 42, 46, 55, 71, 77, 80–87, 89, 91, 92, 113, 125, 132, 133, 135, 137, 139, 155, 158, 160, 163, 178, 179, 209, 215, 216, 217, 221, 233
　attachment, 42
　client–therapist, 162, 176, 178, 180
　dual, 122
　dynamic 18
　learning, 157
　sexual, 122
　supervisor–supervisee, 145
　supervisory, 159, 161, 162, 175
　therapeutic, 17, 24, 61, 63, 71, 82, 85, 122, 145, 177, 181, 215, 223
　trauma 66
research 21, 51, 53, 71, 135, 198, 200, 233
　autism, 20
　on autistic adults 78
　current, 161
　effectiveness of talking therapy 87
　ethics 140
　knowledge 97–104
　with older autistic adults 183
　on practising as a neurodivergent therapist 22
　subjects 124
resilience 89, 90, 94, 152
RSD (rejection-sensitive dysphoria) 156
rule(s) 9, 81, 107, 117, 133, 153, 159, 190, 224, 237
　'didn't get the', 32
　different for autistic people 215
　on how to be human 33
　implicit, 150
　moral, 136
　social, societal, 66, 86, 109, 117

rural 122, 200

S

safety 113, 150, 179
   creating, 177, 182
   environment of, 72
   establishing, 215
   polyvagal exercises for, 114
   -seeking 191
   sense of, 35, 110
   signs of, 112
self 17, 114, 140, 167, 177, 230, 232
   actualising 204
   advocacy 185
   advocating 152
   authentic, 43, 49, 62, 194
   AuDHD, 82
   autistic, 82, 127
   -aware 101
   -awareness 228
   -belief 62
   -concept 138
   creative, 237
   -denying 176
   -deprecating 101
   determination 103
   -development 156
   -discovery 115, 204, 209, 217, 228
   embracement of, 46
   -energy 9, 11, 17, 18, 37
   -esteem 62, 101, 125
   genuine, 147
   -harm 109, 156
   inner, 71, 187
   -judgement 194
   -loathing 113
   normal, 32
   -opinionated 117
   -protective 219
   real, 187
   -reflection 2
   -reflective 162
   -regulation, regulate 110, 111, 193
   rocking, 106
   -scan 211
   sense of, 172, 179
   -soothe 89
   -therapy 32
   -transformation 119
   true, 71, 234
   -understanding 210
   unmasked, 98
   which one truly is 69, 71, 122–131
   -worth 66
   younger, 116
self-care 67, 139, 158, 160, 193, 233
   art journalling for, 59,
   needs 114, 190
   practice 24, 24
self-diagnosis 81, 156
   in autistic community 22
self-disclosure 121–131
   about being autistic 45
   boundaried, 72
   of neurodivergence 158
self-identify 97, 102, 233
sensitivity 61, 65,
   central sensitivity syndromes 196
   hyper, 111
   hypo, 111
   sensory, 197, 199, 200
sensory 25, 43, 52
   arousal 43
   capacity 127
   differences 120
   environment 36
   experiences 9, 53, 156
   feedback 35
   information 12
   joy 227
   needs 37, 45, 102, 222
   overload 16, 67, 111, 200
   overwhelm 64, 118
   processing 92, 167
   regulation (skills) 149, 191
   responses 44
   sensitivities 55, 197, 198, 199, 200
   space 27
sexuality 82, 83, 158
shame 3, 56, 99, 109–114, 134, 160, 163, 184, 234
shameful 34, 179, 194
shutdown 109, 118, 177, 191, 200
small talk 28, 41, 86, 168
social
   activity 120
   anxiety 25, 40
   capital 222

change 237
class 237
climate 37
concepts 184
conditions 237
confusion 55
connections 91
creatures 153
cues 136
development 237
difficulties 102
exclusions 150
experiences 31
field of perception 173
function 34
hierarchies 10, 63, 65, 66, 118, 227
identity 120, 128
interaction 63, 88, 103, 150, 167
investment 221
issue 38, 108
justice 135, 169, 234, 238
life 189
mask 10
media 21, 23, 78, 214
model of disability 120, 167
needs 75, 232
norms 28
rules 66, 86, 117
sciences 62, 89
security 170
separateness 111
services 57
setting 66
situations 20, 26, 31, 39
skills 37, 91, 98, 120
support 41, 232
understanding 216
work, worker 14, 62, 184, 185, 186
socialise/socialising 40, 66, 119, 227
   forced, 224
socially 26
   accepted 67
   anxious 210
   awkward 91, 102
   constructed 219
   imposed 167
solution-focused 54, 163, 235
soundscape 167, 171–174

space 16, 30, 33, 35, 36, 37, 38, 63, 168, 179, 222, 223, 227, 235
   affirming, 176
   allowing, 44
   auditory, 173
   autistic/ADHD-led, 167
   create, 85, 112, 113, 115, 177
   give, 22, 114, 166, 167, 181
   for growth 180
   hold, 49, 119
   live intermedial, 167
   mainstream, 171
   mental, 65
   metaphorical, 139
   need for, 169
   neurotypical, 133
   non-judgemental, 180
   quiet/sensory, 27
   safe, 17, 177
   supportive, 170, 182, 234
   take up, 32
   to talk 45
   therapeutic, 234
   therapy, 10, 24
   three-dimensional, 43
   to unpack 162
   virtual meeting, 166
   within the image 46
Special Interest(s) (SPINs) 15, 31, 66, 89, 91, 98, 103, 228, 234
spectrum 54
   autism, 135, 136, 193
   on the, 119
   wide, 57
spoon theory 120, 190
stereotype 30, 194
   failure to challenge, 207
   harmful, 223
   regarding autistic people 1, 2, 4, 9, 10, 22, 37, 58, 63, 81, 86, 190, 212
stigma 119
   attached to autism 4
   autistic people more vulnerable to, 139
   and misunderstanding 22
   negative, 102
stigmatised 118
stim 24, 45, 108, 151, 171
   autistic, 236

energy found in, 173
socially-accepted, 67
subconscious(ly) 42, 45, 57, 82, 180
  issue 227
  level 84
  system 114
subculture
  alternative, 198
  autistic, 5, 151
suicidality 88, 127, 196
  risk markers for, 131
suicide 53, 90
superpower 27, 164
supervision 21, 23, 24, 26, 146, 156–165, 170, 212, 222, 233
  group 227
  neurodiversity-affirming, iv, 175–182, 223
  neurotypically informed, 146
  non-affirming, 179
  seven-eyed model of, 157, 160
supervisor iv, 4, 22, 23, 24, 26, 27, 49, 82, 93, 125, 145, 155–165, 170, 175–182, 207, 209, 212,
  autistic, 146, 179
  clinical, 232, 237
  supportive, 65

T

tantrum (as opposed to meltdown) 108, 111
therapy 2, 4, 9, 25, 28, 34, 35, 37, 52, 55, 65, 76, 78, 84, 88, 89, 93, 94, 95, 111, 118, 149, 150, 154, 162, 173, 174, 182, 183, 184, 187, 193, 194, 210, 212, 213, 214, 216, 233, 234, 235
  aim of, 80, 124
  art, 40–46, 57–68, 227, 232
  autism in, 11–19
  autistic-to-autistic, 145
  barrier to accessing, 197
  caseload 75
  client-centred, 74
  dance movement, 30–38
  effective, 87, 202
  environments 166, 169
  essential element in, 71
  free, 170
  goal(s) 85, 148, 186
  'good', 175
  group, 65, 227

institutions 141
journey 54
life-affirming, 166
life-enhancing, 217
as meditation 16, 17
modalities 91, 120
models of, 53, 54
online, 2, 123
personal, 41
practice 74
rhythm of, 85
room 1, 5, 46, 56, 63, 178
session(s) 16, 78, 82, 167, 182, 223
space 10, 24, 45
strategies 139
talking, 190
time-limited, 137
trainees 227
training 33, 125, 176, 218, 232
world of, 22
training 1, 3, 10, 51, 55, 57, 80, 82, 101, 111, 118, 119, 122, 132, 133, 148, 149, 168, 170, 179, 189, 197, 205, 211, 212, 213, 215, 218, 222, 223, 224, 225, 226, 232, 233, 236
  art therapy, 59, 62, 227
  in autism 124
  'autism-is-pathology', 77
  as autistic CBT practitioner 20–28
  conformist, 98
  core, 210
  counselling, 156
  current, 207
  dance therapy, 32, 36, 40, 41, 49
  demands of, 94
  formal, on autism 209
  mental health, 153
  on neurodiversity 53
  social skills, 104
  somatic experiencing, 63, 65
  specific, 228
  supervision, 157, 181
  therapists, 214, 217, 223
  therapists-in, 175
  therapy, 33, 125, 181
  to work with neurodivergent clients 56
  yoga teacher, 14
trainee iv, 2, 101, 148, 205
  art therapy, 62

autistic, 224, 225
counselling/psychotherapy, 212
disabled, 226
experience as, 207, 222–228
non-autistic, 27
therapist 210, 214
trainer 3, 77, 99, 176, 205, 207, 224, 232, 236
  autistic, 209–219
trait(s) 20, 54, 136
  ADHD, 84
  of autism 60
  autistic, 59, 61, 161, 199
  human, 164, 193
  managing, 53
  neurodivergent, 175
  personality, 193
translator 148, 151, 152
trauma 3, 9, 12, 13, 14, 17, 18, 41, 61, 76, 89, 93, 94, 98, 102, 128, 162, 193, 197, 198, 199, 215, 234, 235, 237
  acute, 147
  and the autistic therapist 88–96
  'Big T', 92
  childhood, 88
  chronic, 150
  client's, 126
  complex, 66, 92 147–154
  compounded, 154
  developmental, 72, 88, 90, 92, 95
  dissociation through, 10, 33
  effects of, 152
  healing 18, 232
  invisible, 129
  major, 150
  marginalisation and, 88
  neurodivergent, 34
  neurodiversity and, 233
  past, 168
  processing, 58
  reactions 191
  relational, 92
  relationship, 66
  specialist, 43
  symptom(s) of, 13, 37
  therapy, somatic 233
  trigger 152
    warning 147

traumatic 93, 94, 199
  childhood events 118
  events 13, 43, 92
  experience(s) 61, 63, 89, 215
  memory 63
  responses 177
  stressors 88
traumatised 53, 100, 133
  autistic people 88
  teen 9, 11
traumatising
  genuinely, 130
  re-, 94
  therapies 94
tribe
  awareness of, 3
  find your, 187
  in isolation from, 185
  my, 94, 124, 163, 184
  new, 55
  one's, 145
  our, 184
  part of, 4
trust 71, 72, 154, 177, 180, 198
  breach of, 139
  build, 80, 215
  dare to, 43
  intuition 59
  learn to, 111, 177
  my beast 113
  in ourselves 62
  (in) the process 42, 67
  safety and, 72, 215

U

unconditional positive regard 126
unhealthy coping mechanisms 40, 193
unmask(ed) 76, 87, 88
  self 98
unmasking 156, 163
  importance of, 22
unsafety 106, 111
untraumatised 89

V

validation 54, 91, 94, 119, 138, 171, 216
  of emotions 95
volunteer 100, 133, 147, 169

W

weird 40, 89, 124, 133
  child 107
  don't be, 34
weirdness 90
weirdo 155
window of tolerance 139
Wise Mind 149, 150

Y

yoga 14, 32, 23